America's Runaways

America's Runaways

by Christine Chapman

WILLIAM MORROW AND COMPANY, INC.
NEW YORK   1976

Printed in the United States of America.

1 2 3 4 5   80 79 78 77 76

Library of Congress Cataloging in Publication Data

Chapman, Christine.

America's runaways.

Includes index.
1. Runaway youth—United States.   2. Runaway children—United States.   I. Title.
HQ796.04517   1976   301.43'15   75-23274
ISBN 0-688-02986-8

Book design: Helen Roberts

To my mother, Esther Patton Van Ingen
and
To my grandmother, Rose Goodrich

Acknowledgments

What began out of my curiosity and a simple question—why do thousands of children run away from home?—has expanded into a full-length book and a list of obligations I can never repay. So many interested people helped me answer, and ask, the hard questions that it is impossible to thank them individually. They appear in the book as they are: runaways and parents, high school students and teachers, ministers and runaway house counselors, police officers from New York to San Francisco, lawyers and judges, city and county social workers, government men and women, psychiatrists and psychologists.

My debt to runaways and the parents of runaway children is huge, for they trusted me enough to reveal the worst moments of family life. I have changed the names of parents and of every child, runaway or not, except those individuals involved in the 1973 Houston murder case. In Houston, in spite of their grief, Dorothy and Fred Hilligiest and Elaine and James Dreymala talked to me about the case and their sons and gave me permission to quote them.

My own sons, Peter and Danny, enacted before my very eyes the complexities of growing up today. At times they tried to spare me the facts, but more often they set me straight. My

7

students replied thoughtfully to questions I asked them as they confided to me the anxieties of a middle-class adolescence.

I am grateful also to Robert L. Smith, Headmaster of the Sidwell Friends School, for allowing me a leave of absence from teaching to begin the research.

My special thanks for insight into the intricacies of the runaway problem belong to writer Lillian Ambrosino of Boston; Jim Baumohl of the University of California at Berkeley, who gave me permission to quote from his report on street people, *Down and Out in Berkeley*; Eunice Faber of Ann Arbor; Floyd L. Parks, a Maryland lawyer; psychiatrist and professor Dr. Helm Stierlin of Heidelberg, West Germany; and Bill Treanor, founder and former director of Runaway House in Washington, D.C. I want to thank Nick Chriss, reporter for *The Los Angeles Times* in Houston, for sharing his files on the murders with me; Steven Meltzer of San Francisco for helping me interview runaways on the streets of Berkeley; and John Rector and other staff members of the Senate subcommittee on juvenile delinquency for always answering my questions.

I am grateful to writer and editor Lois O'Neill for her early encouragement and to my excellent editor at William Morrow, Hillel Black, for his patience and astute criticism.

· It is my husband, Bill Chapman of *The Washington Post*, to whom I owe the most thanks. He bought the airline tickets and read a dozen rough drafts. He showed me how thorough and painstaking a good reporter is, and how tolerant is the man who lives with a wife who writes a book.

CHRISTINE CHAPMAN

Washington, D. C.
June, 1975

Contents

Introduction

by Robert Coles

They are American children, American citizens, like millions of others, but they are living quite special lives—awful to contemplate, actually we have to do so, have to look at the unparalleled rootlessness that characterizes the wayward youth of the twentieth century, industrial United States. Runaways, the author of this thoughtful and sensitive book calls them—boys and girls or young men and young women who for one reason or another (for many reasons, usually, that in their sum amount to a lifetime's reasons) have chosen to leave home decisively, and all too often, in a way that hurts themselves as much as the parents and relatives left behind.

Not the least of this book's virtues is the author's sense of history, her willingness to connect a desperate boy or girl, hitchhiking toward someplace, any place, with others in the past who left one part of this country (or came here from abroad) in order to find or try to build a new life for themselves. In a sense, America was built by runaways, as we are told in the beginning by Mrs. Chapman. But there was a difference. It is one thing to leave New England, say, in pursuit of a life in Colorado or California as a farmer or rancher, even as, in the literal and non-pejorative sense of the expression, a gold digger. It is quite another matter when a child or youth takes to the road out of fierce anger or overwhelming anxiety or depression that is all consuming—and goes no place, really, but rather wanders around in self-lacerating confusion. The cities of this nation, the highways, too, are now places where such young people stay—a day on the road, a day in this city, a day in the next, and so on. It is sad and frightening, and certainly reason for reflection.

This book provides the reader with all that he or she will need to know in order to begin at least a consideration of what the presence of thousands of runaway children in our midst might tell us about ourselves as a nation. Many but not all runaways have grown up in what might be called "runaway homes" —families that sorely lack stability, solidity, and self-assurance, families plagued by economic jeopardy, social vulnerability, and very important, psychological fragility. They are uprooted or rootless families—even when well off moneywise. They are families adrift—at the beck and call of various crises, which seem interminable. Or they are families ordered about thoughtlessly and arrogantly by bosses, companies, "authorities" who care little for the impact of a vagabond life on children, however buffered by financial support. And, of course, even among those who never move physically there are the spiritually uprooted—those who are at the mercy of the opinions others have, the latest fashion or social trend, or those who have lost faith not only in God, but in everything and everyone, except, really, the so-called "norm." It can be, it is, for all too many in this rich and powerful country, a matter of the blind leading the blind: nervous parents, ever afraid of what others think or believe or spend their time doing, conveying to their children little but the need to conform, or pretend, or oblige—in the interests of social position, economic security, acceptance by one or another "group" or the so-called "peers" we are all supposed to think of these days. Needless to say there are other runaways, children of the extremely poor or the only marginally secure, or the hard-pressed and apprehensive working class. Such children know daily suffering, know that suffering is contagious in this world—a father's lack of work results in a mother half mad with fear, and *that* results in a child needlessly, senselessly brutalized. And always, of course, there are those who inflict harm on children out of some inner or private compulsion that has little or nothing to do with the external "realities" of life, but everything to do with those psychological, private betrayals, and early sorrows that the rich or the poor alike know. All of which is to say that there is no one "type" of runaway, no one sweeping categorization that explains the reasons all of them do as they do, and more existentially, become what they are—a curious and often terribly unhappy version of the wanderer.

As the author, Christine Chapman, says in this helpful and touching book of hers, she is "a teacher and a parent, not a social scientist or psychologist . . ." Thank God for that state of affairs. Instead of offering us theories and more theories, the dense, muddled jargon of the academy, or the arrogant and condescending "interpretations" all too many of us in this second half of the twentieth century dote on as if God Almighty's words have been spoken or written, she offers us wonderfully straightforward, direct language, clear, informative, and strong narration, and suggestive evocations of particular human beings, rich with the complexity and ambiguity of human life. Her humility is an additional recommendation (in an age when various "experts" make the most astonishing and outrageous of claims) but it is a humility, a modesty that the reader will no doubt find utterly unnecessary by the time he or she reaches the end of the book.

Part I
From Hannibal to Houston

The meaning of running away in America changes from one generation to the next. The flight of the runaway mirrors the times. Running away is a rejection and a reaction. The child who leaves his family suddenly may be running from brutality or indifference, from alcoholism, or from his own confusion. The paraphernalia of a technical age seduces children to leave home. The shifting images of a television screen, the whine of an electric guitar, the false lament of a rock singer give off visions that pander to hungry imaginations. With each new runaway the reasons for leaving home multiply until only one is certain: the act of running away is the climax of embattled emotions between parents and children.

The idea of running away from home came, historically, with The Territory and Huck Finn's promise to light out for it. For adults, running away seemed a literary notion. We remembered runaways as adventurers, characters in books, idealists. We forgot the motivation to dwell on the experience. The mystery of our own time and a nostalgia for a past we never knew beguiled us.

My Uncle Oscar ran away from home when he was seventeen. He lit out for the West in 1908 and on an afternoon forty years later he returned with a pocket full of gold coins and a silver six-shooter. He handed out $20 gold pieces and he let me and my brothers fire his gun. Before settling in California, he told us, he had lived with the Indians in Texas and Mexico. He was gray-haired and lean when I met him that summer years ago, but he could spin a tale as slick as the shine on his boots. Oscar Goodrich was my hero of the Western night, and I forgot that he had run out of desperation because his father had abandoned him and his mother was dead.

The epitome of the runaway hero is Mark Twain's Huckleberry Finn. Huck ran not after a glorious adventure on the Mississippi, as dreaming, middle-aged men like to believe, but to save his life. His father had kidnapped him from his foster home in Hannibal, Missouri, and locked him in a cabin in the woods. When Huck left Pap, he was escaping from his drunken, dangerous attacks.

Thousands of poor children have run from the meanness of poverty. Like Huck they leave because they must or because they have no patience with being poor. They flee nasty tempers and the indifference of parents who scrape for a living.

Middle-class children run from the demands that affluence exacts from their parents. They run from expectations fostered by money. Their parents are eager to stake a claim for them, but they must cooperate by getting good grades at school and behaving well. The child who leaves because he cannot meet his parents halfway is running from an economic situation as distorting as poverty. Life for the middle-class runaway is a bargain he cannot keep.

During the Depression running away was an economic necessity. Children as young as fourteen and fifteen left home to relieve parents who were unable to support them. These *Boy and Girl Tramps of America,* as writer Thomas Minehan titled his book about them in 1934, traveled to survive. They looked for work futilely wherever the trains took them. Huck Finn went by raft and by foot; these children rode boxcars. They slept in shacks in hobo jungles. Wistful travelers, they moved south or west when the weather got cold. One boy said: "'I don't care how I go as long as I am going. . . . Any place, I think, is going to be better than the last place, but it usually turns out to be worse.'"

Traveling with these children, Minehan observed: "Practically all the families were hit by the economic whirlwind. 'Else,' as Texas [one young migrant], explained, 'why on the road?'" Thomas Minehan believed that "in every nation, following a plague, an invasion, or a revolution, children left without parents and home became vagrants." In the thirties the plague was poverty, and it was the children who left home and parents.

World War II marked the beginning of a revolution in the attitudes of the family. During 1942, the first year of the war, over eight thousand runaways appeared in America's juvenile courts. The nation was prosperous again, but the family suffered as men went to war; the age of anxiety had set in, and children were escaping unhappy homes to take jobs in a war-rich country.

After the war another runaway captured our imagination and became like Huckleberry Finn the prototype of the American boy. His name was Holden Caulfield and he appeared in the novel *Catcher in the Rye* by Jerome David Salinger. Fifteen-year-old Holden runs away from boarding school, because of failing grades, to New York City, where he meets cruel and insensitive men and women during a bizarre weekend. Depressed, he decides to go West to find a job and lose his identity.

> "What I'd do I figured, I'd go down to the Holland Tunnel and bum a ride, and then I'd bum another one, and another one, and in a few days I'd be somewhere out West where it was very pretty and sunny and where nobody'd know me and I'd get a job. I figured I could get a job at a filling station somewhere, putting gas and oil in people's cars. I didn't care what kind of job it was, though. Just so people didn't know me and I didn't know anybody."

As a literary character, Holden is an exaggeration of adolescence. He is the affluent middle-class child whose parents expect him to develop his capabilities in school. Yet, for him school is a pretentious and savage place. In one private school he sees a boy tormented by other students commit suicide. Holden worries about death and his future, and he fears that he may be mentally ill because he is unwilling to endure hypocrisy and cruelty. Parents and teachers, the middle-class moralists, are insistent that he conform, and they anticipate his cure in psychiatry. The book ends as it began, with Holden in a mental institution.

As the fifties turned into the sixties and Holden Caulfield was studied in schools, we heard about youngsters who ran to San Francisco to live in the Haight. These were the flower children, lovers of beauty who disdained the hypocrisies of a materialistic culture. We read about idealistic boys and girls who left home to join the Yippies and change the world. We read of communal life in New Mexico where youth was trying to create a new social order by sharing food, work, and each other. These runaways were nobody we knew. They were familiar to us only through the books we read or the movies we watched, colorful figures who mocked the era. We watched them wander the city streets in groups and we enjoyed them on the stage in *Hair*. They idealized their own youth by re-creating themselves as rogues and picaresque troubadors. They made being young and on the move an art form, an aesthetic with its own costumes and language and meaning. Running away from home to join the movement of peace or brotherly love was of our time, and understandable, perhaps even admirable. It seemed to us then that these youngsters were running after the dream promised by Thomas Jefferson when he declared the independence of all men and listed their rights as life, liberty, and the pursuit of happiness.

This contemporary image of running away blurred the facts until 1970, in the spring, when we saw the newspaper photograph of a fourteen-year-old runaway girl weeping beside the body of a student killed at Kent State University. Our ideas about running away moved from musical comedy to tragedy.

One winter day in Ann Arbor, Michigan, a friend talked about her son, a fugitive from the campus political movements of the late sixties.

Jonah had dropped out of school when he was sixteen and left home at seventeen. He ran half a mile from his house to throw himself into student protests to end the war in Vietnam. His parents could not prevent his leaving because Michigan law reads that a seventeen-year-old is no longer a juvenile responsible to his parents. In Ann Arbor in 1968, rhetoric and drugs inspired a revolutionary zeal in students and hangers-on to do battle with the government: to demonstrate their belief in peace by marching on Washington and their disdain for materialism by living cheaply. Often the ideals of the movement were corrupted by youngsters who abused the cause.

"Wherever he goes, in Ann Arbor, in Washington, in California, in Aspen, Jonah is arrested. In Washington for fighting with a policeman. For stealing a case of Coke or a pair of sunglasses in Michigan. For being in a university building after hours zonked on drugs. For being picked up as a runaway in a state where he was still a juvenile."

As his mother recited the litany of Jonah's offenses against the state, she sounded matter-of-fact. Through her son she had discovered a strange world. Nothing in her background had prepared her for it.

"We are very typical upper middle-class Jewish parents. My own parents were Jewish immigrants. We believe in work and in education. Who ever heard of police? Of psychiatrists? Of lawyers and jail and being put on probation? What did we know about drugs? And running away to live in a commune?"

Before Jonah quit school, his parents tried to dissuade him. They talked about love and family ties. They spoke of the waste of his intellectual gifts.

"We told him his being a high school dropout was unthinkable," his mother said. "He quit school and he left home, but we thought he would come back."

Occasionally Jonah appears at their handsome and orderly house to see his sister, to get something to eat, to take a shower. He sees his parents on the street, perhaps, or in court. He lives in a separate world from his family. He belongs to the street people, the bands of homeless young people who gather like locusts in university towns.

Jonah was a child of the late sixties, changing times that should have taught us to expect the unexpected. They were times that ripped away the myth about being able to control our destiny and that of our children. Gone was the comfortable idea that the possession of a child for his first three years—or was it his first seven?—makes him ours forever.

As middle-aged parents and teachers, we live in the future we worked toward; yet this future, our present, is a foreign country we are slow to understand because its interpreters are our children. Like the tourist guide who knows our language well enough to point out the buildings, the children are too inarticulate to convey the emotions of their experience.

We did not foresee what happens to children who inhabit two cultures simultaneously: the world we had taught them, our past, and the one we lived in, their present. They grew up dismayed because they realized life was not the way it was supposed to be. Parents separate; children live without a father or a mother. Public leaders are murdered. The government lies; the police arrest children for smoking marijuana.

They became sensitive trying to reconcile two sets of ideals—those they heard at home and those they learned from friends. The conflict of values confused them; often it caused them to withdraw; sometimes it caused them to rebel, usually against the family which has talked of love and loyalty and has asked for achievement and respectability.

They showed their uncertainty by testing the limits of family and state. Like Jonah, many found life easier outside of home and, resourceful, they stayed away. Others, like Taddy, a runaway I met in Houston, were too young to survive without parents. If Jonah was a runaway of the sixties, rebellious and destructive, Taddy typified the unhappy, baffled child of the seventies.

When I met her, she had left her suburban home north of Houston for the fourth time for the beaches of Galveston. Calling herself a "beach freak," she played her guitar for meals and slept where she could. In September, when the hurricanes hit Galveston, she hitchhiked back to Houston to a runaway house and waited to hear her parents say again that they wanted her home.

"I ran away because I was pissed off at my parents. I couldn't stay at home all the time. They're nice people, but they don't understand what's happening and I don't tell them anything."

Taddy was a fourteen-year-old girl puzzled by the incongruities of her childhood. At school once a girl pulled a knife on her because she made a rude remark. Then, her parents sent her to a private school which bored her. Her brother became ill on drugs and her parents placed him in a home for emotionally disturbed children. Her own boyfriend raped her in the woods near her house. A boy she knew died of an overdose. Other friends who used drugs lived in halfway houses or mental institutions. For herself she did not believe in drugs. She gave up smoking pot, she said, because she hated losing touch with reality. Reality was hard enough to handle straight; stoned, it was impossible.

When she mentioned her casual hitchhiking, I asked her if the discovery in August, 1973, of the murders of twenty-seven young boys had not warned her away from the road. The killers had picked up many of their victims while they were hitchhiking.

No, the murders didn't frighten her or keep her from thumbing. They were less chilling than the expectations her parents had for her, less crazy than her solitary suburban life.

"I hate living in the suburbs where there isn't anything to do and no one to talk to. My brother's away and my parents and I never talk. My father's an engineer and he wants me to go to college. My mother wants me to go to boarding school, but I won't. I'll probably end up with a psychiatrist again.

"I want to go home," she decided. "But I don't."

Hers was the predicament of many runaways: she wanted to return to the routine security of home, but she deplored the boredom, the quarrels, the hard work required of her. Like most runaways, Taddy had become sophisticated about the surface of life, but she was ignorant of its complexity and the depth of feelings. The anonymity of being a runaway was soothing: she was nobody anyone expected anything from. Yet, the responsibility of being a lone child running—and the love of her parents—kept bringing her home.

I. Running Away in America

" 'You were never young in the world I'm young in,'
children realize in thinking about their parents today."—
Margaret Mead, anthropologist, at the Sidwell Friends
School in Washintgon, D.C., October, 1973.

The school gymnasium was filled with children and teachers who
had come to see Margaret Mead. Wearing a long red cape and
striding to the stage with a tall walking stick, the famous anthropologist made the headmaster walk fast to keep up with her. The
children thought she was somebody's grandmother. In spite of
her cape and staff, she looked ordinary: short gray hair around
a plain, plump face, rimless glasses over curious eyes. When she
began to talk directly to them, ignoring the adults in the room,
the children knew she was extraordinary.

Listening to the seventy-two-year-old woman, fifth through
twelfth graders heard what they had long suspected: there were
no adults who knew more than they did about what they were
going through. Their parents came from a different world, a
world which had taught them that some things were right and
some things wrong. They, the children in front of her, did not
have the luxury of absolutes. There was a new way of thinking
about ethics, new ways of living which were invented during

World War II. Marriages did not last. Divorce, common everywhere, was to be expected because people lived so long and
children left home so early. The suburbs children lived in were
nightmares of uniformity. Between them and their parents was
a vast expanse, not simply a generation gap; it was a worldwide
ditch, manmade and perhaps impossible to cross, she explained.
The children found an ally in the woman who had jolted the
thinking world with her *Coming of Age in Samoa,* the 1928
study of adolescence in a primitive culture. Margaret Mead implied the irony of family life: children were dependent on elders
who brought them up for a world that no longer existed.

When I heard Dr. Mead that October morning, I had returned to teaching after a year's leave of absence, which I used
to research a book on runaway children and their parents. Immediately before school started, I had left Washington for Texas
to learn why the police in Houston were calling twenty-seven
murdered boys *runaways.* In August they had discovered their
bodies buried in the sand of a South Houston boatyard and in
shallow graves on local beaches. When the press and the public
denounced the police for failing to prevent the murders, the police retaliated. They called the boys *runaways,* suggesting their
delinquency, and they said their parents were neglectful.

By the summer of 1973, when the Houston murders had
become the worst episode of violence in American crime, I had
traveled throughout the country trying to uncover the facts about
runaway children. Coming from the anguish of parents in Texas
to Margaret Mead's blunt appraisal of the modern family, I
began to realize that running away from home was an expression
of despair. What I had turned up in Houston and in other parts
of the country about children who ran was evidence of the
different cultures inhabited by parents and children. As Dr.
Mead described the unusual gulf separating children from their
parents, I realized that runaways did not know how to jump the
gap.

For a long while I had thought something was going wrong

with the children I taught. When the revolutions of the late sixties had dissipated and protesting students settled down in college classrooms to study again, the children in high school continued to react. The political adventure was over and Richard Nixon was to retain the presidency in 1972; yet the reaction to confrontation was continuing among youngsters who did not know who Eugene McCarthy was. They did not remember the trial of the Chicago Seven, and the shooting at Kent State was as remote as the fading war in Vietnam. Still, they were acting peculiarly. I noticed a curious sullenness, a new resentment, that I had not observed before in the teen-agers I knew. They felt uneasy around adults and avoided them whenever they could. Whatever I tried to teach them in English classes, they accepted as the conventional waste of their time. They did not see how the study of literature was worth their attention because they believed that books belonged to history, not to life. Many were polite about sitting quietly and offering mild attention; others were hostile. A few were interested, but even they joined the others in believing that class was not real, that school was in-consequential except as the means for fulfilling their twin goals of college and freedom.

Uneasy, I remembered my own adolescence as boring and embarrassing, full of the ups and downs of emotional excess. These children, however, were like martyrs. They seemed to share a pain or understand a misery that I knew nothing about. Unlike their older brothers and sisters, the voluble activists of the 1960s, they were silent and self-contained. They did not try to explain themselves to their parents and teachers. Perhaps they felt that words were inadequate to express their condition. When being silent became too hard to bear, they acted; they did not talk, yell, shout. They did not only sink further into them-selves, smoking dope and turning up their music. Many ran away from home. By running away they announced that they were coming of age dismayed.

I had taught high school students about those literary runaways Huck Finn and Holden Caulfield. I didn't know that extraordinary American literature was becoming commonplace American life until my own students began to run. A couple of girls ran away with their boyfriends. Another girl I'd taught got into her Mustang and drove miles into Virginia or Pennsylvania to stay away from home for several days. At other times she'd drive into the suburbs where she worked at lunch counters and slept in her car. A tenth-grade boy literally ran out of the school to Georgetown with the dean of students fast after him.

Another student told me that her friend had gone all the way from her home in Cleveland Park, a wealthy neighborhood in northwest Washington, D. C. to San Francisco, where she had lived for a year with her boyfriend. A neighbor whose husband was a government lawyer had visited a spiritualist, thinking that her runaway daughter was dead and hoping for contact. A newspaperman I knew had searched through Berkeley for his missing son who was picked up later by the police in a small Ohio town. The son of one of Richard Nixon's aides ran away from home when the Watergate exposures began to implicate his father.

These middle-class youngsters were not the children who have always run away: the kids from poor families, from alcoholic parents, from broken homes. They were not beaten with electric cords, chased with butcher knives, or hit on the head with pieces of wood; nor were they sexually promiscuous or heavily involved with drugs or liquor. My students belonged to the other America, the safe one, the one that promised its youngsters liberty and the pursuit of happiness. If the public schools were bad, their parents could afford to send them to private schools. If the city got dangerous on their side of town, they could move to the suburbs. My students wore braces if they needed them, they went to summer camp or to Europe, and they aimed with their parents for an ivy league college. They had it made from the instant of their birth. Yet, they too were running from home. They were joining the traditional runaway, the abused child. We were shocked because we had believed the assumptions about class and behavior for so long that our common sense was dulled. The middle-class child was leaving home to protest the condition of his life. His parents, unaware that he had joined an army of defectors, said running was part of the changing times, of a permissive culture where meaning was found on the road, not in the home.

Since Huck Finn lit out for The Territory, fleeing home has dramatized a child's need to assert himself by getting away from oppressive elders. During the late 1960s running away was a political act intended to change the system, usually the one in power at home. In the 1970s, with estimates of runaways reaching the hundreds of thousands, running away has become a symptom of growing up confused.

When I began my research in 1972, the runaway child seemed to me the typical American adolescent, more heroic than his compliant counterpart who stayed at home. Legally, as a *runaway*, he had left home without the permission of his parents. Depending on the laws defining a juvenile in the state where he lived, the runaway was eleven to seventeen years old. The majority of runaway children I met came from the middle class. Their parents worked in the businesses, professions, factories of America. They were airplane mechanics and engineers, saleswomen and shop owners, nurses and doctors and psychiatrists, schoolteachers and college professors, civil employees and elected and appointed political leaders.

I met poor children who were running, but not many of them. I met black children who ran, but not many. As a teacher, I have known runaway children whose parents were the really rich and very important, but I have not met them on the road. Perhaps the Pinkerton men found them first or maybe they went to more exotic places than I did.

I have met more runaway girls than boys. Although some statistics show equal numbers of boys and girls on the road, thirteen- and fourteen-year-old girls run more often than boys that age. Today's runaways are younger than those of a few years ago. Then, runaways were the older teen-agers; today, they are from fourteen to sixteen years old. While many repeat their runaway episode, all learn that a runaway cannot survive alone.

I have looked for runaways in major cities, in college towns, on beaches, and in mountain towns. For three years from 1972 to 1974, I traveled up to New York and Boston from Washington and down to Miami, over to Houston and out to San Francisco and Berkeley, to Denver and Boulder, up to Ann Arbor and back to Rochester, New York, where I lived as a teen-ager. I wandered inside suburban shopping centers where children gather, mingling with their elders and bypassing them, creating an enclave of adolescence where they exchange news, sell dope, hitch a ride out of town.

I found them—the new runaways—around the Tastee-Freeze in the shopping plaza, living in condemned houses in the city or in small, crowded apartments, hiding in pinball parlors in university towns, sleeping in bus stations, living in mountain camps or in runaway houses in the ghetto. When they understood that I was a writer and not a policewoman, they talked to me willingly and often eagerly. I told them I would change their names—to Taddy and Kelly and Pammy and Nina, to Julie and Jody, to Jimmy and Rick, and Katie—to make it easier for them to be honest with me.

They told me they had not one but many reasons for running away. They listed the pressures of growing up—parents, the demands of friends and school, sex—that forced them to leave. They said their parents did not accept them as they were. They needed freedom to grow their way, not as their parents wanted them to be. They talked about unsympathetic stepfathers and nagging mothers, described violent family fights and threats upon their lives. Sure, they had smoked dope, or played truant with their boyfriend, or messed up their grades. So did everybody once in a while. For many the unspoken reason for their leaving home was that they felt unwanted.

The new runaways have failed to measure up to the ex-

pectations of their parents. They have shocked them with behavior which parents do not expect. They know too much about
the way things are without being able to reconcile life with the
way their parents say it ought to be. They run to get away from
the pain of being in the wrong and feeling guilty.

The new runaways contradict the stereotype of the deprived
child fleeing from a broken home. Their stated reasons for leaving—like having abusive parents—may label them as underprivi-
leged, but American runaways are, predominantly, middle-class
children. Across the country the people who know them best
say they represent all classes, but especially the middle-to-affluent
income levels. After they leave home, these youngsters exchange
their middle-class status for that of the wanderer. If they remain
away long, they will become members of the lowest class in
society, the homeless poor.

The runaway child is a contradiction. He may hitchhike
out of state, but usually he stays within it, close to home. He
may be gone weeks, but he returns usually after a few days. He
may beg or steal or sell himself to earn a few dollars to eat, but
he can get along with the help of friends and strangers. He may
be mentally ill, but usually he is a healthy youngster who needs
a change. He may be retarded, but usually he is of average to
superior intelligence. Away from home, he becomes shrewd and
often calculating because he is gambling for the right to control
his life.

If he meets a sympathetic adult, the runaway will conceal
his self-reliance and disguise his cunning. People may take care
of him if he seems weak. He will lie about his age, pretending
to be older than he is if he thinks the police are looking for him,
or pretending to be younger to benefit from child-care services.
Although girls on the run have liberated themselves from their
families, they depend on men for protection while they travel.
Running away implies bold activity, but the runaway is uncertain about what to do and where to go. He is free in a society
that does not recognize the independence of children.

I have written this book to describe running away as a national outburst of indignation. Runaway children are angry and scared; their parents are terrified. They both know that running away is only a temporary solution to the anxieties of growing up. From the summer of 1972 when I began to investigate the runaway issue, through the spring of 1975, when I finished writing the book, I changed my idea of runaways as bold, unlucky youngsters cursed with unusual problems. I learned that the problems runaways had at home and in school with adults and friends were the same troubles all children had. While most of them endured, passively, the unique adolescence of the seventies, many others showed their confusion by leaving home. Other youngsters became silent or drunk or stoned, or, fortunately, absorbed in activity. Others became intimate with a boy, or a girl, who understood their unhappiness, a loyal friend to whom they could tell everything. In different ways, teen-agers everywhere isolated themselves from their elders.

By leaving home runaways selected the most dramatic escape, but they were unaware that it was becoming a national answer. They accepted it as private and personal. It was between them and their parents. In truth, they were crusaders for the rights of children.

I am a teacher and a parent, not a social scientist or a psychologist, but I have interviewed a number of experts. Doctors and scientists, lawyers and judges, guidance counselors and social workers have explained to me their theories. Because I have taught hundreds of teen-agers, I cannot accept the professional points of view uncritically. These general theories portray the adolescent as a social or mental problem. They do not describe the actual children we know. The runaways I will introduce are ordinary American children.

I will introduce their parents, whose names I have changed. They talked about having a runaway child as a stigma, and agreed that running away was a family matter. They defined the child's flight from home as his immediate reaction to a family fight about his behavior. Ultimately, they thought, running away was his rejection of them and their values for the excitement of freedom.

I will describe the children who are running and where they are going, and show what happens to those who try to survive in unfamiliar places and what happens to those who return home. I will explain how to search for a runaway child. Most important, I will examine the reasons for running away in America. They are as complicated as the emotions that bind a family together and as simple as unhappiness.

I will probe the questions which puzzle institutions established to serve the family: What is the meaning of running away from home? What kind of child runs? What kind of parents does he have? Psychiatry is bickering about the nature of the runaway symptom; the law as it is enforced by the police and the courts varies its attitude from case to case; the branches of government, uncertain of their responsibility, are at last aware that a national problem exists.

For three years I have watched the federal government try to determine the extent of the problem. In January, 1972, the Senate Judiciary Subcommittee on Juvenile Delinquency estimated that between five hundred thousand and one million children ran away each year. The committee had compiled the statistics by using the Federal Bureau of Investigation's annual crime reports, which contained national figures on runaways. The figure of one million children wandering around the country endangering themselves was shocking—and misleading.

Statistics are as elusive as runaways themselves. Nobody knows how many children have run from home. Probably no one will ever know exactly how many families worry about a runaway. From my examination of published police department statistics in several cities, I know that the records on runaways are inaccurate. It is impossible to keep score on people who refuse to be counted. Thousands of parents will not report their runaway to the police because they do not want their child's name

on a police record. Thousands of others, relieved that the youngster has left home, will not report him because they do not want
him back. Some do call the police, frantically describing the
child as a runaway because he has not returned home. The
youngster may have run away, but he may be visiting friends,
having forgotten to tell his parents.

Statistics released in 1974 by the University of Michigan's
Institute for Social Research suggested that the number of runaways was lower than we had believed and that the majority
stayed close to home and returned soon after the episode. The
uncertainty about the size of the runaway population continues.
A statistician from the Department of Health, Education, and
Welfare estimated it at three or four million annually! The truth
was not to be found in official statistics.

Laws throughout the country prevent an accurate counting
of runaway children. Each state varies on the legal age of juveniles. In many, a child is classified as a juvenile if he is under
eighteen; in others if he is under seventeen; in a few if he is
under sixteen. Running away from home is an offense only children can commit; that it is an offense is determined by the age
of the runaway and the state's code of juvenile behavior. The
homeless young Texan is a runaway at sixteen; a District of
Columbia resident is legally a runaway at seventeen. A New
York State child may be a runaway at fifteen and subject to a
hearing of the Family Court, but if he runs at sixteen, New York
does not consider him a runaway. However, the sixteen-year-old
Texan who reached New York could appear in Family Court if
he were caught by the police. He would almost certainly be returned to his home state under a section of the law known as the
Interstate Compact Pertaining To Runaway Juveniles.

The law treats runaway children as property. The law's
determination of who, in the current parlance, is a "child in
need of supervision" of the court depends on the parents. The
police and courts judge law-breaking children by the interest
their parents take in them. If parents want a captured runaway

returned to them, the police will oblige. They will either detain the child until his parents pick him up or they will send him home, escorting him to the airport to see that he gets on the plane. If parents want to be rid of the child, the court will try to please them by placing the youngster in a foster home or in a state- or county-run juvenile center.

In a later chapter I will show how the law is unfair to runaway children. I was shocked into realizing the inequity of the law toward youngsters by a Maryland case involving a pregnant girl. When her mother insisted that she undergo an abortion, the sixteen-year-old ran away from home. She was captured by the police and held in the county jail until she appeared in court. In an unusual decision the judge ordered the girl to submit to the abortion partly because she had shown her irresponsibility by running away from home. Although a superior court reversed the decision, the case of Mary Susan Parker, as I identify it, is an outrageous example of the law supporting the parents rather than the child who is searching for help.

The police have shifted their point of view on runaway children. Until recent years, when running away from home seemingly became a national fad, the police considered the runaway a lawbreaker. Contained in local laws are sections which define certain behavior of juveniles as incorrigible or beyond control. Smoking, drinking, the use of vulgar language, truancy, and running away from home are legal reasons to put the child in the hands of the police and the juvenile courts. Running away, whether spelled out specifically in the juvenile code or hidden in a general phrase like "offense applicable only to children," was an offense handled by the police and corrected by the court. Today, because thousands of children are running, the runaway is only a nuisance, not a lawbreaker; and police say they are performing a "public service" by listing the reported instances of missing juveniles in their files.

The confusion which besets a police department confronted with the runaway problem was exposed by the discovery of the

mass murders of young boys in Texas during the summer of
1973. For three years, from 1971 through 1973, a homosexual
and his two teen-age accomplices enticed, then killed twenty-
seven boys without being detected. Their parents had reported
the boys as missing, but the police assumed they were runaways.
So many parents had asked the police to locate their missing sons
that the Houston department believed the murdered boys too
had run away from home. They went through the motions of
aiding the parents but did not search for the boys. They recorded
their names in the missing-children reports of the juvenile division.

When I talked to Houston Police Department officials a
month after they had uncovered the bodies, I heard five thousand reasons for their neglect of these missing children. Each
year in Houston over five thousand children are reported to the
police as missing from home without permission. In a city where
serious crime is an everyday fact, the hardest-working police
department could not cope with the increasing numbers of missing youngsters. In the chapter on the Houston murders of al-
leged runaways, I will explain how the dead boys are mute
testimony to an overwhelming fact: so many children are running away from home in America that the police tend to ignore
them.

The statistics attempt to assess the size of the runaway population; the horror stories magnify the dangers of being footloose;
but the most certain symbol of the steady current of running children is the runaway house. The shelters and counseling centers
for homeless children fleck the map of the United States. In
cities and suburbs coast to coast more than eighty runaway houses
have appeared since 1968, when the Department of Health, Education, and Welfare listed four that received funding from the
Department.

The runaway house is an advocate of children's rights.
Staffed by men and women who fight for justice for children,

the house works as their protector and defender. It expands traditional services for children and coordinates them under one roof. It will act as a mediator between children and parents, as a buffer between children and the law, as a tutor to children who have acted boldly and sometimes irresponsibly by running away. When I describe one of the primary causes for a child's running away from home—the violence done to him—I will explain how the runaway house has become essential to the welfare of the community.

The attention paid to runaway houses within the community signified the seriousness of the problem locally, but the federal government remained to be convinced. The Houston murders appalled the lawmakers. Believing with the police that the children were runaways, Congress decided to investigate the issue. Government leaders woke up to the complexity of running away from home: hundreds of thousands of children were leaving their homes, illegally, to live outside of the law. Within their own states or in other states runaways were a burden on communities unable to take care of them. Workers in the social services, then the police, and, finally, the policy makers no longer viewed such youngsters as a final outburst of the rebellious youth of the sixties. As runaways became an army to be reckoned with, they became a cause unto themselves, as harbingers of social change, as the symptom of social disease. They said to lawmakers that the welfare of American children was in danger, that the changing times had eroded the stability of the family.

Except in the case of the very poor, the federal approach to family matters has been one of benign neglect. Sacrosanct, the family was beyond the intervention of the government. At times the government had advised families on the nature and care of young people with reports from the White House Conferences on Children and Youth, by platitudes issued from the Department of Health, Education, and Welfare, by scientific essays from researchers at the National Institute of Mental Health. Ten years ago NIMH conducted research on suburban runaways and published its findings in a study, "Suburban Runaways of the 1960s." No one gave it much attention.

However, in the early years of the 1970s prophetic men and women who served on congressional staffs suggested that Congress take a stand on the runaway issue. They asked senators and representatives to support a national runaway program. In January, 1972, in televised hearings, Senator Birch Bayh of Indiana introduced a proposal to aid runaways and their families. Runaway children and adult experts testified before the Senate subcommittee investigating juvenile delinquency. The purpose of the hearings was to present running away from home as a national issue which demanded the attention of the federal government. Through the senator's proposed legislation, runaways could be housed in federally financed shelters until they were reunited with their parents. Congress dallied with such legislative proposals for two years until the Houston case shocked the country—and the government—into action. Within the past year the federal government has acknowledged the new social issue with its approval of legislation aiding runaway houses. The story of the federal government's gradual intrusion into the troubles between generations is not melodramatic, nor uplifting. It is a story of ambivalence, of shifting values, and political gain. In a final chapter I will describe the government's changing policy toward runaway children.

In writing what I have learned during the past three years, I recognize that my sympathies have been with the children from the beginning. Once I had interviewed my first runaway, I was caught. She was a wide-eyed girl who left home, she told me, because her parents preferred her younger, prettier sister. Her sister "could do everything right," while she got terrible grades and even burned the soup!

The girl and her sister were both victims of the hopes and expectations of their parents. The runaway failed to measure up; her sister had assumed responsibility for both of them.

My sympathy is double-edged. It turns naturally to children who expect to be loved for being themselves; in the same moment it turns to parents who want success for their children in a time that no longer guarantees it.

As parents we have awakened slowly to the twentieth century. We were unprepared to be parents in a period which nobody has ever imagined for us convincingly. The moral quality of the era affects youngsters and figures in their plans to escape us. It is a practical time and a hedonistic one. The greatest pleasure seems the greatest good and the easiest solution the most practical. Romance has probably disappeared; certainly the romantic chapter of childhood in which running away was a brave plan has vanished. Almost one hundred years have passed since the publication of *The Adventures of Huckleberry Finn* in 1884. In 1971, we were surprised when the American Psychiatric Association published an article in its journal calling running away from home the *runaway reaction of childhood*. The psychiatrists grouped the *runaway reaction* with the major behavior disorders of adolescence.

Huck Finn represented the essence of childhood for us once. Was he a carefree boy seeking adventure, or a case for psychoanalysis? What happened to Huckleberry Finn is happening again to the children of America.

2. Runaway Girl

"Every chick I know is a runaway."—California John in Miami, August, 1972.

The first time I saw Kelly she was dancing in the Sherwood School spring festival. With other eighth-grade girls she was weaving in and out of an elaborate circle. She moved slowly in a modern dance, graceful and clumsy at the same time. Outdoors on the green lawns the dance was only part of the holiday that meant the beginning of the last month of school for all of us. From the youngest, gravest child to the silliest senior each class was performing its celebration of spring. When Kelly and the eighth-grade dancers began, we were weary.

As we watched them, someone started to laugh. A boy, restless on the backless bleachers, had opened his eyes long enough to realize the intent of spring. He passed along his knowledge to a pal and soon the whispering audience was caught by the spirit of the dance. The dancers themselves were oblivious to us. They danced seriously, propelled by the music and the patterns they were creating.

Kelly heard the laughter. She saw the boys grinning and poking at each other. Maybe she noticed the embarrassment of the girls in the audience. I don't know if she knew what was so titillating. She smiled as if she understood.

The dancers wore bodysuits that accentuated their developing breasts. They wore no brassieres and for some of the dancers the freedom enhanced their suppleness. But for Kelly the freedom was devastating. Her breasts were big and the movement of those pendulous breasts swinging free distracted us from the dance, became the dance. The boys looked in wonder as the girls moved up and down, in and out, around and around. The dance seemed endless.

That summer when she was still fourteen years old Kelly was to run away from home with a man with whom she had been sleeping all spring. She moved into his apartment and asked her sister to bring over her bikini and her stereo. Her mother was distraught because of her; her father infuriated. Her sister was glad she had left. She said Kelly was no good.

If there is a typical runaway, it is a defiant girl who refuses to reconcile the commands of her parents and the demands of her school with the image she has of herself. The image shifts with her changing body as her opinions alter with each new influence, but they are changes she is willing to accept. Her parents remain immutable and intolerable. Whatever she tries to do on her own, her mother resists and her father laughs at. Her parents disapprove of her clothes, her friends, certainly of her.

If she is a young girl, she may dye her hair and paint her fingernails. She may begin to smoke. She may try marijuana or liquor. She may skip school to see if she can get away with it. Perhaps she'll neglect her homework. Curious about the power of adults, she wonders how well she can deceive them.

She will want a boyfriend and she may get one if she is bold enough. If she has a boyfriend, her mother worries about what she's doing with him and her father hopes she doesn't get pregnant. If she and the boy see each other often, her father begins to nag at her. He may deny her permission to see the boy or forbid her to leave the house. If she disobeys her father, he is certain they are lovers. If she obeys him, she feels friendless, loveless. She has no control over her parents, but they have complete control over her.

She resents the autocracy of her parents. She must be always careful and dependable to keep herself safe and spare them from shame. She objects to being shut out of life as she thinks others live it. If she has a brother, she believes he has a life full of possibilities because he has freedom to come and go.

If she were a woman, she might agree with the feminist idea that girls are trained to be passive. Because she is young and intrigued by boys, she derides the women's liberation movement. She wants to feel like a woman, a woman who is admired by men. If she does not have a boyfriend, she worries that she's too ugly to get married. She's not even certain that she wants to marry. All she really wants to do, she thinks, is make it on her own.

If her parents continue to interfere with her, she will tolerate them no longer. If her mother shouts at her or slaps her in the face again, she will leave. If her father yells at her or refuses to let her go out, she'll go for good. She is not a child.

Running away from home is her final challenge. The act of running exposes the hostility of her parents and her own determination to end the fights. It states that their demands on her are excessive. She is unwilling to submerge her individuality to their anxiety and dismay. If she does not leave, she believes they will hound her forever.

I found Kelly living in an old house with five boys. She was no longer the voluptuous dancing girl. In her place was a maturing young woman, newly shy, recently practical, and stubborn. Kelly worried about money and the leaking roof. She complained that the landlord made no repairs. She told me the boys had tried to treat her like a servant so she embarrassed them by calling them "pigs." She insisted they help her with the housework. Kelly was eager to continue her schooling and schemed for ways to earn money without working. She explained the necessity for freedom and she spoke of the fear that went with it. She had run a long way from the private school and the suburban wealth of her parents. She had run a few miles across the city to establish her independence.

Kelly was my Huckleberry Finn. She was the child who refused to grow up straight. She was the rogue who lived by her wits. Her father had agreed to her bargain, or she to his: he would let her go if she would not threaten his reputation. Kelly used her sex as a commodity, in trade for security, for someone to look after her. She evaded the law by lying about her age, by acting and looking older. She found a school where she could learn what she wanted and avoid the academic requirements of her prep school.

Kelly defied the controversial child-rearing habits of a middle-class society and did so completely. She had attacked the authority of home, school, and law to control her life. She had run away from home and stayed away.

"Every kid should leave home," Kelly insisted. The words were her banner, her slogan for freedom. She was proud and independent.

"I've never seen a family where the kids aren't repressed. The longer they stay at home, the more repressed they get. The sooner they get away, the better they'll be. I'm not in a pigsty," Kelly said. "I'm not in a rut. It's possible."

Kelly had carried souvenirs of her childhood to the house where she lived with her boyfriend and his friends. She decorated their bedroom with peacock feathers from her father's farm. She pinned a photograph of herself playing with a dog to the wall. She put small green plants on the window ledges and her old schoolbooks on the radiator and on a table. In the living room her stereo was blaring, her dog and cat were curled in the corners by the radiators.

When I went to the house on Meridian Hill, I didn't know

I'd find Kelly. I was going to interview the runaway friend of my niece. It was a nasty, wet January afternoon. A woman had been raped in the neighborhood during the week. Formerly elegant with rows of brick townhouses, the streets looked shabby with their littered front lawns. The black and white poor lived there because the rent was cheap.

The runaway lived in a dilapidated house in a condemned row, my niece had said. The porch was sagging, and over the rotten steps was a plank so a motorcycle could be driven into the house. Nailed to the front door was a poster of Jesus Christ laughing hard. I pounded on the door and a boy answered.

"Yeah?" he asked, surly and suspicious.

"Is Kelly here? I'm Becky's aunt. We have an appointment."

He smiled then and exposed a broken tooth. I looked straight, but I had the right password. He yelled upstairs: "Kelly! It's Becky's aunt."

As I entered the house, the boys were hanging a flag displaying a marijuana plant. They were shouting, arguing about where to put the banner. They looked as if they were college boys instead of dishwashers in quick-lunch restaurants.

Kelly came down the stairs reluctantly. Since she had first told Becky she would talk to me, she thought she was stupid to agree. What good would it do her? She might only make trouble with her parents. She was tall and big-boned with long brown hair, and wore blue jeans and a shirt. I noticed her striking green eyes, but I did not recognize her. She was sixteen years old, but she looked nineteen.

"Becky said you taught at Sherwood. I went there until about eighteen months ago," she added.

I knew who she was then, Kelly Miller, the eighth grader who ran away from home to live with a man. The girl whose father was one of the best lawyers in Washington. The girl whose mother had had a nervous breakdown, whose sister had disowned her.

"Did you like Sherwood?" I asked her.

"No, I hated it. I could burn it down tomorrow."

We were off to a querulous start. To Kelly I represented the authority she had run from, and at first she seemed to me like a spoiled child who takes everything she can, then attacks because she got it.

"Sherwood makes unrealistic demands," she continued as we climbed the stairs to her bedroom. "You have to take certain courses, follow certain rules. I can't believe it."

In eighth grade, the year she ran, Kelly acted distant, even superior, she admitted. Feeling out of place at the private school, she pretended indifference, and the teachers thought she was strung out on drugs. Although she had started using marijuana when she was twelve, she did not smoke it at school. Until she left home, she used only hashish or marijuana. Later she would discover mescaline, LSD, and heroin.

Kelly was no Huckleberry Finn, but she was kin to Holden Caulfield, the disillusioned prep school boy. Still, she was too young to have run to the Haight or traveled on Kesey's bus, much too young to have roughed it with Sal Paradise and Dean Moriarty. She'd been up so long it looked like down to her. She was sixteen years old going on thirty-five, a minor character in a major novel about the collapse of American society. She hadn't left home to live with her boyfriend. Her parents knew that she and the boy were lovers. She ran when she realized her mother and father did not want her. They wanted a daughter faithful to their idea of a successful family, an attractive girl who would graduate from school and go to college. They got a rebel, a girl who refused to go along with them. They gave her everything generous parents can buy. She gave it right back to them.

Kelly had had a nursemaid and had spent weekends in the country and summers in New England. She remembered digging her toes in a sandbar, looking for shells, and gathering clams. When she was three years old, ill with fever, her mother came into her room and held her, rocking her to sleep. Her father had given her a horse to care for and they had spent days on their farm in Virginia. He built a free-flight cage for his birds and she collected blue feather tails from the peacocks. Her parents promised Kelly and her sister trips to Europe and ivy league colleges.

She promised them nothing but trouble. She caught venereal disease and ran away from home twice. She picked up boys in the park. She defied her mother and fought with her sister and father. She threatened her father with the police when he struck her.

"Three or four nights before I left home," she told me, "I said something snotty to my father and he threw food at me. Then he slugged me and knocked me down. He kicked me hard in the ass. I screamed at him, 'I'll call the cops on you.' He said he'd commit me to the courts as incorrigible, as a juvenile delinquent. I ran away when I was thirteen for three days and stayed with my boyfriend, not Ken, a different boy. Later that week I left home for good with Ken.

"That night my mother wanted me to cook dinner. I burned it and my father said, 'Can't you do anything right?' Then he asked me: 'Do you want to do just what you want when you want to do it?' 'That's exactly what I want!' I shouted. Then he said: 'You don't belong here.'"

Kelly and Ken took their money out of the bank and caught a bus to New York, then to Chicago. They traveled to a small town in Iowa where Ken's grandparents lived. They stayed with them for a month and Kelly got a job in a corn factory. She cut the black ends off the ears of corn and saved her paychecks for traveling money. Ken bought his grandfather's car for sixty dollars, and they talked of going to California, Mexico, Texas. Instead, Kelly called her parents. They said: "We want you to come home." They sent her fifty dollars and promised to tell the police she was no longer a runaway if she would return. Later, Kelly learned that her father had never reported her to the police.

"When I got home, we sat around talking, my parents and

Ken and I. They asked me what kind of life I wanted to lead. I told them I wanted more privileges and no household responsibilities. My father said that wouldn't work out. He told me I could leave home if I fulfilled his conditions. I had to find a job because I couldn't ask him for money. I had to enroll in a school and find a place to live. I had to promise to make no scandal for him."

She glanced at me to assess the impact on me of her father's new deal. I agreed that the conditions were difficult for a fourteen-year-old to meet. She smiled.

"I did it. All in one week. They didn't give me anything when I left. Not even my clothes."

Kelly went home anticipating reconciliation. Although she was a child under the law and to her parents, she had proved herself as capable as an adult. For a month she had lived safely, working, saving money, planning her independence. With the month as evidence of her maturity she returned to her parents expecting acceptance on her terms: to live together as equals. They surprised her. Recognizing the strength of her will, they used it against her, to turn her out. They wanted a daughter who agreed with them, not a commander who had defeated them.

So Kelly moved in with Ken and joined him on the job. Together they built and delivered water beds, earning enough money to pay the bills. When the company went out of business, Kelly modeled nude for private artists and commercial galleries. She became a full-time baby-sitter for women who worked. Although she had enrolled in a free school in the District of Columbia, she attended classes infrequently because of her jobs.

When I talked to her, she was back in school, studying and selling marijuana.

"I'm living off Ken and going to school mornings," she said. "I'm dealing a pound of dope to earn some money. I paid a hundred and eighty dollars for the pound. I'll sell it by the ounce. Fifteen dollars an ounce. Five dollars for a third of an ounce."

It sounded like an offer, but I shook my head. She shrugged

and complained. "People at Sherwood are so unaware of what's going on outside. They don't know what it's like not having money. That school shelters the kids."

I asked her what she thought of freedom, having known it for almost two years.

She looked at me as if I were from another world, the world of her family and the school where no experience exists without its lessons. But she was a child of that world and she answered me politely.

"Before, at Sherwood, at home, I couldn't even imagine the lifestyle I'm in now. Freedom? It's really scary. It really is. There are times when I don't think I'm going to make it anymore. I've been held up, robbed, and raped. It's been a really hard fight. I don't know how I made it."

Raped. She said the word slowly, then she hurried past it.

I asked her how it happened.

"A friend and I, another girl, went out at three in the morning to steal a flashing light from a street barrier. We were walking near the bridge on a street where Ken and I used to live. This Spanish guy came out of the woods with a knife. My friend ran and he pulled me into the woods. He held his knife on me. When he was finished, he let me go. I went home and cried all night long."

As I began to know Kelly, as she began to allow me to see beyond her indifference, I understood how much her sexual freedom troubled her. She never talked about sex, but once, showing me through the old house her free school used, she pointed to a closed room and called it *the fucking room.* Since I looked puzzled, she explained: "It's the room we go to when we want to fuck."

When Kelly talked about Ken, she did not refer to love. She talked about a relationship, which was more than the coupling of two lonely kids and less than the lifetime contract of her parents.

After I had talked to Ken one afternoon, she walked me to

the front door with him. He said to Kelly: "I told her all about our sex life."

He was teasing her, but she became anxious and stern.

I assured her that he had not.

Sex was important to Kelly. It was nothing to joke about. Sex symbolized her power over her family and it was the basis of her friendship with Ken. Sex was the weapon with which she threatened her father and dominated her mother. Her familiarity with sex set her apart from her schoolgirl friends. It had cast her out of the family and into a world where it was as valuable as dope. Sex did not cause her rebellion; in the beginning of her awareness it was her rebellion.

"It's much easier for a girl to be a runaway than a boy," Kelly told me. "She doesn't have to look farther than a block to find a pig male who wants to live with her."

Kelly found Ken in a park in Washington. He was nineteen years old, she was fourteen. Playing a cool guitar in a pretty park, he drifted into her life in the spring. She was an eighth grader in a private school, he worked as a janitor to earn his room. He was an army brat, a high school dropout, a boy who had left home when he was eighteen to travel up and down the East Coast.

"We spent the night together," Kelly had said about getting to know Ken.

Kelly and Ken were lovers with permission. Ken described the scene they played with her parents to obtain sexual privileges. Kelly refused to sneak around to sleep with him, she told him. She wanted to tell her parents, to get their permission and their reaction.

"One day we confronted Kelly's mother," Ken said. "Kelly said, 'We want to sleep together.' 'Oh, oh,' said her mother, very confused. 'You'll have to ask your father.' Old man Miller was in the house. When we told him, he was very cool about it. He said, 'You can't sleep together in this house. You're going to have to find your own love nest.' Then he throws the bummer—the responsibility trip. 'Here's what you do to enjoy it. Birth control,' he tells us." Ken enjoyed reliving the scene.

"Her father wants to control everything," Ken explained, "but so far he hasn't done anything except talk. He's a know-it-all who dominates the family; the mother's a baby. She makes unreasonable demands like a child."

Ken lighted a cigarette, pleased with his description of Kelly's authoritative father and her ineffectual mother. He measured the man who had threatened him and found him weak.

"Her father gave me cheap shit about having me put in jail," he added. "He told me I was responsible for Kelly's leaving. He tried to get me mad, make me fight with him, play his game with his rules. He judges people by how successful they are and gives his daughters a rough time if they don't live up to what he expects. Kelly's parents were always telling her she was too fat. They put both their daughters on diets so they wouldn't reflect bad on Donald Miller. 'Don't eat too much,' they told her. 'Don't eat any potatoes.' When they looked at her report card, they looked at the record of her weight. They had a fight over potatoes! Well, one night, she grabbed some things and split with me. 'We'll go somewhere,' she said. I always wanted to run away as a kid. I thought somewhere else was better.

"Boys and girls all run away and they don't know what the hell they want," Ken decided. "They really want someone to take care of them, but there's no one there. Out on the street they're desperate and vulnerable. Their expectations are crushed. Grownups are boss, no matter how crazy they are.

"I guess I wanted to get Kelly to love me and take care of me. And she wanted me to take care of her. We need each other, but it's been rough all the way. When we started living together, Kelly was in a spot where she turned all her anger on herself. She cut her wrists. We've pulled ourselves out of that hole, but we fight and threaten to leave. The only way we've been able to deal with each other is through bioenergetics."

Kelly had explained that her participation in a bioenergetics program had saved her relationship with Ken. In spite of her father's disapproval, he had signed a medical statement so she could join the therapy group. The method Miller disapproved of included exercises to break down physical blocks formed in childhood. A group of men and women lived together for three weeks to exercise and talk, to respond to each other, to feel again, to become unafraid.

"Kelly couldn't love me without having good feelings about herself," said Ken of the benefits of bioenergetics. "Now she's dealing with my problems where I used to deal with hers. I've got to catch up with her."

Ken was to begin his three weeks in bioenergetics therapy later that afternoon. He had scraped up enough money for a down payment.

"Did she tell you about the rape?" he asked.

I nodded.

"There was no rape."

I returned to the Sherwood School to interview the young women who were close to Kelly while she was growing up. Going back after a few months away from the school, I felt awkward and displaced. I was stepping back into a familiar setting that had become unnatural to me. Watching girls and boys move through their schoolday, I understood why Kelly had found the routine unreal. Being a student, like being a teacher, meant fulfilling somebody else's expectations hourly. Students and teachers produced on demand for every class.

In the library I met pretty Louisa Levin, Kelly's best friend. Kelly had told me that Louisa always understood her feelings without her having to explain them. Louisa was petite and quick, sensitive to people and willing to please them.

"I was shocked when Kelly told me she'd run from home," she admitted. "I'd been in Israel with my family all summer so I was surprised when she called to tell me. She said her father had literally kicked her out. He was always arguing with her about how lazy she was, what a big baby she was. Kelly said he hit her and called her 'irresponsible' and 'selfish.' "

Louisa was discreet in describing Kelly's parents. She called them more tolerant than her own mother and father, for they had allowed Kelly to associate with older boys. She discussed their anger when they discovered that their thirteen-year-old was no longer a virgin. Kelly—and her parents—learned from a physician that she had a mild venereal infection. Her father was furious; her mother felt "let-down," as Louisa put it. The girl had betrayed them.

"They were never calm or rational about her," Louisa said. "When they worried about her, it came out as anger."

"Kelly was reluctant to tell me she wasn't a virgin anymore," Louisa remembered.

Trying to be honest and still loyal to Kelly, Louisa hesitated to talk about Ken. His background and expectations were foreign to her.

"I think he's very, very nice," she began. "I'll be frank," she decided. "I think he's sort of dull. Oh, he's fairly intelligent, he's not a fool. But his expectations aren't really high. He has no goals. He doesn't want to get anywhere."

Louisa belonged at the private school Kelly had abandoned. Although she was bored with the routine, she was ambitious, aiming for Yale or Barnard, then a career in law or the arts. She wanted all the chances at success her parents desired for her. She could understand Kelly only up to the point where she had run away. She could not understand her staying away.

"I've thought of leaving for a few days, but nothing like Kelly's doing," she said. "When you're younger, it's easier to mix with people who are different from you. Kelly's more refined, more intelligent, more worldly than the people she's living with. After a while, she'll be bored, and she'll need more money. For the people we associated with, Kelly is unusual. What she did was very extreme."

In the private school Kelly attended from kindergarten through eighth grade, parents paid to avoid extremes. They spent thousands of dollars in tuition to insure the careful nurturing of their children. They wanted to protect them from indifferent teachers and undesirable classmates. They paid for, and received, special attention for their children.

"Everybody in Kelly's class was special," her sixth-grade teacher told me. "I loved them all, but Kelly was a leader. She was fascinating and very grownup. A friend and I took her to the movies to see *The Wanderer* and *Easy Rider*. Later I wondered if I should have let her see the drug movie, but she liked *The Wanderer* better. It was a fantasy about a kid in an enchanted forest."

By the time Kelly was thirteen the enchanted forest had become a nightmare. She was fighting constantly with her parents and with her sister. She dated boys she barely knew, one after another. She was trying drugs. She rebelled in school daily yet she turned to a young teacher for advice.

Sally Tyrone looked like a serious and thoughtful student. An unpretentious woman, she seemed uncertain too about the way the world runs. She accepted Kelly on her terms, unconditionally.

"I wasn't going to condemn her or judge her," Sally told me. "I'm not easily shocked. One time Kelly said: 'Let's put it this way, I'm not a virgin.' She wanted information on birth control and I told her where to get it. 'I know my friends would be shocked,' she told me. They would have been," Sally added.

"'I'm bored with school,' she told me. She talked about dropping out in the eighth grade. 'I want to leave.' She talked about running away, but she said her father would find her and it would be worse at home. At this point, she said, 'It's not worth it to run away.' She had nothing to run to," Sally said.

"I pushed her to go to boarding school, but she told me her parents refused to let her go. She said they needed her and her

father felt she was too young. I'm not sure she even mentioned
boarding school to her family. She thought it would cause more
trouble."

I wondered if Kelly believed then that her parents did not
want her. If she tested them by suggesting boarding school, she
might learn what she discovered that summer: her mother and
father were as unhappy living with her as she was with them.

"I remember her crying several times," Sally said. "Once,
she was all shaken up about a boyfriend's death in an auto acci-
dent. I didn't feel she knew him that well. Did she make it up?
Usually I believed her because her actions made sense based on
what she had said. She was not necessarily lying, but I wondered
what was left out."

While Ken was living with the bioenergetics therapy group,
I met Kelly for lunch at the Golden Temple of Conscious Cook-
ery on Connecticut Avenue. Operated by the disciples of an
Indian guru, the restaurant served wholesome, natural foods,
Kelly explained, that would be good for me.

"I took my parents here for dinner the other night. They
really liked it."

Kelly had moved out of the house on Meridian Hill in a
hurry. A new woman had moved in with her seventeen-year-old
brother. He and Kelly had fought, physically. He was psychotic,
Kelly said.

"I went home, but I told my parents it was only temporary
until Ken and I found an apartment. They're being nice. My
father's not saying much. My mother's been buying me clothes
and helping me sew cushions for my new apartment. She wants
me to come back. To go to an acceptable high school. To graduate. To go to college.

"I'd like to go to college, but I can't live at home. I don't
know what I'll do."

I asked her about the rape.

"I was down that day I talked to you," Kelly apologized. "I

wanted you to feel sorry for me. I wasn't raped. Just scared I would be."

Had Kelly lied, or changed her mind? Was the rape story only a plea for sympathy? When she first described the incident, she told me she cried all night after the man released her. I believed her because her anguish was real. Sex was her weapon against the hostility of her parents. Making love, she felt loved. When she realized sex was a commodity in the runaway's world, she wept for herself.

Kelly was an abused child, abused first by her family, later by the rest of us. We had not loved her enough to keep fighting with her, to prevent her from hurting herself. Her running away and her imaginary rape were the only attacks against her which she had controlled.

A peaceful girl brought us hot bowls of the good soup. Hungry, quiet people ate their wholesome lunches. We began ours.

Since we talked last, she said, she had gone back to Sherwood to visit her old friends. She felt at home, she smiled, because one of the boys she liked ran up to her and hugged her. She went to classes with Louisa and met her teachers. Everyone was being silly in math and lunch was as awful as always.

"If I were still there, I'd be a sophomore. I can't believe it."

3. Victims of Violence

"My mother hit me on the head with a log from the fireplace. She wiped the blood off her refrigerator and the floor before she gave me a towel for my head. She wants to get even with me for something. She came after me once with a knife. I beat her up and then I got out."—a fourteen-year-old runaway girl at Runaway House in Washington, D.C.

In the web of reasons for Kelly's leaving home is the violent one she shares with many runaways: a parent who hits to hurt. The tangle of cause and effect of cruelty against children is a Gordian knot with a simple strand. If parents get angry enough, they will hit the child who disobeys them. According to Kelly, whose lawyer-father hit her with his fists and his feet, she had infuriated him. She drove him wild with her nasty temper and rude language. In spite of his intelligence and his position, he beat her.

Like Kelly, other runaway children reported parents who yelled, screamed, shrieked when they were angry. If they were enraged, parents would hit, beat, strike, choke. In my interviews with runaways from wealthy families as well as from poor and middle-class families, I heard often of the sudden attack. Most of the youngsters had been struck by their parents; some of them severely; many of them frequently. They have all been shouted at, derided, deplored.

Although we may deny it, each of us is capable of hitting children. We would like to believe that only the bitter, drunken poor like Huckleberry Finn's father lose control of themselves and act like savages. But, if we are honest, we know that we can speak harshly, angrily, to a child. We can threaten. We do demand. Sometimes parents strike. With hands, belt, cord. With feet, fists, sticks, venting anger against a demanding society on children who are learning about growing up.

Yet we are appalled to read in the papers of a particularly gruesome case of child abuse. We become self-righteous at the accounts of children tied to their beds, burned, starved, broken.

Many behavioral scientists will imply that only poor people strike their children, that such violent anger is a result of poverty. They will say that the middle class talks more, hits less, and uses the psychological approach in disciplining children. They have, however, more reports of child abuse among the poor and non-white minority than from the middle class. Reporting procedures are biased against the poor because their use of public services puts them under the close scrutiny of welfare personnel.

However, adding to the shame of child care in America is the underreporting of child abuse. There are no national statistics for any class. In my interviews with runaways who were beaten and with adults who treated them, I found no correlation between a parent's economic class and the severity of the punishment he dealt out to his children. The wounded runaway is classless.

Social scientist David G. Gil claims that the entire society is guilty of abusing children. In his book *Violence Against Children* published in 1970 by the Harvard University Press, Gil proves that Americans believe in rearing their children with the rod.

Gil disagrees with the premise that the abusing parent is a deviant, personally maladjusted. He suggests that the demands society places upon its citizens and those the citizen places upon himself make him angry. Competition attacks him. Provoked to anger, one victim chooses another. The adult, subject daily to a dehumanizing society, lashes out at the child who irritates or disobeys him.

A Brandeis University professor, Gil based his analysis on national surveys of child-abuse incidents reported during 1967–1968. He used almost 13,000 of those incidents. He supplemented the surveys with 1,400 case studies from 39 cities and counties; with interviews with 1,520 adults taken across the country; with a six-month survey of newspapers and magazines published throughout America. He discovered from the public-opinion survey that nearly 60 percent of adult Americans thought that "almost anybody could at some time injure a child in his care." The survey indicated that several millions of children may be physically abused every year. A few hundred die because of the violence.

The age of abused children extends beyond early childhood. Over 75 percent of the victims were older than two; almost half of them were over six years old; and one-fifth of them were teenagers. Those facts in Gil's study supported my findings that violence against them caused children to run.

According to David Gil, for every age under twelve boys who are beaten outnumbered abused girls. However, among teen-age victims the girls outnumbered the boys. Often the police and runaway-house counselors confirmed my discovery that runaway girls outnumbered the boys, two to one or three to one.

Hurt children avenged themselves on their parents by running away from home. Some of them retaliated by stealing from them, others by hitting them back. They had learned a lesson of violence by violence.

When I began my research on runaways during the summer of 1972, I spent a week interviewing the children at Runaway House in the District of Columbia. They introduced me to violence as a primary cause of running away in America. Eve, soft-voiced and gentle, was still being beaten by her stepfather, although she was seventeen. Jody, nervous and irritable, had run away from a mental hospital where he was regularly strapped to a bed or table. Nina's father beat her because she would not obey him. Julie's mother whipped her with an ironing cord because she smoked marijuana. Big Bob's mother had a boyfriend who punched him in the face when he came home. Wonder's mother slapped her hard for disobeying her. Pammy's mother hit her over the head with a log because she ran away to meet a boy.

Violence was the sharpest connection between them. These bruised children came from homes in which two parents lived or, in the case of Bob and Wonder, where the mother was rearing the children by herself, but they all came from homes where they were hurt. Their parents' jobs ranged from that of filing clerk to government lawyer.

As runaways, they had each left home at least twice. Pammy held the record: she had run away from home seventeen times. Big Bob had gone the farthest: from Maryland to California where he lived with the Hell's Angels for a few weeks. Jody talked most like a street kid with his stories of panhandling in Washington's Georgetown and selling dirty comic books to the freaks and the long-hairs. At twelve Nina was the youngest; Eve the most innocent; Julie the prettiest, whose story of rape was terrifying. Wonder, a slender black girl, was the most well-read and the most determined to go to college. Pam, who was fourteen, was already the most cynical and the most philosophical. She traveled with a knife and, having already fought with her mother, she was not afraid to use it.

"Kids are hell, really hell," Pam declared. She was the girl whose mother had cracked a log over her head after her last runaway episode. "They want more freedom than their parents give them. They want to get out at night to see their friends and mess around. Parents nowadays should stop hanging on the kids. You can't stay just one way all your life."

Violence at the hands of their parents marked them with

bitterness and shame. They were not the battered children the
newspapers wrote about because they were old enough to run for
their lives. Their beatings usually left no permanent physical
damage, but they wore the psychological scars openly. They
were shyly withdrawn like Eve, who refused to look me in the
face. They flung themselves around the room, erratic like Jody,
whose parents betrayed him when they changed the locks on
their apartment door to keep him out. They pouted, sullen and
suspicious, like Nina, who wanted to return home to see her sick
mother. Her father had said no. They talked tough like Pam,
whose mother encouraged her husband, Pam's stepfather, to discipline by hitting.

Like Kelly, they had provoked their parents into beating
them by being rude, unruly, irritating. They had misbehaved
and disobeyed. They had embarrassed the family. They had en-
dangered themselves. They begged to be taught who was boss.

"I love my children and I use the switch," the mother of two
girls, ages twelve and sixteen, told me. "That's the way I was
raised."

"My mother thinks she's a big shot, big boss," Wonder
complained. "We fight and fuss and she hits. She says, 'Get out,'
and I go."

When he reaches adolescence, the future runaway will
chafe against restrictions more fiercely than his acquiescent
brothers and sisters. He disobeys parents' repeated demands because he feels demeaned by nagging. He wants equal time for
his point of view, and he rarely gets it. His formidable will
matches his parents' assertiveness.

As Jody explained the conflict: "When you're younger, you
seem to take the hassling because there's not anything else to do.
When you get older, you get your head together. I ran away
when I was fourteen because I was getting older and they were
hassling me more."

Jody returned home, but he left again because of attacks by
his parents. Since he could survive away from home, he refused

to tolerate the clash of wills. Even his casual eating habits riled his stepfather into striking him.

"This one time I was in the kitchen eating and my step-father said: 'Did you ask your mother if you could get something to eat?' 'No, you dumb-ass!' I shouted at him. He slapped me so hard I fell down. Who asks if he can get something to eat in his own house?"

Parents and children are inevitably contestants. Jody and his stepfather, Kelly and her father, all the runaway boys and girls are fighters, combatants in a contest which often ends in violence. Vehemence is certain if neither side understands that the change from childhood to adolescence is as grave as the metamorphosis into middle age. For the child, the intellectual, emotional, and physical transformation may start as early as twelve or thirteen.

As Pam, the philosophical runaway, figured: "Thirteen or fourteen is the hardest time for kids. It's hard on the parents to have a teen-ager, but it's even harder for the kid to be one."

During the teen-age years the child's intellectual capabili-ties expand. He is able to make connections between ideas which were alien to him earlier. His mind can leap about the landscape of ideas, but he is usually unable or unwilling to explain himself. His emerging feelings about himself, his friends, his parents also lack focus, and tongue-tie him. At home, where he is most often called on to defend himself, he can say only no or else nothing at all. He is ever on the defensive to protect his budding sense of self.

Confusing also is the physical change: the boy grows taller, the girl fuller. While parents anticipate the transformation of their children into adults, they are still surprised by its speed. The maturing body of their son delights them. They are proud of his manliness. The altering body of their daughter frightens them. Her transformation is sexual too, but it is a change full of danger for her, shame for them. In their minds her adolescence is aggravated by sex. If she has matured quickly, they imagine a sexual precocity which she may not possess. Yet to her parents her actions seem centered on sexual freedom. By setting strict curfews and refusing her permission to go out, they hope to curtail her opportunities to meet boys. Finally, they may use force to deny what has already occurred. Her body flaunts the fact that she is a woman. Her age reminds them that she is a child.

The girl who matures early physically carries trouble with her if she runs away. A premature knowledge of her sexual power, gleaned from her parents, shines from her eyes, asserts itself in the way she moves her body. Everything she says or does seems erotic. She becomes a prey for sexual adventurers. She is a natural companion for the libertines of the road.

Such a runaway was Nina when I talked to her at Runaway House in the District of Columbia. Nina was petulant and voluptuous, a presence in the house. She dressed like a gypsy queen with a long skirt and a full blouse and jangling bracelets and chains. Her dark hair was long and curly, her eyelids smudged with blue shadow, her cheeks were rouged.

She told me that she was seventeen years old, and I did not doubt her. She moved imperiously. Nina told everybody she was seventeen. Everybody believed her, she said, as she admitted that she was twelve, almost thirteen. She giggled, and I believed her. When she spoke of her parents, she pouted.

"My parents never wanted to agree with me. I never got my side. They beat me sometimes and they didn't let me go out just to make me mad. They got down on me for staying out until ten thirty even on the weekends, for the way I dressed, and for coming to Washington for the Peace Vigil."

To go with her independence, Nina had acquired a new name and Freedom, a biker boyfriend. Nina had met the nineteen-year-old biker from Atlanta on one of her escapes to Washington. He was demonstrating in front of the White House at the 1972 Quaker Vigil for Peace. He had named her Stardust and had danced with her on Pennsylvania Avenue.

"We're very extraordinary people," said Nina-now-Stardust. "We do crazy things in front of the White House like the boogie.

He asked me if I wanted to get a Quaker marriage. It's not legal. We got one at the Peace Vigil. They read a piece of paper."

Almost thirteen, Nina had run away six times from home, from a detention center in Virginia, from men who picked her up while she was hitchhiking. The boys who befriended Nina went to bed with her. The men who picked her up on the road did not fare well if they tried to force her.

"I don't like to hitchhike, but it's the only way I can get around. A friend and me were going out to Maryland. An old man about forty picked us up and offered us ten dollars apiece. We said no. He let us out, but some of them grab at you. I carry my lighter fluid and I spray it in their eyes. Then they can't see at all. It burns and their eyes are sore for a couple of days. It gives me a chance to get out of the car.

"The first time I ran away I didn't mean to. I met some guys in a shopping center near my house and they asked me to go to Williamsburg. I like to visit places," she added.

"I want to go home." Nina broke her monologue with a wail. "I want to go home, but my dad doesn't want me home. My mom does."

Nina's father was an airplane mechanic. He tried to make Nina behave, to stay in nights, to stop picking up or being picked up by strange boys, to help at home. He tried to correct her, but she began running and kept running when his rules displeased her. Finally, he put her in a detention home.

"I hated it there. There was no radio, no stereo, only cards. It was worse than school and school is boring. I can't get into it. I skipped sixty days last year, but I was never busted for skipping."

Nina wanted to go home, but she didn't want to stay there. She wanted freedom, but she was too young to handle it. She disliked school, but she was considering a boarding school that Runaway House recommended for her.

Because she was a child she expected others to take care of her. Because she used her sexuality like a woman that became difficult to arrange. She was learning how to defend herself, but she was puzzled at having to. She did not understand that her sexuality separated her from other children and from adults. It put her into limbo, where she was neglected by her family.

Nina and Kelly were runaway girls from two different classes of society. They were both outcasts in a world they explored too soon. Because of their sexual precocity they had angered, then shamed their fathers. To their fathers they represented a failure of the flesh, a failure of control. Both men had used beatings and tongue lashings to discipline their daughters. When they failed to control them, they wanted to be rid of them. The lawyer told his daughter to get out. The mechanic put his child in a detention home. The lawyer threatened his daughter with filing a petition in court against her. The mechanic refused his critically ill wife a visit from their daughter.

In Dr. Gil's study, *Violence Against Children,* the father figured as the antagonist in about 40 percent of the cases. However, when their children anger them, women can be as violent as men. In nearly 50 percent of the child-abuse incidents studied by Gil, a mother or a stepmother did the beating. Gil's statistics show that over 70 percent of the children were mistreated by natural biological parents. Only 14 percent of the children were abused by a stepparent.

Mothers who strike their erring daughters are quick to tell them why they are angry. They do not hedge with words like *responsibility* and *discipline* and *self-control* as their husbands do. They name names—*bitch, drug addict, tramp*—and tell the girls they're *boss.* When they're provoked, they grab what they can get their hands on—a stick, a log, an ironing cord. They slash and they scream.

As Julie, another girl I met in Runaway House, told me: "My mother was always screaming at me: 'You're the oldest. Set an example. What will the neighbors think, you bitch!' She beat me with an electric cord."

Julie was fair and pretty. She had the high cheekbones and

slim figure of a cover girl. When I met her, she was humming a song she was writing: "The story of my life/can be summed up in a song,/It's about a jigsaw puzzle/that was put together wrong."

The picture that emerges from Julie's jigsaw puzzle is the nightmare of every American parent with a teen-age daughter. It shows a boyfriend who starts her on drugs at fourteen and on sex at about the same age. It shows a gang of kids sitting around smoking dope in a small town where there's not much else to do. It pictures the daughter running away from home to the city after many fights with her mother. The father, a salesman, is hardly in the picture because he travels so much in his job. There are several scenes of the girl at foster homes. There's a scene of Julie's shooting up and another of a melodramatic escape from a state reform school. The puzzle is not complete: there's a rape scene which symbolizes all the violence of her life as she is forced to do what she does not want. She is sixteen years old.

When Julie ran away from home the first time, she was fifteen. Her parents filed a petition with the court declaring her *incorrigible*.

"I was their drug-addict daughter," she explained. "The guy I was going with was dealing dope and gave it to me. I've never bought drugs. It's a waste of money. I've done acid and mescaline, but I haven't done a drug now since May."

Since her parents had signed papers stating that she was beyond their control, she was sent to court when she was found. The judge gave her a warning. The second time she ran away and was caught, she was sent back home on temporary probation. After her third attempt, Julie found herself in a foster home. According to Julie, her foster mother threw a butcher knife at her. At a second foster home the woman tried to throw her down the steps. The court placed her temporarily with a minister.

"It was great," she sighed, "but it lasted only three weeks."

The court in North Side sent her to Washington's Florence Crittenton Home. The home, known for its care of unwed and pregnant girls, has a residential treatment program for girls "who have some impulse control." Julie was supposed to learn to develop that control.

"I ran away from there too," she admitted. "The girls beat me up and threatened to kill me. They said I was a hippie. I was using drugs that I got in Georgetown."

When Julie ran away from the Home, she came to Runaway House, where she stayed for several weeks. She was to live with a counselor in a commune until the House had an opening for her in one of its residences. She got tired of waiting and decided to return to North Side.

"At first it worked out okay," she said of living with her family again. "My mother wanted me to stay home and not hang around with 'D.C. trash.' Then the fighting started again. She said I was too independent for my own good. That I wanted to be eighteen. She's such a bitch. I returned to Runaway House for two days."

As Runaway House continued the process of trying to place her, she decided "not to go through the whole rigamarole again." She left for California and made it to Indianapolis. She called Runaway House and learned that there was a place for her in Second House, a group foster home.

"I came back hitching," Julie said, "and I was picked up on the outskirts of Columbus, Ohio, by the police. They put me in a juvenile-detention home. It was hell for two days. The matrons beat up a little girl who fell asleep when she wasn't supposed to. I was sent by plane to Washington. My caseworker was waiting for me at National Airport. She took me back to North Side, where I stayed at a farm, a foster home, until I went to court."

In court for the fourth time, Julie was surprised when her court-appointed lawyer recommended that she be committed to the state reform school for girls, Bon Air.

"He started adding up all the money I had cost the state in the past six months and he said it came to twelve hundred dollars. The Florence Crittenton Home cost four hundred dollars a month. Our hanging judge sent me to Bon Air, but first I spent three days in the county jail. Like a hardened criminal. Then I went to the diagnostic center for six weeks where they observed me and gave me all kinds of tests. When the psychologist talked to me, he said I was intelligent, that I had strong areas like English and science. I really like to learn."

After six weeks at the center Julie was removed to Bon Air where she stayed three weeks before running away again.

When Julie decided to run from Bon Air, she made her plans with four other girls. They would wait until evening when the girls were in the showers and in their pajamas, then they would very casually walk away from the cottage toward the briar patches, where they would hide until dark. After dark when the excitement died down, they would try to reach the highway to get a ride into Washington.

"We figured if we left when the girls were in their pajamas they'd have to change to catch us. We walked around in back of the cottage, then ran into six-feet-high briar patches. We heard the other girls and we lay in those patches for two hours until it got dark. There were rats and snakes all around us. We could hear them. We heard the state police cars and saw the spotlight going through the woods. I decided that since they were expecting us to run through the woods our best chance was to take the main road out of Bon Air to the highway. We were scared, but that's what we did. We just walked down that road to the highway. We split up then, two of us going one way, three the other. A car came along and two really nice guys from West Virginia picked us up. We were lucky because the next car belonged to the state police."

Julie's luck did not last. Dropped off by the West Virginians, Julie and her friend got a second ride and the escape melodrama turned into a horror story.

"This dude picked us up. He said he'd take us into D.C., but he had to stop at his house first to call his friend. He took us to his house and called him. Then he whipped out a gun. His

friend came over. The dude was about twenty-one, his friend was
older. They got into a hassle about whether they should do it to
us or not. I don't think the older guy wanted to. He held the gun
while the dude raped me. He got me down on the floor and did
it to me. My friend was watching and screaming.

"It was so different," Julie said. The rape was not her sexual
initiation. Then, she said: "I was pissed."

That night the two men took the girls to Washington. Julie
returned to Runaway House. She remained there as the counselors worked with the courts to gain custody of her. Now she
acts as a junior counselor to other runaways, listening to them,
telling them what happened to her, hoping that they will be
luckier.

They were articulate children, these runaways. Perhaps
they had learned the hard way that it hurts less to talk than it
does to suffer in silence. They had shown me their wounds and
had talked about the others, psychological and physical, which
they had taken. They had described what they had done to
retaliate, what they planned to defend themselves. They were
living in a world where the cunning, the shrewd, the quick survive, and they had learned the rules from their parents. If you
are hurt, hurt back. If love fails, hate. If freedom is thwarted,
leave. Julie and Pam and Jody, Nina and Kelly were victims of
the war between parents and children which nobody wins.

Runaways whose parents beat them should not be forced
to return home. Nobody of sensibility will disagree with that
simple conclusion. Yet, daily, adults in authority are returning
runaway children to the families they have escaped from. The
aim of institutions concerned with runaways as a social problem
is to reunite the children with their parents. It is a small matter
if the child prefers not to go back. If the parents want him home,
home he goes. The purpose of the social services is to remove the

youngster from a seemingly dangerous situation like the street and return him home where, it is assumed, he will be safe and kept sound. The police work toward that end when they find a runaway; they use the Interstate Compact on Runaway Juveniles to extradite children whose parents have filed a petition in court for their return. Public agencies like departments of health and social services are determined to reconcile families; family and juvenile courts act for the good of the community by insisting on the unity of the family. The basis of the Runaway Youth Act, which was approved by Congress, is to reinforce the family. Tradition insists on the sanctity of the family. The institutional response to unconventional runaway behavior is to return the child to his rightful place, his home.

But the countercultural by-product, the runaway house, puts the child's preferences before those of his parents. The child comes first in the philosophy of American runaway-house staffers because they have seen too many abused children to accept the idea that parents know best. While they realize that many children run only as a temporary relief from a disturbing situation, they also know that the repeating runaway is a child who needs more than a vacation from routine pressures. He is a child who is unwanted at home. His proof is the bruised face, the welts on his arm, the healing wound in his scalp. He needs an advocate and he has heard that the runaway house will help him.

The runaway-house movement began in the late 1960s when children left home to emulate their older road brothers. In 1966 Huckleberry's for Runaways opened in San Francisco; in 1967 in Boston Project Place started; in 1968, during the summer of Resurrection City, Runaway House began in Washington. In places popular with traveling youngsters because of their mecca mystiques, unorganized hostels called *crash pads* sprang up. Some were what they seemed—a room to sleep in for a night or two. Others were a seduction, an offer of food and bed in exchange for the child's cooperation in selling drugs or in prostitution.

As more and more children used running away from home as the answer to their problems, many communities became pressed to house them and feed them. Sympathetic ministers would open the basement of their church or find room in the parish house. College students in university towns offered space. Finally, when communities realized that running away was not a fad, they began to support the respectable, shoestring housing. Through the cooperation of church and local activists or through the coordination of the social services, shelters for youngsters on the run gained financial and emotional backing.

The houses were staffed with young people who remembered how difficult it was to be fifteen years old; the runaway house became the homing ground for many children who had no place to go. It also became a center for medical, legal, psychological assistance. In the runaway house the fleeing child would find a bed, food, friends, and good listeners. He met other youngsters whose troubles were worse than his own. He found counselors who heard him out, then asked him what he wanted, and how he expected to get it. Children found something new in runaway houses—respect and acceptance.

The first shelter for runaways I visited was Runaway House in the District of Columbia. During 1973 Runaway House had sheltered 707 children. By early 1974 the total number of runaways who had stayed there since it began was 4,000. Up to 1974 the house operated on an annual budget of about $25,000 which came from private foundations and individuals, churches, social-service agencies and federal money. Three full-time staff counselors earned $75 a week. Several volunteers worked part-time as counselors. With the new federal emphasis on runaway programs the D.C. residence received a grant of $47,500 from the National Institute of Mental Health in June 1974.

Runaway House is a three-story residence near DuPont Circle, a small green park in a busy midtown section of Washington. It is in a mixed neighborhood—both black and white, both disrepair and elegance. The house was comfortable and bright:

tie-dyed curtains at the windows, newly varnished floors. Four-letter words painted on the walls formed rhymes and revelations: *Don't change Dicks in the middle of a screw/Vote for Nixon in '72. I fucked two girls and I didn't get caught. We are the children our parents warned us against.*

They are: A girl sitting on top of the piano. Another doing macramé. Another lying with her guitar across her stomach.

I sit in the living room, watching, waiting to talk to Jay, the counselor in charge. I have been in and out of the house for a week and the runaways accept me by ignoring me.

A handsome blond boy flicks his cigarette ash in a grocery bag and asks one of the girls: "Are you really going to California?"

Another boy, jumpy and frightened-looking, comes in spooning a bowl of cereal into his mouth.

"Lunch!" the girl on the piano shouts. "Give me some. I haven't had anything to eat all day."

The girl in the leather jacket asks someone to sign her autograph book. She wears green fingernails and calls herself Sunshine. A camera hangs around her neck. She's going to California with Pammy, the hungry girl.

Pam jumps down from the piano and slides across the room. She kisses the wall. "Oh, Runaway House, I love you!"

She hears her song on the radio. "Be quiet, everybody! I've waited two days for this song."

Everyone is quiet. When the song is over, Pammy announces: "We're off to California! Let's find Wonder," she says to Sunshine, "and say good-bye to Jay and go."

They climb the stairs to Jay's room on the second floor. They knock quietly and he lets them in.

"Are you going to California?" he asks them.

"Yes, do you have a list of crash pads?"

"You'll have to copy them from the runaway book."

Pammy, dimpled and excited, hoists a laundry bag to her shoulder. Bottles clink together.

Jay hugs them both and wishes them luck.

"Send me a postcard when you get there. Or better yet, send me a postcard when you cross the District line."

They leave, smiling good-byes, and he notices that in their hurry they forgot to write down the addresses of runaway houses.

"They won't make it," he told me. "They'll be picked up once they leave the District."

Later, the next week, I will see them again. Pam and Wonder came back to Runaway House, anxious for its help. They told me they had reached Pennsylvania, where Sunshine remained.

Referring to Pam, the constant runaway, and to Wonder, the black girl who had run from a detention center, Jay said: "We get our hard-core runaways in the summer. Maybe it's easier to run from reform schools and mental hospitals then. In the other months we get more kids who run away from their homes. Last February when report cards came out in Virginia we had thirty-three girls in the house one night!"

Jay was a surrogate parent and a good friend to runaway children. Before our interview, he had gone to the District's Receiving Home for Children where he visited a young girl who had been staying at the house until the police arrested her on the street for running away. Placed in the home and locked up overnight, she had asked Jay to come see her. He had also begun to arrange Nina's placement in a church-run boarding school. He had talked to a young man who thought he wanted a job in Runaway House and he had interviewed a new client, a suburban runaway, who arrived that afternoon. Although Jody had accused Jay of hassling, he had supervised the boys as they cleaned their dormitory.

"Jody gets along with the women better than he does with me," Jay smiled.

After Jay graduated from Georgetown University, he accepted the counselor's job in Runaway House for two reasons. He wanted to work with teen-age children and he needed time

to decide his future. His experiences at the house were so reveal-
ing that he had enrolled at Georgetown University Law School
for the fall term. He was convinced that injustice toward children was common.

As runaway-house counselors everywhere have told me:
"The kids are being screwed! They have no rights."

Runaway-house staffs have learned that the rights of children in trouble are secondary to the wrongs they may have committed. Controlling children is the aim of the community, not
protecting them or respecting them, the counselors say.

Former war protestors and political campaigners, many runaway-house workers are activists who are using their energy and
passion to reform institutional attitudes about children. In my
visits to several runaway houses, I have always been impressed
with the dedication of the young men and women who staff
them. They are sensitive about children and cynical about their
chances. They are realists in the battle for children. In the
United States today there is no other organization besides the
runaway house which fights daily for children's rights.

The *National Directory of Runaway Centers,* the runaway-
house list Jay referred to, is published by the National Youth
Alternatives Project of Washington, D.C., and is the runaway-
house bible. It sets forth the philosophy of the houses, stating that
the main goal of the runaway house is not to reunite families but
to help a youngster understand why he is running, then to find
alternatives to living at home for the child who cannot return
safely. The immediate purpose of the house is to give the child
shelter. If it is a counseling center only, it will place the runaway
in a foster home temporarily until his case can be resolved.

Runaway-house staffers advise the child to reach decisions
about his future. Perhaps it is obvious to both counselor and
youngster that he will return to his family. Then, the house will
serve as a mediator to open discussions between angry parents
and upset child. If it is possible and safe then the house will work
with the family to effect a reconciliation.

The counselor will act as an advocate to help the runaway. He will deal with his parents, the law, and the social-service organizations of the community. If the child wishes it and the parents consent, the house will try to place him in a foster home, a group home, a boarding school, or in private living arrangements. If the parents refuse to relinquish guardianship of the child, the runaway house or counseling center will ask lawyers to assume the legal problems. If the child is ill, the house will call on doctors to cope with medical or psychiatric problems.

Over the past several years residential houses such as Washington's Runaway House, Huckleberry's in San Francisco, Boston's Project Place, and Covenant House in New York City have increased their services to running children. Two houses which began in the early seventies, Focus in Las Vegas and Pathfinders for Runaways in Milwaukee, are now two of the busiest centers. Within the past two or three years smaller cities like Rochester, New York, and Grand Rapids, Michigan, have opened runaway centers; suburban areas like McLean, Virginia, and Hyattsville, Maryland, are providing runaway shelters for children who leave home. There are eighty-one runaway houses across America, but according to the 1974 edition of the *National Directory of Runaway Centers,* "there are still 21 states which have no centers to house runaways and no programs to provide short-term housing."

The houses face their own problems from parents and the law. According to state and local laws, a runaway house must inform parents of a child's whereabouts and ask their permission to house him. If they ignore that regulation, they may be liable for harboring a minor. If the counselors do not comply, they endanger the trust the house has accrued in the community. If they do comply, they may jeopardize their work with the child.

If they refuse the parents entry to the house, as many do, the police may appear with a search warrant or a court injunction against them. If they allow the parents to come in, the child may leave by the back door. As Pam and Wonder and Sunshine did, children even run from runaway houses. Victims of violence, they distrust adults. They are also victims of the runaway culture, a way of life which many adolescents share and which the parents of runaways will not understand.

4. The Runaway Culture: Sex, Dope, and a Declaration of Independence

"Typically, she [the runaway] will be gone two weeks and will have had a ball, and you can put it down as almost certain that she experimented with sex or drugs, and usually both."—Julie Cochran, assistant to the chief of police, De-Kalb County, Georgia, August, 1973.

The public imagination suffers from time lag. Titillated or shocked by the lives of runaways, imagination lingers on details and denies the metaphor: the runaway explosion dramatizes the diffusion of new forces in adolescence. Growing up today pits the traditional rites of passage against the newly avowed respect for all men, regardless of race, color, creed, sex, or age. The youngster's desire for sexual knowledge and the teen-age acceptance of drugs chafe against his status as child. He is confronted with making decisions that end his childhood prematurely. In many places how a child handles an invitation to smoke dope determines his acceptance by the group. Smoking a marijuana cigarette, like drinking beer, is his gesture for recognition. At other times, in other places, stealing—and deceiving salesclerks and shop owners—becomes a proof of cleverness. Drinking, then

74

bragging about the amount, continues as a test for manhood. Spending the night with a friend may begin the child's sexual initiation.

Whether they submit to these conditions of adolescence or choose to delay them, children are faced with questions. *What do I do* becomes compounded with *how do I get away with it.* The ancient dilemma is theirs: knowledge in the form of experience is forced upon them whether or not they want it. The apple has become a joint, a tablet, a birth-control pill, and they learn at their peril. If they join the adolescent adventurers, they become members of a fugitive world where what they do is against the law. Like criminals they lead a double life: the private, secret life of their teen-age friends and the public role of school and home.

Meanwhile, parents guess at the details, but they are reluctant to follow their surmises to conclusions. Perhaps they prefer not to abandon their simple vision of childhood. Perhaps they cannot imagine that their children have absorbed the freakish counterculture and have made it theirs. As parents, they worry about sex because the dimensions of sexuality have expanded. They include the idea, popular everywhere, that sex is cool and pregnancy no longer a danger. The pill, available for the asking, is ubiquitous. Bisexuality, publicized into fashion, is intriguing. The easiness of hitchhiking is a constant threat to safety. As dangers increase, parents tend to protect youngsters. In their zeal, they may become repressive. One father told me, talking about his daughter, that he supports detention, "holding them tight," at home or in an institution. A mother explained, "We believe in strict discipline. We use the belt if it's necessary."

Children who run away are not libertines or cultists. They're running from a society that refuses to admit the gravity of adolescence. Adolescence has become a period of pessimism. One of my students, a seventeen-year-old girl, told me: "Nothing is hidden from us. With the breakdown of moral codes, children are exposed to almost everything existent from pornography to violence. There's a new philosophy that says everything in life is educational and nothing should be kept from a child. We see the future as pessimistic, not optimistic."

The public must accept two facts: the life of many adolescent Americans is inescapably linked to drugs and sex. And, these adolescents believe that they deserve the rights of adult Americans to be heard, then treated fairly. When they introduce these facts of life at home, their parents may smell revolution in the air.

To adults the children's revolution is philosophical, not practical. To children the revolution is real. It is a daily fight to alter their position, a matter many are unwilling to leave to chance or time. Runaways frequently desert their homes to protest unfairness.

Many parents of runaway children deny discussion and reject compromise; they insist and demand. They cut off privileges and they punish severely. The child who runs retaliates in kind.

A very pleasant and attractive twelfth-grade girl whom I taught last year described her repeated runaway episodes as power plays. In an essay, she wrote: "The first few times I ran because of my parents' refusal to show any interest in my thoughts and experiences. Soon it became a way of showing them I didn't care where I was and that I could handle myself. Running was a way of arbitrarily punishing them as they did me. I was flaunting my independence against their readily accepted ivory-tower values. I forced my parents to try to understand me and ask me what I felt."

Her parents finally heard her and she stayed home for longer intervals. When I knew her, she was to graduate with her class in the spring and attend college in the fall. I would never have guessed that she had been a runaway if I had not asked my students to answer a few questions in writing. In a quiet way she was gracious and self-confident and not distrustful of adults. She spoke tentatively, but she was not afraid to voice her opinions.

Running from home does not signify an irreparable breach between generations. Yet, runaways are evidence that parents have failed to come to terms with modern history and old-time biology. The evolutionary process belongs in the books, they think, not in the home.

In August, 1972, during the Republican Convention, I went to Flamingo Park in Miami Beach to find the runaways who believed in independence and wanted to change the system. I was sure that in those tents, in those packs of kids who shuffled through the dust of the park, there were young people whose politics differed from their parents' and they had left home to prove it. The park was a county carnival of causes and I expected to meet runaways lined up in front of the tent of their choice.

I was wrong. I met reformed runaways who had returned home. Like my student, their runaway experience was past, probably for good. Their adventure was important to them, but it had served its purpose. It had alerted their parents to their dissatisfaction and confusion. They worked within the system now rather than outside it.

When I reached Flamingo Park, I was new to the cause. First I tried the Women's Liberation tent, where I saw a young woman lettering a sign. Within the tent her sisters were having a consciousness-raising session.

"We don't have any runaways staying with us," she said. "You'd think the girls would come here, but they don't. They find some fellow and shack up with him. There may be runaways in the park, but they're not here. Try the big meeting," she suggested.

"Hey!" she called after me. "The best thing for you to do is get a fellow with long hair to go around with you. Then maybe the others will tell you something."

I went to the morning meeting and saw hundreds of kids

hunching together trying to hear the speaker. The meeting had moved to the shade away from the sound truck, and nobody could hear anybody. The camp directors were shouting out orders for the day, where to go and what to do to hassle the rich at the Fontainebleau.

When I asked three or four different campers if they were runaways, they were suspicious or irritated.

"Listen," a girl said. "I'm here for some real serious political action."

I tried the information table of the Miami Conventions Coalition where I lined up behind a boy who wanted to know if Jesus was really a Jew. He thought the people at the Jews for Jesus tent were putting him on.

"You can try the Zippies," a harried organizer told me. "They're younger and wilder than the other groups. If there are runaways here, they'd be with them. Or with the American Pot Party."

The American Pot Party was stationed under the shade of the biggest tree in the park. Boys were stretched supine on the limbs of the tree. Others reclined under it. They agreed that runaways would be crazy to come to Flamingo Park.

"It's the last place I'd come," a boy said, hugging his shade.

"Maybe there's one runaway in the whole park," his buddy Jerry said. "The police are checking the ID's of kids who're trying to get down here. A lot of people never made it."

Jerry had made it to Florida with the Zippies. He was cadging a joint from a friend under the big tree when I came up to them. He told me he was eighteen.

"Runaways are afraid of the pigs," he said. "I was stopped twice myself in Florida, once for hitchhiking, another time for loitering. The pig said to me: 'I'm gonna remember your face so when I see you at the other end of the stick, I'm gonna work you over.' Yeah, I expect to get gassed, clubbed, jailed."

After Jerry got his joint, he agreed to walk me over to the Zippies. I asked him why he'd come to Miami Beach.

"Look, I'm really only sixteen, but I'm not a runaway. My mother knows where I am. She doesn't care. I ran away last year during school, then when I turned sixteen, I dropped out. I went back to school in Illinois, and they suspended me for smoking a cigarette. The whole damn school was in the middle of a race riot and I was busted for smoking a cigarette!"

In March Jerry had run away to California from his home outside of Chicago. With him he took his girlfriend, who was on probation for running away. The girl had spent the night with Jerry and when her parents found out, they disowned her. They planned to put her in a home for girls.

"We split to California, to L.A. I had money for two bus tickets and I got a job out there. We broke up in L.A. and I moved into Hollywood. I called my parents after a couple of weeks. They were upset, but they said, 'Take care.' I had some money to live on from my father, my real father. He was killed in Korea. But I returned to Illinois in a month."

After completing the eleventh grade, Jerry dropped out of school and left home for Madison, Wisconsin, to join the Zippies. He wanted to belong to a politically active group.

"History's being made every minute, and I want to be part of it," he said. "Here at the park the movement's not what I expected it to be. There's a lot of apathy, but our presence means we'd like to change things."

The young activists at the Zippie tent claimed a runaway named Judy. One went looking for her while the others passed around a joint and talked about their action at the Fontainebleau Sunday evening. They had helped block off the entrance to the hotel where a money-raising dinner was scheduled. Chanting, "Keep the rich out," they managed to stall traffic and force some of the rich to climb a high fence to get to the dinner on time. They tussled with irate Republicans and brought out the National Guard.

"It was a beautiful demonstration of a people's victory," a young woman gloated. Her name, she said, was Honey and she didn't want to talk about it, but when she was sixteen she was a runaway and a hooker.

"I had to eat," Honey said.

Suddenly someone shouted: "Rip-off!"

A man raced past the Zippie tent. Two dozen campers chased him, shouting at him to stop.

"They want to kick ass," Jerry said.

"Stop running through the camp!" another, older organizer screamed.

"That's what they used to shout in my high school," Honey said. " 'Stop running through the halls!' It's just like high school."

The Zippie returned without the runaway. "Maybe she split," he explained. "We try to discourage runaways because they're security risks for anyone who puts them up. Everyone is very political here and runaways are not mature enough."

I left Jerry and Honey and the helpful Zippies to continue my search. I joined the gawking tourists, strolling through the park, watching the protestors wake up.

Past the Vomitorium and the Lobotomy Machine, home exhibits to capture the attention of the media, was the Gay Alliance tent. Out front two boys were discussing their high.

I stopped to ask them if they were runaways. Sure enough, when they were younger, they had run and discovered sex.

Jimmy, a handsome, bare-chested sixteen-year-old, had run away from his wealthy North Miami parents when he was fourteen. "I didn't go far, just to a friend's house. The friend, a girl, was having a gay party, girls in one room, boys in another. I wanted to sleep with the chicks, but they made me sleep with the boys. I got raped, darling," he said, sounding like a young boy's idea of a big-city homosexual.

"How does the song go? 'You made me love you, I didn't want to do it,' " he crooned.

"You can't fight the feeling," his friend and lover Rick said.

Wearing a towel around his head and zinc oxide on his nose, Rick looked like a desert sheikh or a Miami Beach lifeguard. He ran away from his home in North Carolina when he was twelve. He hitchhiked to Orlando, where the police picked him up and held him in a detention home. When he told them his name, they called his mother, who came for him.

"My mother has this nasty habit of marrying rich old men," Rick said. "She's done it four times. The third one was pretty nice though."

"My parents wouldn't let me go to a Janis Joplin concert," Jimmy explained. "They were afraid I'd get mixed up with dope. I ran away and the only dope I'm mixed up with is my lover and a little pot, darling."

Jimmy calls himself *gay* and says his parents don't know about him and Rick. "They're very strict Jewish parents and very nosy, darling. They would kill me if they thought I was gay. I'm very butch at home. I'm bisexual really. I'd like to marry a black girl and have two children."

"I was going to leave home again a few weeks ago and I told my mother," Rick added. "She asked me to give it another try and I did. I would like to continue my ballet lessons. I want to be another Nureyev. My mother knows I'm gay. She's a Cherokee Indian and we believe that life is a unification process."

" 'Life is a cabaret, old chum,' " Jimmy sang to Rick. " 'Come to the cabaret.' " He flung his hips out, imitating a saucy Liza Minnelli.

"You're too fem to play Liza," Rick protested.

"All I need are the breasts," Jimmy insisted, cuddling up to him.

He looked at me and smiled. "I haven't run away since I was fourteen. I've got my lover now."

Jimmy stuck his fingers in Rick's mouth. Rick nibbled at them. They began to pet each other and I moved on.

Jimmy and Rick were characters out of a farce. They were comics in the theater of the absurd, and the Gay Alliance tent, Flamingo Park, Miami Beach, was the perfectly right, perfectly bizarre setting for their mock passion. They were foils for each other. Rick was melodramatic, serious, the straight man to his friend's clowning; Jimmy was high-spirited, making fun of himself and enjoying his outrageousness.

For them running away from home was one piece of the costume of adolescence; the other parts of the whole were the twin masks, sex and dope. Dope and sex, interchangeably sly and smiling, glum and morose.

The boys were smart enough and vain enough not to upset their minds or their bodies with destructive drugs like heroin or the amphetamines. To be different, they chose to dally at homosexuality. They assumed the poses and the nuances of real actors; they imagined a partnership of the sexy Minnelli and the soulful Nureyev. They were entranced by play. They reminded me of little boys dressed up as cowboys, trying to outdo each other with their cleverness. I didn't take them—or their sexual ambiguity—seriously.

They wanted a special identity and they took one from the gay-liberation movement. The homosexual was proclaiming his right to be seen and heard after years of discrimination. He found courage in the freak scene, the colorful counterculture, where the ambiguous motto "Do Your Own Thing" didn't fool anybody. Sex was alive among the renegades. Now everybody was getting the news, high school teachers and high school kids, Catholic priests and United States senators, closet kings and queens. Sex was liberated, and the children were curious. The joy of sex was public property.

After the Houston murders of 1973, parents of runaway boys worried that their missing sons might be victims of the homosexual killers. Before Houston, they discounted sexual rebellion as a reason for a boy's leaving. They may have wondered whether their son had made his girlfriend pregnant, but they never mentioned his seduction. The parents of runaway girls, however, always spoke to me about their fear of sexual assault.

They veered away from their suspicion that the girl was out making it with a boy she met at McDonald's. They dreaded the idea of her being raped and wondered if she knew enough about birth control to keep from getting pregnant. A mother whose fourteen-year-old was missing for a week said: "After three days I thought a maniac had raped her and thrown her into the woods." Her father said: "She's pregnant. I know she's pregnant." The girl told me she was really angry at her father for thinking that; her mother knew she had her period when she left. She didn't have a boyfriend. She had run away because of a punishment she didn't think was fair.

In the minds of newspaper readers the road life of the runaway is filled with sexual excess. Newspaper and television reports underline the sexual situations runaways can encounter. Male or female prostitution. Orgiastic communes and crash pads. Sexual license for all comers. In an interview for *The National Observer* Julie McCall Cochran, assistant to the chief of police in DeKalb County, Georgia, talked about the sexual behavior of runaway girls. Mrs. Cochran, a former investigator in the youth division, reported that most of the missing children were white girls.

"I think the reason more runaway boys aren't reported missing is because, frankly, parents don't have to worry about their sons losing their virginity. This particularly terrifies fathers.

"But when we start checking on a missing girl, we usually find another missing girl, perhaps someone she has a phys-ed class with, or some other place where their paths crossed. Maybe the other girl thought she had a good reason to leave, so she says to her friend, 'Come on, there's an apartment on Buford Highway where we can crash! They often leave with no money, no extra clothes.

"Typically, she will be gone two weeks and will have had a ball, and you can put it down as almost certain that she experimented with sex or drugs, and usually both. Occasionally she'll rip up her clothes on the way home so she can yell 'rape' if she thinks her father is excessively angry. She has almost always been molested, quote and unquote, but rarely against her wishes."

To viewer and reader the dramatic news story of the runaway sets the norm; the life of a runaway may seem an orgy, or a wild story of perversion. The young women around Charles Manson were identified as runaways. At first the twenty-seven boys killed in Houston were described as runaways. Even the dignified United States Senate exaggerated the sex life of runaways to call attention to legislation to help them.

In 1972 the Senate put runaway children on the witness stand before television cameras. They appeared during the Senate Judiciary Committee investigation of runaway youth by the juvenile delinquency subcommittee. Several witnesses testified about the pressures on runaways to prostitute themselves to earn their room and board. There was this exchange between Sen. Birch Bayh, chairman of the subcommittee, and a young man from Greenwich Village who searched for runaways:

Senator Bayh: "Let's envision an imaginary fourteen-, fifteen-, sixteen-year-old girl or boy that reads about the glamour of the Village and runs away to the Village and is initiated into one of these crash pads. What has it been your observation will happen to that girl or boy?"

Jerry Cagiao: "At first they will be taken into the crash pad on a friendship basis; for like two or three days, they will feed them, take care of them. But then after that, they say, well, you have got to go out and sell drugs and prostitute yourself to support the crash pad. So they go out and sell drugs or a girl prostitutes herself."

Later the senator questioned a fourteen-year-old runaway girl who lived with a sect of Satan believers in Phoenix. Trying to determine whether she was used sexually, the senator asked her: "Did they ever order you to do things or make you do things that you didn't want to do?"

Miss B: "No."

Senator Bayh: "Or felt you had to do?"

Miss B: "They would try to talk me into it, but they wouldn't make me do it."

Certainly a girl exposes herself to casual sex when she runs away. Maybe she pretends she's running away for sexual freedom, but she'll discover that the road is not a speedway to love as she imagined it. And, she will not necessarily or automatically agree to sexual relationships unless she thinks they are fair trade for a meal or a room. The crude road expression "a bed for a bang" suggests the economic necessity of sex on the road.

"Once a girl gets into the runaway culture it is difficult for her to avoid sexual relationships," a psychiatrist told me. "She may need to pass her body around to survive.

"However," he emphasized, "even runaway girls will respond to family values by *not* becoming sexually involved."

Most of the runaway girls I've talked to knew boys at home or met boys on the road with whom they fell in love. Most proved their love by having sexual intercourse. Many of them spoke of it indirectly by saying, "I met this guy, and he's really cool and we make it together." Others were blunt: they had *fucked* or *screwed*. Some caught a venereal disease. And, of course, some of the girls were still uninitiated sexually. Like the fourteen-year-old whose father feared a pregnancy, there are many children who return home virgins.

One day I visited the psychologist of a suburban Maryland high school to hear his ideas on runaway children. I wanted to discover whether his students in a large public high school were more or less sophisticated about drugs and sex than those I knew in a smaller, private school. He confirmed my opinion that runaway or not, public school or private, high school and junior high school students were the Walter Mittys of society.

"What about sex?" I asked him.

"Everybody's into it," he said at first. But as he talked, he modified his pronouncement. Sociable children, youngsters with many friends, had more opportunities for sexual behavior than

shy, withdrawn children. It isn't the quiet child we worry about
these days, he laughed. It's the active, outgoing youngster who
gets around and knows a lot of people.

"Socially active kids are into more sexual behavior than
kids who keep to themselves. For active kids sex follows a pro-
gression," he explained.

He described the ludicrous dilemma of the boy and girl who
fall in love and want to have intercourse with each other. At
first they're timid. Then, they make love, but they're still nervous. They are not afraid of each other or of getting caught.
Rather, they fear pregnancy and the possibility of abortion. They
talk about it and they decide she will go to the school nurse.
She does and the nurse prescribes birth-control pills. The girl
continues to take the pills and love her man until the romance
is over. Then, she frets and comes to the school psychologist for
advice. Should she stop taking the pill, or should she continue?
She might meet somebody tomorrow. She might fall in love over
the weekend. What does the psychologist advise?

He smiled. "I ask her what's involved in the decision, what
are the consequences. She may meet somebody soon, she says.
She doesn't like the idea of abortion. Abortions are hard to deal
with. A fifteen-year-old girl has a lot of guilt after undergoing an
abortion. Often, girls run away from home to get an abortion.
They 'do a runaway' to cover their absence. They feel it's
better for their parents to think they've run away from home
for a few days than to tell them they're going to the city for a
saline solution."

For adolescent children the sexual revolution has arrived.
As a teacher, I have watched the high school sexual scene for
twelve years. In a girls' boarding school where I taught in 1963,
the girls could not go downtown shopping without a chaperone,
who was usually a house mother. The boys who wished to call
on the girls had to be approved by the girls' parents. If they received approval, their names were placed on a list. This list was
always checked before the telephone operators put their calls

through to the dorms. Security was tight. At the iron gates to the school, guards checked all cars, going and coming, for contraband boys. A beautiful southern girl evaded the prohibitions on her sex life practically. She left regularly for weekends with her lover. The man, thoroughly approved by school and parents, was her father's friend.

Four years later I was teaching in a private co-educational school. The class of 1967 was thrilled by the first class marriage in June, soon to be followed by the first class baby. In 1970 the seniors were collecting money for the first class abortion. In 1971, preparing a biology project, students were conducting a survey on the sexual life of the school. I wish I had the results, but the project was stopped because the surveyors were reprimanded for the use of words like *fucking, screwing, balling*. ("Well, what do you call it?" the dean of girls was asked.)

Is *everybody into it* as the psychologist said?

Imaginatively, yes, everybody's into sex through the activities of friends and classmates. The romances, pregnancies, abortions, early marriages of some feed the imagination of children whose experience is based on conjecture. What would I do if this happened to me? Would I keep the baby, get an abortion, get married? How would I handle it if my girl got pregnant? Would I marry her or pay for the abortion? Would we run away and live together? Pregnant girls do run away with their young lovers; or they run alone to an abortion clinic. Some will defy their parents and attempt to keep the baby. Many will marry pregnant.

Pregnancy among teen-agers is increasing, as Zero Population Growth reported in a 1974 survey. One in ten teen-age girls has a baby and 17 percent of all American births are to teen-agers, fifteen to nineteen. ZPG, the national organization which supports reducing the present rate of population growth, stated that half of all teen-age brides are pregnant at their weddings.

Young girls will run away to look for boys. They want to be where the boys are. In Ann Arbor on a winter afternoon at

Ozone House, the runaway shelter, I met red-haired Katie, a lover of good times, free dope, good-looking boys, and the excitement of the road. Only after her fifth runaway did she admit that she was becoming weary of the hazards of illicit travel.

"The first few times I ran away, I thought it was great, but it gets old. You're going someplace new and meeting people. Then you start getting tired of doing it. You get hungry and cold. You worry about a place to stay. You worry about getting busted. I always think the police are looking for me."

At Ann Arbor's runaway shelter, I found her, wrapped in a blanket, a fourteen-year-old girl from Florida. The heat was not working, and people coming in and out did not close the doors. She shivered with cold as she watched the snow. Snow was as new to her as running away was old. Before Ann Arbor, she had traveled the southern circuit to New Orleans, to the beaches in Florida, back to New Orleans. In coming to Ann Arbor, she followed the advice of a boy she liked and lost on the road.

"While I was staying with him, the police came to bust the house for drugs. I hopped out of a window to get away from them, but they caught me and put me in a detention home in Pensacola. I ran from the home after two months, but the police caught me again and put me in jail. I'd been living with my mother and stepfather, but they didn't want me, and I hated living with them. When I went to court, my father appeared for me. They released me in his custody. When we went back to the jail to pick up my things, the matron told us I had VD.

" 'I can't have her,' my father said. 'I don't want her.' "

In the legion of runaway children, Katie was a *throwaway*, a girl nobody wanted. Disowned by her father and her mother, she lived as she could. When she stumbled into the ragtag army of the runaway ranks, she felt at home. Accepted by other outcasts, she adopted their habits. Taking drugs and having sex were as vital to her place in that society as getting good grades in school were to other children. Katie was only fourteen years old, but she had sampled the life of an exile and pronounced it satisfactory. Even at fourteen she knew the drawbacks, but she was powerless to prevent them. She had moved into the routine life of the aimless runaway because her parents were ashamed of her.

Although Katie had smoked marijuana since she was twelve, she was not running in search of it. If there is a connection between dope and running away, it may be a family argument over the child's use of marijuana, especially if the parents call the smoker a criminal. Teen-agers everywhere flaunt their independence with marijuana as well as with alcohol.

The adolescent's use of marijuana is the one feature of juvenile delinquency which has increased dramatically over a five-year period, social scientists have discovered. Late in 1974, the Institute for Social Research at the University of Michigan published a study entitled "Changing Patterns of Delinquent Behavior Among Americans 13 through 16 Years Old: 1967–1972." The paper was the second national survey of youth which the Institute had conducted. Its purpose was to compare the delinquency of teen-agers in 1972 to those in the 1967 survey. They defined delinquency as illegal behavior and the delinquent as a juvenile who knows that he is breaking the law. The interviewers questioned 1,395 children, representatives of all levels of the population. They based the results of the study on the answers the youngsters gave them, considering them more reliable than official statistics.

Directors Martin Gold and David J. Reimer drew conclusions which might surprise naive adults. The most startling finding of the study was that the use of marijuana increased nine times from 1967 to 1972. While there was no wild upswing in the rate of other delinquent behavior, drug use jumped from the low incidence reported in 1967. The report stated: "The increased use of drugs is most marked among 15- and 16-year-olds; among girls the increase is probably limited to that age group. Adolescents from all social strata gave evidence of the same trend, but the increase in the use of drugs seems most sharp among boys of middle status. Rural boys and girls do not seem to have participated in this shift to drug use."

Stressing that the main drug used was marijuana, the scientists tried to explain its popularity. They stated that parents allowed their sons more freedom in 1972 than they had in 1967. Marijuana was part of their youngsters' social life. Like the high school psychologist, scientists claimed that marijuana accompanies the social activities of both boys and girls. Girls smoked dope and drank alcohol when they dated boys who did; boys used marijuana more frequently when girls were not with them. Among girls and boys the use of marijuana was understood as a "normal adolescent activity." In 1967, marijuana had symbolized rebellion; in 1972, it had become "an aspect of typical adolescent activity." Drug users were not outsiders.

The other drug popular with children is liquor. The rise of alcoholism among teen-agers was reported by the National Highway Traffic Safety Administration in a study released in December, 1974. The study reports that half of America's adolescent children attend drinking parties at least once a month. Youngsters have admitted driving an automobile while they were intoxicated. They have been passengers in a car whose driver had been drinking. The study of the drinking habits of high school students reveals a motivation similar to the marijuana smokers: they drink because their friends drink. They are gregarious youngsters who fit easily into the group. "They are not far out, dropout, alienated or underachieving types," the report stated. "On the contrary, they represent all levels of scholastic achievement and aspiration."

To their parents the appeal of beer, wine, or booze is understandable because they use it themselves. Many parents condone, tacitly, their sons' drinking but object loudly and angrily to their smoking marijuana. They may imagine the dope smoker as a spaced-out freak, for as a student of mine described his parents: "They find it impossible to believe that intelligent, functioning students use drugs."

For many adolescents marijuana and alcohol like soda pop and potato chips have become social amenities. "You don't have to be a creep anymore to be using dope," a police officer said. "You come across kids who look straight—like Mom and apple pie—and they're doing their thing every day."

The high school boys I know who smoke marijuana agree with scientists and psychologists. They smoke "because everybody does it." "It's available." "I like the way it makes me feel." A boy from Andover, the New England prep school, explained his reasons for smoking pot in an essay in a collection called *High School*. School, he said, stifled creativity. The use of drugs and sex freed it. As the main reasons for drug-taking, he named the "need for social acceptance and the desire to escape." Perhaps marijuana is a runaway experience. Or perhaps dope, like beer or wine, is fun to share with friends.

Today boys and girls don't need to leave their neighborhood to smoke a joint like the runaways of the sixties. The runaway culture is available to all children. It exists as an alternative to being straight all the time. For children who feel estranged from their family or detached from the routine of school, the runaway culture thrives wherever they get together. After school, over the weekend, at parties or simply with friends, they emulate the life of a runaway as they talk and smoke and listen to music. The talk is both tough and wistful—of the future and the past; the present, so full of teachers and parents. They speak of being free to live the way they want, near beaches or in an apartment in the city. They talk of travel, working in the wilderness, not needing money to live, sailing, and saving the environment, living with a beautiful, sensitive sex partner. Of being honest with people.

The runaway culture is the other side of adolescence for American teen-agers. It's fugitive alley where no adults live. No

authority, no school rules or schoolwork, no pressure, no demands invade it. The runaway culture is feeling independent
and being completely immersed in self. It means trying everything they have ever imagined without hurting themselves—sex,
drugs, and freedom. Unless they know the monotony and the
fatigue of the real runaway life, it is their fantasy, their escape
into irresponsibility.

Marijuana, alcohol, and casual sex are the playthings of
children who yearn to be independent. Controlled at school, misjudged at home, the youngsters assert themselves with friends.
Their vision of the adult society as restrictive and authoritarian
is akin to Orwell's in *1984*. Big Brother is always watching. The
child who does run away fulfills the fantasy.

5. Hassled Children:
School and the Runaway

"The boy . . . did not have the right stuff in him; and exactly as it had shown itself in his not keeping decently up with his studies, so it showed itself in making him quite unable to do his work on the team. I want to see each of you play hard when you play; and I want to see each of you work hard, and not play at all, when you work."—President Theodore Roosevelt at the Friends School Commencement in Washington, D.C., on May 24, 1907.

School. It never changes. It may be the single point of certainty in a child's turning world. School is the machine that promises to leap forward and backward in time, but it freezes time for hours, days, years. Parents and philosophers may wrangle about the innovations of contemporary education, but the children know: there is no change, only interruption. The curriculum adds new courses; the faculty admits new teachers; new buildings go up, but the days get longer, the desks get harder, the expectations become more intense. For most children the real world is always beyond the school grounds. For the runaway, school is the real world.

School is the ally of his parents, the enforcer of their expectations, the final judgment on who he is and what he can do.
It is a continual test of fortitude and an endless examination of
self. When a child runs, he is running from his place in school
as well as from his life at home. In his imagination he transforms
school into life. If he is a loser in school, he fears he will lose
at life. If he succeeds in school, he objects to the relentless pressure of success.

In my interviews with runaway children I have never talked
to one who said that school alone was the reason for running
away. School aggravated and fueled the fights with their parents, but by itself it was not the machinery that set them in
motion. They run from home, not school, unless like Holden
Caulfield, they are escaping an institution which contains them.
I met dozens of runaways who talked about the importance of
school to their parents and, if they would admit it, to themselves.
In spite of their quarrels, these runaways and their parents had
agreed about one issue: school determined their success in life.
It was not a stopgap, a breather, a moment to hold off the future
and enjoy the present. School was an early measure of their future. From report cards through scholastic-aptitude examinations
in grades eleven and twelve, school outlined their capacities for
success and failure. Two kinds of runaways in particular would
have agreed with Teddy Roosevelt that the game at school took
grit: one was the boy or girl who was not a capable student; the
other was the extremely competent student and school leader.
Competing was not worth the score to one; the score was not
worthy of the effort to the other.

To the poor student, the child who gets C's and D's on his
report card, school exposes his ineffectuality in a dozen ways.
His boredom, his apathy, his unwillingness to cope with detail
spring from one source: his fear of competition. School does not
reject the weak student, but it classifies him. It does not always
condemn him as ignorant or incompetent, as stupid or lazy, as a
fool or a freak. He only thinks it has. By the attitudes of teachers

and classmates he becomes aware of himself as unfit. The report card judges him. Teachers tolerate him. Awards and honors which pass him by insult him.

A runaway girl told me: "I had the feeling that something was wrong with me. I never fit. I was uncomfortable and my parents were uptight."

Among runaways, the girl who does well in school, whose grades are A's and B's, is not rare. There is an irony here that mocks the theories. Many students run to flee frustration, but why does she leave? School rewards her, but she calls it boring. She works hard and it pays off in academic honors, club offices, and college acceptances. One day the pressures from home and school come tumbling down on her, and she thinks that the rewards are empty compared to her effort. If she runs, she's rebelling against a society that has slotted her for production.

Children run in a technical society because of an inability to produce or a reluctance to join it. In Japan the Tokyo police pointed to schools and mothers as the reason for runaway boys and girls. A news story in *The New York Times*, in April, 1973, datelined Tokyo, stated that Japanese children were running away from home in record-breaking numbers. The police blamed the pressures of education and home to excel in school as the dual reasons. They called the mothers of runaways "mama monsters." According to the news story, mothers make their children study long hours outside of class to prepare for entrance examinations. In Japan good scholastic records are essential to get into the universities, to get decent jobs. Even an applicant for kindergarten must pass an entrance test. Mama becomes the monster who makes the child study.

An assistant inspector of police who handles runaway cases was reported saying: "Underlying this is the pressure of the mother who expects more than the child is really capable of doing."

In Japan school semesters begin in April and September. According to the police, these are the months when the runaway rate is high. In the United States some runaway-house workers and policemen claim that May and September are the months for running away from home. Their idea is that children run in May before final examinations start and in September before school reopens. Other runaway-house counselors and police officers disclaim the tie-in with the semesters. They say children run from the pressures of home and school all year round.

The connection between a child's schoolwork and his running away is revealed by government-sponsored research into the runaway issue. The study "Suburban Runaways of the 1960s," published by the National Institute of Mental Health in 1967, attempts to relate the runaway's grades to his parents' goodwill. The report states: "Parental dissatisfaction with the child's school performance often led to nagging and disciplinary measures which, over time, became conflicts in their own right."

When I began to teach in Washington in 1963, Robert Shellow and his associates in the Adolescent Process Section of the Mental Health Study Center of the National Institute of Mental Health were undertaking a survey of suburban runaways of Prince George's County, Maryland, and their nonrunaway counterparts. The Shellow Report described anxious children running from home because they had trouble coping with the demands of their parents and schools. Assuming that "school is a trouble spot for most adolescents, whether runaways or not," the report found "school as a special problem area for runaways."

About 731 runaway children from ages ten through seventeen were studied through interviews, police and court records, and school reports. Two-thirds of the parents reported that the runaway had had trouble in school. To compare the reaction of runaways and nonrunaways to school, a questionnaire was administered to 1,350 students in eleven junior and senior high schools. Again, about two-thirds of these nonrunaway students admitted having difficulties in school. The survey also showed no distinctions in scores on intelligence tests. The intelligence of runaways did not vary from national norms. The differences between the two groups as students, the runaways and the comparison group, occurred in three ways: in grade averages, absences from school, and in retentions, that is, being held back.

The runaway child gets a bad report card. As the study states: "Eighty-two percent of the runaway children had grade averages of C or below for the grading period closest to their reported absence." Only 32 percent of students in the comparison, or nonrunaway group, reported such low grades. Grades of runaways for the period around the time they left home were then compared with an earlier set. The grades preceding the runaway period were lower than the others. Grades of the comparison group dipped in time too. The tedium of repetition affects all students. However, the grades of runaways started lower than those of nonrunaways and dropped more sharply.

The runaway is a truant. He averaged nineteen days absent from class during the academic year of the report. The median of absences in the secondary-school population is thirteen days, according to the Shellow researchers. My guess is that skipping school is habitual with runaway children before they decide to leave. Nina had told me she was absent sixty days one year—and nobody spoke to her about missing so much school. However, the child who cuts class or skips school frequently is not necessarily a potential runaway. He is probably bored with school and tired of going to classes too, but the runaway may feel that no one cares whether or not he is there.

Being held back a grade for failing is an embarrassment and a guarantee of boredom. Nearly half the runaways interviewed in Prince George's County had been retained in school. About 20 percent were older than the norm for their grade; in the comparison group only 7 percent were overage.

The runaway changes schools more often than the nonrunaway. Contributing to being kept back in school was the fact that runaways interviewed for the study moved often. More than two-thirds of the families of runaways had changed their addresses at least once. Only half the comparison group had moved.

When a family moves, the children usually attend a new school. In the shift from one school to another, they may be placed in a lower grade level. Because of the change, schoolwork may suffer and report cards will show it. Junior high, with its uncertain seventh-, eighth-, and ninth-grade years is a crucible for runaways. Many of the school transfers for Prince George's runaways took place in junior high school.

The runaway is not a school dropout at the time he runs, the study reported. "Only 58 of the runaways were school dropouts at the time of the runaway, about one-fourth of the runaways old enough (over 16) to have dropped out legally." The rate was no higher than that for the general school enrollment. However, the boy who repeats his runaway episode because of school may become a dropout. Running away could be a prelude to his giving up on school. The report concludes that the runaway with school problems is usually a boy.

A boy with a poor report card, which may also record his unexcused absences, may indeed run from the anger of his parents. Ten years ago when the research on the Shellow Report was completed, boys held the lead among runaways *reported to the police* of Prince George's County in a sixty-forty boy-girl ratio. But today the runner is as likely to be a girl as a boy. For the eight months from July, 1973, to February, 1974, Prince George's County police reported that 56 percent of the runaways were girls, 44 percent boys.

One gripe common to both runaways and nonrunaways was the bias in favor of the college-bound. "The major problem appears to lie with those students—and they are in the majority—who will not go on to college." The child who thinks college is unattainable is the odd man out. Most schools overlook him because he is thought not to be serious.

The Shellow Report reproached the school system for its prejudice against the child who is not competitive scholastically. He endures the frustrations of school until he plays truant or withdraws in the classroom. He may not run physically, but he escapes into his daydreams. The report sympathized with the academic runaway, but it neglected to consider a premise upon which most schools are based: book learning is a prerequisite to getting ahead in America. Learning for its own sake is hardly the point in most American schools; classes and homework are only exercises in endurance. Training the character becomes more important than training the mind, as schools expect ambition and determination to develop during the high school years. If these qualities do not appear, schools seem to give up on the resistant child. As the report observed: "Truancy and dropping out psychologically, which appear on the surface to be a child's rejection of school, might, in many instances, be better seen as the school's rejection of the child, especially the one who does not accept academic values."

The child does not always reject academic values; often he delays them. The indifferent student may realize the importance of a diploma when he decides to get a job. The good student has already accepted the academic values of his parents. Like the Japanese runaways, American boys and girls object to intensive schooling. Whether or not they plan to attend college, most children think school is a hassle, a pressure, which they must bear daily.

The child who does everything right reaches a point of being unwilling to continue. He runs from great expectations.

Such a runaway was April Drake, an attractive blond cheerleader who loved God and her parents and who excelled in school. April was not a "normal runaway," her mother insisted. She had left home because of tensions she created for herself.

"April pushed herself in the worst way," her mother told me. "There was a demand on her every day. She never had a chance to date or to think. April ran away from home, basically, because of the pressures of society."

In the spring, when runaways become conspicuous in the cities, newspapers report the story much as they do the natural disasters of the seasons. Early last May, I read about April's running away on the front page of *The Washington Post*'s city section. "PARENTS AGONIZE OVER MISSING GIRL," the headline proclaimed. April was one of ten thousand children between fourteen and seventeen years old who were running away annually in the Washington area, the subheadline continued. The story about the sixteen-year-old featured the note the girl left. The paper reprinted her photograph from the high school yearbook. She was a very pretty girl with long blond hair and a sweet smile.

Her note to the family said how sorry she was to hurt them. "I really have to get away. I can't stand it. I really can't. Please don't worry because I know God loves me and will protect me. I'm sorry."

When I called her mother, she cried: "April's coming home! She's coming this weekend to visit. We hope she'll stay."

For two months April had worked as a secretary in New York City. She shared an apartment near Central Park with another girl and earned $115 a week at her twelve-hour-a-day job. Tall and poised, she had told her employer that she was eighteen, two years older than she actually was.

During her second month in New York, April telephoned her family and friends without speaking to them. She would dial their number, then hang up after someone answered. Her mother said she was certain it was April. She primed everyone whom April was calling to say: "Please speak to me, April." Finally, one evening the girl began to talk and cry. She was homesick. She missed her friends and family. She missed her boyfriend. She was working so hard even homework seemed easy. She wanted to go home for a visit, she said, and her parents begged her to come.

Once she had returned to her family, she decided to stay. In her first evening at home in four hours she made up two months of homework in her Statistics and Probability course.

"April always took advanced courses," Mrs. Drake explained. "She picked the best and the hardest teachers. She was in an advanced college push class. This year, her junior year, she took six major subjects as well as a commercial course. I advised her to take some secretarial skills in case she ever needed to support herself. She agreed and took the double course, the straight college and the commercial. She was also a cheerleader and always busy with school activities."

I asked about April's boyfriend. Mrs. Drake admitted that he had upset the girl. "She broke up with him because he was rough with her and he drank. He became obnoxious one night and April broke it off. When he started dating another girl, she felt bad. She tried to get back with him, but it didn't work. It's all or nothing with her. The night she left she thought of going to his house, but she hitchhiked to New York instead."

Mrs. Drake considered the part she and April's father had played in the girl's decision to leave home. Perhaps they had controlled her too tightly, or seemed too ambitious for her.

"We are strict parents, but she was a perfect child. She's accepted everything we've told her always. We made all the decisions and they were okay with her. We believe in discipline. In a curfew and knowing where the children are. That's the way I was raised."

In New York April had proved herself not a child and no longer perfect. She had run away from home, hurting her parents, but she had earned her way honestly.

"Now we're treating April like a young adult," Mrs. Drake said. "When she came back, I asked her, 'How could you forget about yourself for the future?' She understood and she agreed with me. Since she wants to go to the University of Virginia, she is back in school, plugging away."

I teach students like April Drake. I teach in the school to which President Roosevelt delivered his famous "American Boy" speech at graduation in 1907. He was talking to children and parents that spring day and, although almost seventy years have passed, his advice affects parents and children still. The child of ambitious parents drives himself hard. He must do well. His parents expect it and he expects it of himself. He thinks he needs A's to make Harvard or Yale; B's are mediocre. He is tense and self-critical. A middle-class child like April believes he can become anything he dreams if he practices the virtues President Roosevelt advocated in his speech—work, perseverance, courage, determination, decency, and usefulness. If he will buckle down and grow up straight, he may, one fine morning, wake up to find his dream come true.

A child is a great dreamer. His dreams are more real to him than his efforts to achieve them. His shortest hours are spent dreaming of what he will do. If he is like April, he will try to bring about the dreams, first, by following the directions of his elders. Like April and other runaway children, he may learn sooner or later that determination alone will not get him what he wants.

A runaway girl I knew well said: "The sixties taught us that nothing we do matters. We want too much."

What they want is what April wanted: the intangible, the unattainable. April thought she should have love as well as good grades and high school popularity. When her romance with a boyfriend was unsuccessful, she wondered why she bothered trying to be perfect. She acknowledged futility by running from it. When she returned to her family, they were able to persuade her to accept the future she had momentarily refused. As her mother described her, April was "a child reaching out." Like every child, she wanted to believe in possibility.

Twenty-five years ago when I was a student in a public high school, John Marshall, in Rochester, New York, was a neighborhood school with about eight hundred students in grades nine through twelve. We had the best swimming team in the city, a very good basketball team, and a professionally equipped radio workshop. In classes we did what we had to, or more if we wanted to get grades good enough to make the National Honor Society. Algebra and Latin were tough, history was a bore,

English and Spanish usually lively, and Health Instruction a joke. In English we read the old-timers: *Silas Marner, David Copperfield, Julius Caesar, Ethan Frome, The Vicar of Wakefield,* poetry and plays, and *Essays Old and New*. During the day we moved to bells that jarred us out of the classroom reverie every forty minutes. We saved our spirit for after school as we tried out for plays and put out the newspaper and screamed at pep rallies in the auditorium. We dressed like adults and wore our hair like movie stars. In the winter we went ice skating at Maplewood Park, to sock hops in the gym; in summer on hayrides where the boys acted sophisticated with a bottle of wine.

Many of us wanted to go to college on scholarship, and some of us did. Some married their high school sweethearts and spent the first year or two on an army post where the young bride became pregnant. Some became pregnant first, then married their high school sweethearts.

I didn't know anyone who ran away from home. I knew girls who became pregnant and boys who got drunk, but no one who smoked marijuana. A boy I knew was suspended for smoking a cigarette in the boys' bathroom. Two girls were reprimanded for swearing and warned that if they used such language again they would be suspended. All in all, the times were tame, and we could only be good kids.

As the 1973–1974 school year was about to begin, I returned to John Marshall High School to learn how it had changed, what the students were like, and how they were meeting the shocks of modern adolescence. Downtown on Alexander Street, The Center, an advisory agency that coordinated programs for city and county high schools, was initiating the Runaway Advocacy Project. The young Center staff planned to provide shelter and counseling for local runaways. Counselors had estimated that the Rochester area had about 130 runaways a month, 80 who were reported by the police and at least 50 others who went unreported. They told me that children came to the Center for help rather than go back to the schools, which they distrusted.

At Marshall the high school day had not changed: classes were still forty minutes long, bells rang, the grading system was based on letter grades. English classes were reading books like *The Gang That Couldn't Shoot Straight* and *Panic in Needle Park*. If students disliked reading, they could see the stories at the movies or wait until they ran on television. School spirit was dead. Apathy replaced pep. Assemblies were canceled. Nobody put on plays and the radio workshop was defunct. According to one student, "Kids think school is bad. They don't want to have any more to do with it than is required by law."

As the previous school year had ended, white students with several outsiders had stoned a bus carrying black students home. Although the incident appeared to be racial, children and adults at the school said it was a way to avoid final exams. Marshall got fifteen minutes on the evening television news and examinations and classes were canceled as school closed early for the summer.

For the past several years Marshall had enrolled over 1,850 students in grades seven through twelve. First, integration, then a reorganization plan brought children to the school from the city and the suburbs. Citywide integration was being achieved through voluntary busing. After the chaos caused by compulsory busing, the Board of Education reorganized the system for the 1971–1972 school year, adding seventh and eighth grades to city high schools. There were several comprehensive high schools with certain schools designated to specialize in the arts, or science and mathematics, or technical and vocational programs. John Marshall retained its academic emphasis while it continued to offer students programs in business, home economics, and industrial arts as it had twenty years earlier.

"We're no longer a neighborhood school," Ann Turula, Dean of Girls, explained. "Children attend Marshall from all over the city. A few years ago we knew the families, but today it's impossible."

I was fortunate to find Ann Turula, for she was the Girls Counselor during my high school years. Her title had changed, not her efficiency. She was adjusting student schedules before classes began. As we talked, she was nervous and hesitant to name the anxieties which have invaded city schools throughout the country. At Marshall as a new year was to begin, the principal's slogan was: "Wise Adult Leadership"; the principal's worries were: Will school open on September 5? Will the teachers strike as they were announcing? Will the school erupt, again, in racial fights? How many girls will become pregnant? How will dope be brought into the school this year? How many parents will call to wonder where their runaway children are?

To Ann Turula, running away from home reflects the fears of children caught by problems they cannot solve.

"Fears—real or imagined—send them off. Their parents threaten them with court action if they don't toe the line. The children say they're not being treated fairly or that no one's listening to them. They're afraid that we'll call home if they skip school."

At John Marshall young girls run away every year, often repeating the runaway episode. According to the dean, they are students in grades seven and eight. They run frequently, but not far. They may stay in a friend's home for two weeks while their parents do not know where they are.

"Parents are afraid too," she said. "They call the school more than they ever did. Children know more and learn facts sooner these years. The child is the same emotionally as he was twenty years ago, but the problems are so great that he can't cope. Sex problems start in elementary school. Girls as young as twelve are getting pregnant. Also, there's more drinking among young people than when you were in school. Marshall students are not so deeply involved in drugs as children are in the suburbs.

"Students reflect society, but schools have not changed with the youngsters," Ann Turula decided.

Hurrying off to a meeting, she introduced me to a girl for whom the schools have adjusted. Linda, an eleventh grader, was a smart girl. Quick, bright, and eager to be finished with high school, Linda would graduate as a junior because of a program for accelerated students. By June she would complete the studies required for a New York State Regents' diploma and enter college in September. She assured me that she liked school, but she hated its demands on her.

"I'm what they call 'a good kid,'" she grimaced. "I really like school. The only thing I don't like is all the pressure they put on me. From teachers and my parents I got a lot of hassle to keep up my *A* record. When I go to college, I want to go as far away as I can get."

In order to get her freedom, Linda accepted the bargain of her parents and teachers. She was willing to push herself for the benefits of a middle-class education, and curtail her independence.

Another successful student, a boy in one of my classes, condemned the pragmatism of schools when he said: "Teachers, like parents, have an incredible desire to classify us and shut out aspects of our personalities that don't fit the mold. Either they underestimate us, or they overwork us. We're not as smart—or as stupid—as they think."

Most students understand the price of success in school. The cost of doing well by working hard and being 'good kids' is expensive. They pay in energy, loss of freedom, and sometimes with their self-respect. For many children the price is too high.

6. The New Runaways: Children and Parents

"Runaways are local—that is, more often from within the metropolitan area than outside the region. They generally stay within the region too, rather than going long distances." —*Runaway Youth in the Washington Area,* a report by the Metropolitan Washington Council of Governments, October, 1974.

Talking to runaway children in San Francisco and Berkeley in June, 1974, convinced me that the trip away from home has changed during the past few years. California was a microcosm of the runaway world. They were all there: the reluctant runaways and the radical, the throwaways and sunshine runaways. I formed my definitions of the new runaways in Northern California, but I needn't have gone so far. On the streets of Berkeley, in the Haight-Ashbury neighborhood of San Francisco, near the ocean at Huckleberry's, anxious children in California reflected their counterparts throughout the country.

Today's runaways are not leftovers of the sixties. Most children running away today stay close to home because they want to go back to it. Or, they stay close to home because they are too young to get far without being stopped by the police. They may travel within their state, but probably only the adventurous minority criss-cross the country.

The majority of runaways still leave home, simply and seriously, because of trouble with their families. But most I met wanted to be reconciled with their parents. Their plans differed from those of their forerunners who trekked west in 1967. For that modern migration "Love, Peace, and Dope" was the rallying cry. Today the runaway is looking for love and peace for himself at home. He wants hope for a future in which he and his parents will coexist. Without being flamboyant, these children of the seventies represent a movement toward independence that grew from the history of running away in America.

In California in the sixties runaway children made history and became history. To the new runaways their predecessors are characters out of the past, precursors of a revolution in manners. Chasing after love and freedom, the avant garde pointed their thumbs west and reached San Francisco with a flower in their hair. The hip chose Haight-Ashbury in San Francisco to pursue pleasure; the politicos picked Berkeley and the energy of the university to correct the system. Then, being a young fugitive in California meant rebelling against the ties that bind one to the materialism, tradition, and conformity of the family. The youth revolution introduced the idea that no one need live by the values of the past.

The new runaways were inspired by the liberation movements of the sixties to take a stand against their historical role as property. Even the word *runaway* evoked images of the fugitive slaves of the nineteenth century fleeing from their masters.

In 1974 San Francisco was no longer the promised land. Runaway caravans do not unload their cargo in Golden Gate Park; the new runaways may never pass outside of their home state. So many runaways had told me that their goal was California that I imagined they ran west still. In their dreams maybe they did, but the California runaways I met were Californians.

Phase One of the revolution was over. The Epoch of Rebellious Youth had evolved into the Era of Personal Protest. These new runaways have no cause but their own, no underdog but themselves. They are split into solitary cells, but their combined mass constitutes a movement for human rights.

In the Haight and on the streets of Berkeley I talked to California runaways. Like those I met elsewhere, they had left home because they always came out losers in fights with their parents. They did not intend to sever ties, but they wanted equality. They wanted to make their own decisions, to talk to their parents without quarreling, to end being belittled. They wanted self-determination. They wanted their parents to yield their inflexibility and they yearned for respect and the tolerance that goes with it. By running away they demonstrated what they were unable to say.

"I was into total revolution," declared a boy I met at Huckleberry's for Runaways in San Francisco. "I wanted to do something about the government, about school, about home. What I did was get loaded in school, then come home and watch TV and stuff my face and make a mess. My mom was right when she said I needed discipline."

What they want and what they get—these new runaways—are worlds apart. To parents running away from home is rejection. They read bravado as belligerence and sometimes it is both. If the child repeats his runaway episode, parents are convinced of his hatred. Right or wrong, they interpret the running as a decision to be rid of them forever. The running becomes the final act of aggression, instead of a blatant plea to negotiate. As a result of their pain and confusion, parents repudiate the child. If there are new runaways, there are new parents, who are beginning to refuse officially and openly their role as guardians. If the rebellion of youth has entered a new phase, the rebellion of parents has only begun.

The defiance between generations has moved from the privacy of home to the public domain. Many parents are using the nation's social and legal systems to pluck out the bad seed, their runaway child. If they file papers with the court stating that the runaway is *incorrigible* or *beyond their control*, they are petitioning the court to assist in his upbringing. They are assigning the runaway child to the juvenile justice system. He becomes a *throwaway*, the child no one wants. Other parents, like the Caulfields of *Catcher in the Rye*, place the runaway under observation in a mental-health clinic or in a state hospital. If they are leery of courts and clinics or fearful of their reputation, parents may send the runaway to live with relatives in another city. Understanding the runaway episode as a demand for change, parents are ensuring that change with drastic measures.

When I arrived in San Francisco, I headed for Haight-Ashbury. A runaway boy had told me: "A lot of kids think the hippie movement, Haight-Ashbury, is still happening. A lot of good people live there who want to help you out."

We may remember the Haight of the late sixties as television portrayed it for us: a charming carnival where the merry-go-round never stopped whirling. Botticelli-like Venuses padded down the street barefoot, sweet-looking baby hipsters panhandling for spare change or free dope, giving off gentle smiles of love, chanting of peace, and winging high on acid. The neighborhood was a meeting place for seekers of nirvana through chemistry. It was also a dumping ground for adulterated drugs and unadulterated scroungers. The men and women who carried out the runaway program at Huckleberry's remember the tawdry side of the carnival. In 1974 they published a report about the expansion of the house into youth advocacy. Entitled *From Huckleberry's for Runaways to Youth Advocates* the booklet describes the Haight as it was.

At night the tourists and reporters went home, exhilarated by the crowds and gaiety of Haight Street. Then "the bikers" moved in. They were men without motorbikes, tough guys with no focus for their energy. They stopped traffic; they threw empty bottles in the street, paving it with broken glass; they banged on garbage-can lids and shouted until five o'clock in the morning. Finally they moved on, as did many other early residents. The report depicted the farewell scene so:

"As the last of the early settlers left at the end of 1967, they tried to point out to everyone still there that as far as they were concerned it was all over. To make that plain, they carried a cardboard coffin painted black down Haight Street and to the Panhandle.

"Along the way people would toss in bits of what Hippie had meant to them: coins, joints, sodden Kleenexes, a guitar pick, caps of white lightning, fallen leaves and a little poster that said *Speed Kills*.

"Then it was all burned in a big bonfire.

"*Hip Is Dead*, reported the Berkeley *Barb*.

"But the straight press didn't catch on, so nobody told the kids or the tourists still back in Cleveland or Boston.

"The Haight went on for them."

The mystique lives, but today the runaway child is an anachronism in the Haight. Huckleberry's has moved out of the neighborhood and into a Mediterranean-like setting five blocks from the Pacific and miles away from the Haight. The Haight is struggling to become respectable. Next door to communards live professional men and women engrossed in their careers, raising families. The Panhandle, the narrow end of Golden Gate Park, is desolate. No love children smile from under trees.

On the gray June morning I walked through it, a solitary jogger bundled in a ski parka ran with his dog. Facing the park, near the corner of Oak and Cole, was my destination, a three-story house, the home of the Good Earth Commune. The communards were a collection of young people who operated a food cooperative and other small businesses in the neighborhood. They were kind to outcasts of all ages. The street gossip told me: "There may be a hundred of them and they're rough people. They're paranoid, they've been busted so often for dope. They take in runaways, they'll take in anybody."

Their house was an old apartment building which seemed to have survived a siege. The door was boarded and pieces of wood were nailed to the windows. I pounded hard until a sleepy young woman opened the door a crack and peered out at me.

I began explaining what I was doing and that I wanted to talk to any kids who might be living there who had run away from home.

"Runaways mean trouble with the pigs," she interrupted. "The family isn't looking for any trouble with the pigs."

I promised her I wasn't a pig.

"Wait a minute," she ordered. She disappeared down the dark hall behind the door.

The morning mist had turned into a downpour. When the girl returned with a man and a dog, I was almost soaked and ready to leave. The man, whom she introduced as Terry, was scowling, and the dog was stiff with suspicion.

"We don't have any runaway chicks here," Terry said.

I apologized for bothering him and turned to leave.

"You can talk to Eileen. She's been sleeping here all week. Her father threw her out. Technically she's probably a runaway, but she called her father to tell him she'd come home if he wanted her to."

When I told him Eileen sounded just right, he went to get her. I was stranded with a sniffing dog in front of the forbidding house.

Suddenly Eileen appeared. "Are you the lady who wants my life story?"

She was plump, vivacious, friendly. About thirteen—"just fourteen"—she smiled and said: "I have a very mature mind."

She led me into the dark cave of a house down a long hallway to a small room at the back. A couple of mattresses and a pile of magazines furnished the room. Its one window was boarded up. A floor fan was beating dead air. I sat on one mattress, she stretched out on the other.

"They're cool people in the house. Paranoid but cool. A guy from my neighborhood brought me here after I had a fight with my father. We've been getting into too many fights. He always yells: 'What's the matter with you?' He hits me whenever he can catch me."

Eileen lived with her father, a widower, and her religious, Catholic grandmother. The father was a heavy drinker, but he shouted about his daughter's friends and her pill-popping, dope-smoking habits.

"We live in a mixed neighborhood near Fillmore, and he doesn't like me to go out because most of my friends are black. My Spanish friend Maria died from being beat up by two black girls with their steel combs, the cake-cutters. She was smart-mouthing them and they didn't like it. They attacked her and she died from internal bleeding.

"Her death made my dad real strict. 'Black and white don't mix,' he said. 'Why do you always want to go out with black people?' They're my friends," she told me.

"Whatever I do is not good enough for him. He read my diary and found out about the junk I do, the weed, bennies, you know, dope. He doesn't trust me."

Eileen left because of a fight with her father. Frightened by Maria's death, he had told her not to go out into the neighborhood. But Eileen left the house and returned later than she should have.

"He was really pissed. 'Get your ass up here!' he yelled. 'Fuck you!' I answered. 'What did you say, you bastard?' he yelled. 'I never want to see you back here!' I was scared, but I was laughing, too."

The commune bored her. The closed doors and boarded windows were meant to deter contact. Eileen missed the zest of the street.

"There's nothing to do here all day. It's okay, but I'm not

into anything. I want to go back home to be with my friends. My father wants to get me out of the neighborhood because he can't stand blacks. If I go home, and I probably will, he's going to send me to Idaho this summer to visit my sister. He doesn't understand where my head's at."

Eileen's father knew where her head was. It was on Fillmore, San Francisco's meanest street. Eileen wanted the excitement of being with her gang on Fillmore. She was both an onlooker and a participant in their fights.

"I fight pretty good," she told me.

She dropped acid and smoked weed. She drank booze and behaved like her idols, the dudes of the street. Although she was distressed by the death of her friend, she was awed by her nearness to danger. For Eileen life or death was a daily matter. Her grandmother's religion and her father's discipline were inconsequential to her survival on the street. She had learned how to get along.

"I don't talk sarcastic to my black friends the way Maria did," she said. "We get along good."

Because Eileen was a success on the street she was a threat at home. She was tough enough to frighten her father and so defiant that he ordered her to leave. By running she behaved as he expected a rough street kid to; by returning she proved she needed his care and her safe place at home.

After the Haight I took a trolley-car ride to North Judah, a long street leading to the ocean, where Huckleberry's for Runaways has shelters. Allied to the youth revolution since 1967, Huckleberry's had housed hundreds of children coming to the Haight for the Summer of Love. Started by the San Francisco Branch of the Bay Area Social Planning Council, it developed from a minister's idea of finding runaway girls before the police or pimps picked them up. The house at Number One Broderick, a block off Haight Street, which became Huckleberry's, housed three hundred children during the summer of 1967. According to the Haight-Ashbury Research Project, those three hundred runaways represented only 1 to 2 percent of the fugitive youngsters then in the Haight.

Today Huckleberry's provides services for children whose families will not help them. The counselors also continue their efforts to reconcile children and parents who do desire to be together. I talked to two boys, local youngsters like Eileen, whose running away from home had precipitated their leaving it permanently. They were grateful to Huck's.

"They treat you like a human being here, not a juvenile delinquent," said Danny, a wholesome-looking boy from San Bernardino. He had a remarkable mushroom head of hair and wore a white thermal underwear shirt and faded jeans, patched with odd, pretty pieces of material. As he told me his story, which began with his running away from his divorced mother, he sounded like a latter-day Huck Finn. He had camped in the woods of Marin County and had lived in shacks in Eugene, Oregon, with an older brother. He spoke of the adults he had known in three years of makeshift living as if they were people who made mistakes, not monsters who sought to destroy him.

Danny was the boy who agreed with his mother that he needed discipline—three years after he had run from her dictums of cleanliness and hard work. When he kept disobeying her, she decided to send him to military school. Leaving the school, he returned home for his thirteenth birthday, but his mother insisted he go to live with his sister, who had joined a group of vegetarians in San Francisco.

Despising the raw fruits, nuts, and vegetables that his sister ate, Danny left her to roam with an older brother from one crash pad in Eugene to another.

"I stayed in school, but it was a bad scene. In the summer we'd find farm and lumber jobs. In the winter we didn't work. We began dealing acid. We'd sell about one hundred hits of acid a week, making just enough money to the cent to make it."

Leaving his nomadic brother, Danny came to the Bay Area,

where he found work with an artist and his family in Mill Valley. He learned how to make block prints, and for his board and room he did housework. But Danny began to feel that his apprenticeship was slavery. When the artist said that Danny was more valuable to him as a maid than as a printer, he moved out.

"The whole thing was a mind-fuck because I was totally enslaved. I moved up into the woods in Marin County and built a fort. I kept it a secret, but then the artist's son, a kid about my age, came up to find me. When I left, he had to do the housework!"

At first life in the woods was idyllic. Later, when the novelty diminished, it began to pall. As Danny explained: "We liked living in the woods at first. We'd fish, then scarf-up a big fish dinner. We almost started a revolution. Kids sick of their parents decided to live at the fort. But, pretty soon I'd find myself sitting around all day with nothing to do. I came off the mountain around Christmas, 1973, and went to Huck's. I've been coming here off and on for housing. It's the only place I know that has the legal help I need. I'm waiting for placement in a ranch up north."

As the youth-advocacy services of Huckleberry's would place Danny in a boy's ranch, so it was trying to find an alternative for a young artist to live outside of detention centers and mental hospitals. Peter was living at the Greenhouse, Huck's short-term residence for youngsters who were managing without their parents. His parents had assigned Peter to the care of the court and the court had placed him in a home for boys.

An intelligent boy, Peter was talented as an artist and a musician. Huckleberry's had advised him to apply to the city's art institute. When I talked to him, he was hopeful of entering college in the fall.

Although he said his parents were "very well-off in a big house in San Francisco," they had not offered to pay for his education. Peter had become a leader in the family in a way that grieved them. His brother, the second oldest child, followed his example and left home. His thirteen-year-old sister threatened to run away, but Peter dissuaded her.

"It hurts my mother that her sons have left. Once in a while I see her and my father and we talk. We don't talk about why I left home, but now my mother's taking it easy and listening more. She expected so many things of us."

Born in the Philippines seventeen years ago, dark-haired and fine-featured, Peter had moved to San Francisco with his parents and younger brothers and sisters when he was eight. His father, a navy officer, was stationed in the Bay Area; his mother, a teacher, directed her children like a military unit. She expected discipline and she demanded respect.

The Philippine family tried to set themselves apart from American customs. The parents deplored the attitudes of American parents and children. They disapproved of the looseness in disciplining children and the lack of respect for parents. They insisted on absolute obedience to their code of behavior and to their Catholic religion. When the children were young, they attended Roman Catholic elementary schools. When Peter entered public junior high school, he began to rebel against the family.

"When I was sixteen I ran away from home because of a fight with my mother about everything from religion to hair." Peter said his mother hit him with his tennis racket, a hiking staff, a broom, a wire, and nagged him constantly.

One day while Peter was trimming a tree with electric shears, his mother ordered him to be careful, to cut it more here and there, to be neat about it. He told her to leave him alone. He'd do the job his way. She wouldn't stop calling instructions to him. He became fiercely angry and cut the tree to the ground.

"She shrieked and shouted at me. I told her to shut up or I'd kill her. I threatened her with the shears. She ran to tell my father and he kicked me out of the house."

Peter stayed with friends and returned home after a few days when he realized how rash he had been. He apologized to his mother. She didn't answer him.

"My father acted as a referee between us. She thought I was crazy and she wanted me to have psychological tests and be placed in a home. She got her way."

Once Peter's parents had petitioned the court that he was beyond their control, the court sent him to the San Francisco Boys Home, where he stayed for nine months. Hating the confinement, he became belligerent. "My psychological tests labeled me homicidal, suicidal, schizophrenic, and paranoid," he admitted.

Here he smiled: "They were much more creative in name-calling than my mother. They worked on me for a while, then they sent me to a mental-health clinic, which planned to send me to Napa State Hospital. I called my father and he interceded. He called the public defender, who got me out of the institute and into the Youth Guidance Center, a juvenile hall, really a jail for kids. I stayed there one month and was released to Huck's. I'll live at Huck's greenhouse until I'm eighteen. Then with Huck's help, I'll be set up with a job, an apartment, college."

Later, over the bridge in Berkeley, I was to meet other runaway children whose parents had retaliated by placing them outside of the home, often in the custody of the court. Like Peter and Danny and Eileen, these children ran from the house, but not far from home.

In 1974 the runaway rush to Berkeley had subsided from the days when youngsters streamed into the university town. Then, in the late sixties, ministers like the Reverend Raymond P. Jennings of the First Baptist Church opened their doors to the rebelling young. Dr. Jennings's Berkeley Runaway Center was now part of the larger Berkeley Youth Alternatives, an organization similar to Huckleberry's in its shifted emphasis toward children who need a friend in court.

When I talked to Dr. Jennings in Berkeley, he too remarked on the fact that the new runaways were local children. In November, 1974, the Washington, D.C., metropolitan area's Council of Governments would release a report which corroborated him. Runaways were local kids, native to the area.

Dr. Jennings speculated that fewer out-of-state runaways were coming to Berkeley because many places have their own hip center.

"The kids don't have to come so far now to find the counterculture. I was in Kansas last summer, and even Kansas has a counterculture," he laughed.

When I spoke of searching for runaways in Berkeley, he announced that the street had changed. "Runaways are underground now. They're not visible. They live in collectives. People take them in and take advantage of them. There's no doubt about it. The kids are coming, but they're invisible."

I met one of Berkeley's invisible runaways on the day Berkeley Youth Alternatives was moving from its church offices to the old Wonder Bread factory on Bonar Street. The invisible boy, like the invisible man, was black. When he heard me coming, he had bolted under a desk in the church.

At sixteen Duane had spent six months in a California detention center for running away from home. Recently discharged from the juvenile hall, he was helping the youth organization, which had agreed to supervise him, move to its new quarters. When I asked him why he ran away, he told me: "My mother was too nosy and too strict."

He and his mother, a nurse, had moved from Los Angeles to San Francisco and later to Berkeley after his parents had separated. Alone with his mother, Duane disliked her domination. He missed his friends in Los Angeles, so he ran back to the suburb where he had been reared to visit them and to escape his

---

mother's inquisitions. From Los Angeles, Duane ran to Texas, then up to Oregon and back to Berkeley. After Duane's second runaway escapade, his mother rebelled. When he returned, she asked the court to place him in detention. He was, she informed the judge, beyond her control.

When I told Duane that he was the only runaway I knew in Berkeley, he scowled. "I could show you five hundred of them if I wanted to, but I don't want to. I was talking to some of them last night, runaway girls."

Without Duane, I found the runaway girls of Berkeley after spotting the corners and crash stops of the university town: the obvious like People's Park, the porch of the Free Clinic, the corner in front of Cody's Bookstore, the storefront of the Garden Spot Market on Telegraph, and La Val's Pizza Garden at Euclid and Ridge; and the invisible, often illegitimate hangouts like somebody's garage, a ramshackle house that poses as a school for boys and allows boys only to crash, some boy's apartment that sleeps runaway girls, some areas in the hills around Berkeley.

One June evening I walked along Telegraph Avenue hoping to encounter the runaway followers of the street people who inhabited Berkeley. A cold wind blowing down the avenue had driven them away from their corners into shelter. The street was deserted except for two men who were trying to panhandle the price of a bed at the Youth Hostel. One of the spare-change hunters, a bearded drifter, offered to collect some "runaway chicks" for me to interview.

I waited in a restaurant and soon he returned with a green-eyed girl who looked about fifteen years old.

"What do I get for it?" she asked me.

When I suggested supper, she agreed. As she did every evening, she had eaten at five at the University Chapel's food project.

"I eat whenever I get the chance," she apologized, tossing her dark hair out of her face.

Born and reared in El Paso, Dinah had been on the road

for two years, first running away to Colorado when she was fourteen. Cool guys she knew had talked to her about Boulder '72, and she wanted to make the scene. Her parents never listened to her, she said, and after she was busted for dope, they became really strict with her.

In Boulder she was arrested as a runaway and returned to El Paso. Her parents filed a petition with the court, labeling her *incorrigible*, and the State of Texas assumed custody. Dinah was sent to a welfare home which housed fourteen other children. After two weeks she ran away, going first to Dallas, then Denver, then down to San Diego.

"I bummed around for a month living on the beach and looking for a job. I didn't get one, but I met my old man and we thumbed up here. We sleep in front of the Free Clinic and I hold down a corner on Tele and ask people for change."

Dinah could not get a job. She was a runaway well on her way to belonging to the street people who survived in college towns. She was uncertain about her future, but going home was not part of it. She would probably keep moving. If she avoided police and social workers for another two years, at eighteen she would be free of the legal restrictions placed on children. With her "old man" or a new one, she would move on to another university.

The bearded collector of runaways returned with an attractive blond, poised and self-assured. "This is Shelley," he announced. She looked younger than Dinah, yet her poise suggested maturity.

"I'm no longer a runaway," she told me. "I live in Berkeley with friends and I'm sixteen years old. My parents live in Oakland. When I was thirteen, I ran away. I hitchhiked to Colorado, where the police stopped me. My mother flew to Colorado and gave me enough money to finish my trip. My school guidance counselor advised her to give me the money and permission to travel. He said, 'She's going to run away again if she comes back. Why not let her go? She'll come back when she's tired.'

"He was wrong. I never did go home to stay long. My parents and I are good friends now. I had a great time on my trip and I learned a lot. I hitchhiked to New York, New Orleans, Ann Arbor, and then I settled in Berkeley. I'm going to college in the fall, but I've learned more about life traveling than I ever have or will in school. I can teach the flute and I make and sell leather bags and belts. I get jobs baby-sitting and waiting table."

Shelley seemed to be an *emancipated minor,* a term the law uses to describe juveniles who live away from home with the permission of their parents. She was *a radical runaway,* a child who preferred the hazards of the road to living at home, the child whose extended absence was the indication that life at home had become meaningless to her. Most of the radical runaways I have met possess a flamboyant self-confidence, unusual in children, which they have acquired in living by their wits. Unless they are extremely frank, they will not admit to feeling unwanted at home. Radical runaways stay away from home because they believe their parents do not want them. Although they have earned their self-possession the hard way, they signal their unease about their parents by not talking about them. Shelley knew that she and her parents became friends only after she had moved out. She could not trespass on their friendship by returning to live with them.

Duane was *a reluctant runaway,* a child whose running was intended to serve only as protest against the rules of his strict mother. He ran from Berkeley to Los Angeles to see friends and to prove his independence. When he traveled outside the state to emphasize his manhood, he literally went too far. His mother needed to teach him a lesson, to reassert her authority, and Duane spent six months in detention.

Eileen, the San Francisco girl, is a clear example of *a reluctant runaway.* She ran only a few blocks from home and wanted to, indeed would, return to her neighborhood, where she belonged. Her running away was spontaneous, her reaction to a fight with her father. Because she and her father communicated primarily through fighting, the act of running away was a political move, not by any means an ultimatum but a swift coup d'etat aimed at taking the opposition off balance. Reluctant runaways leave purposely and they may return hesitantly, but they are loath to leave forever. Unlike radical runaways, they are unwilling to assume full-time responsibility for themselves.

Some children may run away from home purely for adventure. They are the *sunshine runaways* who leave in the summer for the beaches or rock concerts. And, although I have met children who say they have run in order to see the country, I do not believe wanderlust was their sole reason for going. In leaving home, they are asserting independence and dissatisfaction with demands made on them. They "can't wait to get out of the house," sunshine runaways admit.

Dinah, and Peter and Danny, the boys I met at Huckleberry's in San Francisco, were *throwaways,* children whose parents had given up custody of them and placed them within the juvenile justice system. They are children who are outcasts, children who are physically, psychologically, or socially abused. When she was Assistant District Attorney with the Juvenile Court of Philadelphia, Lisa Richette described them in her book *The Throwaway Children.* She damned their inhuman treatment first by their parents, then by overburdened social workers, welfare personnel, court people. "Affluent or poor," she wrote, "these children have one thing in common: they are about to be cast off because society has run out of answers."

If he can run away from the institution or foster home that contains him, the throwaway may become a radical runaway. He will run as far as he needs to go to be anonymous. He knows the futility of imprisonment and the despair of being unloved. How can street life be worse?

The radical runaway is searching to belong somewhere. At the same time he may seek vengeance against the family he feels has rejected him. His revenge may be unconscious and un-planned, but it stings nevertheless. By leaving home, he punishes his parents. The longer he remains away from home, the more he prolongs their torture. By running he hurts them; by staying away he defeats them. Like Kelly, the radical runaway can achieve independence and revenge in one stroke, as she mocks her family's beliefs in loyalty, chastity, legitimacy.

The radical runaway of the middle class who wants revenge has three other choices to set him outside the family. To flaunt or distort their values, he can join the tribes of street people, the nomads of college towns. He can become a prostitute. Or he can convert to an eccentric religious order. Outcast emotionally, he may choose to be an outcast in deed.

In California I met a graduate student who talked about the malaise of the American middle class. As he described the affluent white runaway from Boston who was hooking for a black pimp in San Francisco, he chortled.

"What better way to stab her parents than to go off and hook for a black pimp! That's the classic revenge of the middle-class daughter," he announced.

Classic revenge it may be, but ultimate revenge it is not. The final revenge of the middle-class child is not running away and becoming a hustler or a hooker, a dealer in flesh and fan-tasy, but staying away and choosing an alien way of living.

Following the teachings of Jesus Christ, or of a guru of the East, the fleeing child finds something he feels is valuable: sacrifice for love, not achievements and acquisitions exchanged for love.

The child who runs to an ashram or a religious colony is bedeviled by his worthlessness. If he tried to articulate his emo-tions to his parents, he might say: "You have convinced me. I am worth less than everybody else. I don't see the value in going to school and college to get good grades so I can have a career that will make me lots of money. I want to find a meaning that ex-tends beyond home and school. I want to be happy, not feel guilty. I am trying to become myself, someone who is free from self."

In Houston, in 1973, I drove to the Children of God colony which was housed in a simple one-story rambler many miles from downtown Houston in a suburb that still looks like country. The colony is the only house along a dirt road. It seemed an ordinary brick house to me, and the sight of a baby buggy near the side door was comforting. A pickup truck was parked in the driveway.

I rang the bell and went in smiling, assuming a confidence I did not feel. I had read newspaper stories on the brainwashing techniques of the Children of God.

I had heard, too, of the fierce determination of parents to reclaim their children from this sect. Under the motto "Free Children of God," some parents had hired Californian Ted Patrick to kidnap their children, who were already of age legally. Patrick undertook to reverse what he saw as the indoctrination process. The deprogrammer, as he became known, supposedly had recovered over 138 devotees of various cults, including COG, which he claimed exercised mind control over its members.

The Children of God, calling itself "founders and leaders of the Jesus Revolution," had received the most publicity among the many orders offering salvation in a troubled world. Founded by David Berg, or Moses David as he called himself, at Huntington Beach, California, in 1968, the Children of God claimed over three thousand members in colonies in North and South America, Europe, Africa, and Asia. In the United States the two states having most of the colonies, or communal homes, were Texas and California.

As I entered the living room, I saw three young women and two men sitting side by side, listening to a lesson read by Jasper, the leader of the colony. Referring to a booklet of anecdotes, homilies, and plain talk called *Letters from a Shepherd*, written by the founder, was a handsome man in his early twenties. He

smiled at me with genuine confidence and asked me to join them
as he finished the lesson. His brown eyes sparkled with pleasure
as he read David Berg's words: " 'We're like little rays of light in
this city that's so dark! Even a few rays of light can make some
kind of impression! Don't ever think because there's so much
darkness, that it's no use to have just a little light, because even
one candle can be seen a mile away when it's dark!' Just like us,"
Jasper said, smiling around at his friends. "We shine like dia-
monds of dust!"

"Shall we sing our song for Christine?" he asked his group.
"Oh yes!" they said as Jasper played his guitar. They sang the
catchy rock tune "You've Gotta Be a Baby"—to go to heaven.

Ah, I loved it—the good time, the gay music, the happy,
shining, pretty boys and girls, at ease with themselves, the attractive leader who smiled like a movie star.

"We love you," Jasper said to me. "Don't we?" he encouraged them. "Oh yes! We love you!" they sang out to me.

"And I love you too!" I smiled back at them, no longer
afraid. There was no hostility here, only love and goodwill. I'd
been in the colony for ten minutes and I was already brain-
washed!

Going around the circle, I met the five boys and girls—
Deliverance, eighteen; Hope, nineteen; Bethesda, eighteen;
Jacob, twenty; Micah, nineteen; and Jasper, twenty-three, who
had found God in a half-hour "miracle of rebirth." Each had
a job to perform within the colony. Deliverance and Jacob
were in charge of buying food and planning meals; Hope wrote
the reports of their missionary trips and took care of the laundry;
Bethesda wrote the daily logs; Micah was the general overseer;
Jasper paid the bills and made sure everybody was taken care of.

Their purpose was spreading the message, "witnessing" for
God, showing nonbelievers God as the answer to their problems.
"Our main vision," said Jasper, "is to reach the whole world with
love of God. To witness we go to shopping centers, rock concerts, football games, many events in the Astrodome. We talk to

people who need somebody to talk to, give them literature and our telephone number. We go out on weekends and for two weeks at a time on missionary trips. We have brothers and sisters who are on the road, who don't live in the colonies. We really believe that America has turned away from God."

I asked whether there were older people in the Children of God.

Jasper said elders, called *shepherds,* did teach them, but that the sect was run by the youth, who had a 100 percent dedication to Jesus.

No one had an outside job, Jasper explained. "We share our wealth, cars, money. We get new income from disciples, through donations for our literature and from our parents. Sometimes it comes through real miracles on our weekend faith trips."

A tall girl, wearing a peasant blouse and a long skirt like the other girls, came in carrying a baby to show Jasper. The girl was Love, the shepherdess of the colony, wife to Jasper, mother of three-week-old Christiana. Love had been assisted by Jasper at the natural-childbirth delivery of their daughter at the colony. Jasper was proud of the child, proud of his wife, who as shepherdess was in charge of the girls.

Jasper told me that the sect did not believe in dating or in premarital sex.

"God will show man and woman who their mate is. Just seek God and He'll show you who it is."

Jasper had been approached by two brothers of the Children of God in his sophomore year at St. Thomas University. Within half an hour he was reborn, he said. He left college to dedicate himself full-time to Jesus. His parents, who lived in New York City, were surprised. They didn't know what to think, he told me.

"When they saw how happy I was, they approved," he said simply.

"Do all parents approve so readily?" I asked.

"We invite parents here, and that helps them understand

us," he answered. "Those who've never been with us have a fear of the unknown. They've been influenced by distorted publicity. So many parents are not supplying the needs of their children. Kids are hungry for love, godly love. God's trying to teach them that by not giving love to their children, they're killing them."

Jasper flashed his warm smile. "Most people are asleep. God has left their lives. That's why they're so miserable."

I asked what happened if a member changed his mind about living in the family and how they got their Biblical names. And really, I wondered to myself, were they as good as they looked, as self-possessed as they sounded?

"We choose our name," Jacob explained. "It helps us forget our old bad characteristics."

"We're not sinless saints," the forthright Deliverance said. "We have problems like everybody else. We try to give our worries and our hangups to God. We don't have much time to think about ourselves."

"It's a hard life," Jasper said. "Staying close to Jesus, maintaining a personal relationship with Jesus, is too hard for some. If they feel the hardship, they leave the colony. We have associates who don't live in colonies. These are our brothers and sisters too."

"You have to realize that you're nothing," Deliverance insisted.

Jasper smiled on us, nodding in agreement with Jacob, laughing at Deliverance, loving us all. "It's mostly the kids who are seeking for a new way of life."

He did not want to offend me. He smiled broadly on me and said: "We love you. Don't we love her, brothers and sisters?"

"We love you!" they echoed him.

7. College Town, Street People

"I wonder where all the flower children have gone."
—a volunteer at Huckleberry's for Runaways, *Youth Advocates*, the 1973 report.

Ann Arbor. Atlanta. Berkeley. Boston and Cambridge. Chicago. Dallas. Denver. Detroit. Honolulu. Houston. Los Angeles. Miami. Minneapolis. New York City. Philadelphia. Portland. San Diego. San Francisco. Seattle. Washington, D.C. These are the cities which the new runaways live in or run to. These cities contain the greatest number of children arrested by the police for running away from home, according to statistics of the Federal Bureau of Investigation and reports from the Department of Health, Education, and Welfare. In these cities runaways continue to gather like weeds, a different mixture from the late flower children.

For the radical runaway, the child who refuses to go home, the city is too expensive and too cold to stay in. Serious runaways have shifted with time from hip city centers to university towns. In temperament they have altered from altruistic rebels with a cause to sad children full of private misery. The flower child has grown up. The happy hippie has disappeared. He has packed his bongos and guitar and slipped out of the Common in

Boston, away from Wisconsin Avenue in Georgetown, D.C., off
the Haight in San Francisco. The woebegone street freak has
settled in and the runaway child is a Johnny-come-lately to a
lost era.

In the cities the youth revolution is dead. In San Francisco
in June, 1974, I found that the cultural upheaval of 1967 and
1968 had evolved into a hundred causes with one theme, the
elevation of self. Its philosophy was a metaphysics stressing the
release of the mind through knowledge of the body. The dedication to self was so strong that any runaway looking for a cause
could participate only as an acolyte, as a sexual servant.

In the college towns, however, the runaway is the center
of attention at social-service organizations staffed by university
students. He is the reason drug-crisis centers, hotlines, and shelter
houses receive funds from local, state, and federal agencies. Runaways pour into towns already worried about the welfare of students and street people. The runaway strains the facilities of the
town, but because he is young he gets attention.

Police officials in college towns say runaways blend so well
into student crowds they are difficult to detect. The problem is
complicated, too, by the youth ghetto, the enclave of nomads who
settle in a campus area, passing as students. Street people, as
they are called because they live, often literally, on the streets,
welcome runaways. They break the monotony. They may bring
dope and they can serve as new sexual partners since most of
them are young girls traveling with older boys.

Runaways to college towns reflect the changing national
portrait: they tend to be girls more often than boys; younger,
fourteen or fifteen, rather than older adolescents; local, from
within the state or the immediate area, rather than from out of
state. Even in Boulder, Colorado, site of the university and a
former hip mecca, I discovered that most of its runaways, like
those in San Francisco, were local youngsters. Out-of-town kids,
sunshine runaways and backpacking tourists, arrive daily to camp
in the mountains, but Boulder's heyday was 1972, the year the

love ship was to land on Sugar Loaf and take everyone to a new world. The love ship never came, but the believers did, pilgrims who were willing to wait to be saved.

Like the small religious colony, the university town attracts youngsters seeking asylum. By running away from the family to a university setting, they are searching for the privileges of a society that is established for youth. They want freedom and protection, friendship and anonymity. They want to get by without adults ordering them around. Whoever they are, wherever they come from, if they stay, most radical runaways become street people.

The distinction between street people and runaways is a legal one: runaways are children, street people adults. By definition runaways belong at home, either with parents or in institutions with guardians. They are not legally free to travel where they choose, to live as they wish. Beyond age there may be no distinction: the runaway child and the street person have both left home to make a life outside of the traditional structure. If they intend to stay away as street people, they must learn how to exist without money. They must expect to enter the lowest level of society, for they will have no education, no home, and no job. According to a report from the University of California titled *Down and Out in Berkeley*, they resemble the migratory poor of the Depression.

Young travelers have made Berkeley their mecca because it is the cradle of their liberation. It is the birthplace of Counterculture, the Hip Capital of the Western World. The history of Berkeley lures them: the Free Speech Movement of 1964, the People's Park confrontation of 1969, the protest riots of a feisty decade. They come to appreciate, and if they are runaways, children with no purpose but escape, they become dupes of another legend.

The glory days of Berkeley are dead: when hippies and student radicals marched together down Telegraph Avenue, when the freaks of South Campus, the ragtag street people and the middle-class dropouts, met the students of North Campus by the fountain in Sproul Plaza, to shout down the war lovers, when those who had nothing to lose joined those who had everything to gain. Then, the street people were called *hippies,* a different sect some say from today's vagabonds, and their presence was changing America's complacency. The exhilaration of realizing that together they could affect the system was a rush of democracy, a high of brotherhood. Those predecessors of the street population believed they belonged to the town; the drifters on Telegraph today know that the packs of campus dogs rate more consideration than they do.

On Telegraph Avenue in the late spring, I identified two distinct populations: street people and university fellows, freaks and philosophers, the vulgar and the precious, town and gown, down-and-out and up-and-rising. There, on both sides of the Avenue, the two rub egos. In front of shops and restaurants and bookstores are the traveling young, the runaways, the backpackers, the drifters, the poor, the displaced, the homeless, the ruthless and their victims, side by side leaning against the wall, playing a flute with case open at their feet to catch the coins. Pushing down the street were visitors from the privileged caste, shoppers and gapers, some just strolling for the ambiance, others because they needed a composition by Sarasate for a violin lesson. The gapers fended off the beggars, young men with outstretched hands who asked for a dime or a quarter. The shoppers moved on purposefully, anxious to finish their business and get off the street and back to Woolsey or Prince, where the bougainvillea covers the house with its purple bloom and the geraniums grow like trees.

The street people, whose numbers include runaway children, are the outsiders. The businessmen deplore them, townsfolk try to ignore them. Undergraduates avoid them; graduate students examine the migrants to analyze them and create theories about a new class of estranged citizens. They can learn firsthand about the drifters by working as volunteers for local agencies. They are intent on alleviating their misery, but they will not associate with them. To the students the street people are bums.

Although students and street people together reclaimed People's Park in 1972, that was their final collaboration. Today the students call the park a "junkie's paradise." The University of California newspaper, the *Daily Californian,* ran a comic strip, "Life on the Ave," showing street people as lazy freaks, mindless on drugs.

To those on the street the students are the middle-class rich, and they have nothing in common with them. They may go to the same rock concerts, but the students pay their way and the street people sneak past the gate. Although each group smokes dope, each buys and sells within its own enclave. They inhabit two separate worlds.

Because of its reputation, Berkeley has spawned a youth ghetto of inestimable population. The number of men and women on the street varies from year to year and season to season so that it is impossible to obtain an accurate count. University researchers take statistical samples and attempt to guess at the size of the group. According to a recent study, there may be eight thousand, or five thousand, individuals living precariously each year on the streets.

Although for an outsider the glamour has faded from Berkeley, wanderers live there because they can. In any season the weather is not extreme. The city police are benevolent if the travelers look older than eighteen. The Berkeley Youth Hostel provides inexpensive lodging. At five o'clock at the University Lutheran Chapel, corner of Haste and College, a thirty-five-cent meal is served to the waiting dozens. Dope is easy to get in Berkeley, but not work. If the wanderers cannot raise the dollar for the hostel, there are people who will take them in, or they can sleep on the porch of the Free Clinic, or in doorways of apartment buildings, in parking lots, or up in the hills. After a time, however, Berkeley will feel to the runaway like other towns and cities. Without friends, without money, the romantic stories of Berkeley are only free entertainment on a slow evening on the street.

The street has changed too, and runaways are the first to realize it. A salesman in a bookstore on Telegraph Avenue told me: "Most kids who are running away are not as sleazy as the scenes they'll get into in Berkeley." Since the late 1960s, early 1970s, the street has shifted from high to low, from with it to without it, from cool and easy to hot and hard.

An astute observer of street life in Berkeley, Jim Baumohl, a twenty-four-year-old graduate student at the university, explained the street's mood as a barometer of the new times.

"There's no euphoria now. The street scene is down and angry. There's stealing and violence and alcoholism is on the rise. The people don't want to be on the street."

Baumohl knew the streets of Berkeley and the Haight during 1967 and 1968. When he was a freshman at the University of California in Los Angeles, he was enchanted with the Haight, visiting his friends who'd dropped out of college to live there. He spent much of his freshman year in San Francisco and he transferred to Berkeley to complete his undergraduate studies.

"I was a tourist thrill-seeker," he told me one afternoon in his Berkeley apartment. "My role was that of the wide-eyed, eighteen-year-old, dope-smoking, acid-saturated idealist."

Later when he was an undergraduate in Berkeley, Jim began working with runaways and street people. After he graduated in 1971, he took jobs as a warehouseman, a bicycle messenger, a cashier. "My degree in creative writing was quaint and worthless and I did shitwork ad nauseum. In my spare time I started the Berkeley Streetwork Project, a program that opened in May, 1972, to counsel street people and to help them find jobs."

Jim is a respectable survivor of his journey into hip. Idealistic and articulate, he sees himself as a combination of the middle class and the counterculture. Settled with his wife in an attractive apartment, he wears the costume of neo-hip, overalls and blue cotton work shirt, as he talks about his doctorate at Berkeley's Department of Social Welfare. Mulling over his commitment to education, he reveals a compassion for the underdog. He hopes to incorporate the values of the counterculture, he says, into the mainstream.

Jim has already begun to affect the mainstream. In May, 1974, he and Professor Henry Miller of the University of California published a study of local street people, *Down and Out in Berkeley*. Baumohl initiated the research through the Berkeley City Council. He wanted to survey the transient population scientifically to prove his experience and test his intuition. He wanted to give the city information of the migrants because he believes that America wastes lives by excluding men and women from obtaining education and employment. He believes men and women suffer because of unfair welfare practices.

"We tend to create and perpetuate misery," Baumohl said. "Then we stick the victim with the bill."

Jim and Professor Miller interviewed street people during the dinner hour at the Berkeley Emergency Food Project for one week in March, 1973. The transients they talked to included runaway children by chance, not on purpose. The fact that they surfaced in the survey reminded me of the Depression. Those *boy and girl tramps of America* went on the road to live like many men who were out of work. By implication *Down and Out in Berkeley* describes a revival of those hard times.

Before the monograph was published, newspapers and wire services announced the seemingly changed street scene. Even as the stock market dropped, the papers reported that *hip was* (finally) *dead* and the hobo revived. "THE BLOOM IS OFF THE 'FLOWER' ERA" said a headline in *The Washington Post,* and "NEW AMERICAN HOBOES TRUDGING STREETS OF COLLEGE TOWNS."

For the report Baumohl and his researchers interviewed 295 people; 239 men and 56 women. The majority were unemployed

young white men, with black men and young white women in
the minority. One-fourth of the women were under eighteen
years old. And one-fifth of all those interviewed had left home
when they were under eighteen.

Although *Down and Out in Berkeley* is a limited study,
as Jim Baumohl admits, I consider it important to the description of runaways in America. The report reveals what happens
to children who run to college towns and do not go home, children who escape detection by the police.

Except for two boys interviewed by the researchers, the children on the street were girls, radical runaways trading on street
attitudes toward women, living off men and the garbage of a
wealthy town.

"Typically, the women quit high school and ran off with
somebody," explained Baumohl. "Then they split and she didn't
want to go home again, so she picked up with another guy and
so on. But the street's not a big sex scene. The opportunity's not
often there."

In *Down and Out* Jim records the techniques of a seventeen-year-old runaway girl he calls Annie Peters. In a few sen-
tences Annie gives a how-to-manage guide for runaway girls:

"When I come to a town I usually go to the long-hair part
and look for a place to crash. It's not usually much trouble. If
I'm with a dude we can usually panhandle or score some acid to
deal. . . . Markets throw out a lot of food, and you can live
off that and out of garbage cans most of the time if you don't
have any money. . . . Usually people are concerned about me—
'specially if I'm alone—and they turn me onto things. But I'd
rather travel with a dude, because a lot of time he'll know somebody somewhere we can stay with. . . . When you travel alone
you get pushed into all kinds of weird sex trips and shit. When
you travel with a dude, for a while you may ball him, but at
least you know where he's coming from."

When Annie was thirteen, she was arrested for smoking
dope in a park and she ran away from home because of her

parents' rejection of her as law breaker. For them she became the bad example, the oldest child whose arrival at adolescence confounds its parents. Annie has two brothers whom she telephones on their birthdays, but she has no plans to go home. As she told her interviewer: "My parents figure I'm a bad influence, and they'd just as soon have me out. . . . I guess I'd rather fuck up here where my parents won't find out about it unless I get busted. I'm pretty careful about that now."

Annie came from a two-parent household, and so did over 61 percent of the men and women considered in the study. The report pricks the myth that erratic youngsters run only from broken homes. It also shakes the prevalent assumption that runaways and drifters represent minority groups as strongly as they do the majority, for the street population is white. Blacks, Chicanos, Indians, and Asians together constitute only 17 percent. The families of street people live in cities and suburbs in every state of the union, primarily in the industrial areas of the Middle Atlantic region and the Pacific Coast.

The street ages its inhabitants quickly. A seventeen-year-old like Annie may look thirty in a few months. Hustling is exhausting and debilitating, but aging has one advantage; the police will ignore those who seem old enough to be out there.

I wondered how many runaways have escaped the police by looking older. Baumohl found several.

"Many of our subjects had been runaways," he said, "and they're still on the street."

"Then they've made it," I observed.

"They've survived," he corrected. "Runaways grow up. They turn eighteen. They're no longer runaways. They're faced with problems they didn't have to think about before, like getting jobs."

Down and Out in Berkeley focuses on the drifter's difficulty in getting a job. The statistics describe men and women who are unprepared to live in a technical country. In contemporary America this makes them not only outsiders but losers.

While only 6 percent of the transients are under eighteen, 70 percent are between eighteen and twenty-five. Young and hungry, they are bitter because they can't get work. Their parents are blue- and white-collar workers whose educations surpass those of their nomadic children. Thirty-four percent of the fathers had graduated from college. Nine percent of their children had. Thirty-two percent of the street people had failed to complete high school while 25 percent of their fathers had not.

As one would expect of inadequately educated gypsies, nobody wanted to hire them. Almost 87 percent of the street people in the university survey were unemployed. By their admission they wanted to work. They had looked for jobs and had been turned down. Many of the would-be workers claimed to have a skill, but they overestimated its selling qualities. They could mold candles, trim hedges, or work a cash register. They knew how to repair a sagging porch, but the requests for such jobs were few.

Lack of training and of education are two strikes against street people. The third is their very nature. In academia they are dull, apolitical scroungers. In a community which romanticized the hippie, these people have nothing to offer.

"Hippies, some of them, were committed spiritual seekers," Baumohl insisted. "You could get articulate thinking from them. They were coherent and persuasive and capable of astute political analyses. The sentiment was *Journey to the East*. It was an odd agglutination of Kerouac and Hesse."

The 1976 street person is inarticulate, if not mute, according to Baumohl. He is neither political nor religious. While his drug involvement is intense, he uses drugs to avoid boredom, not to attain nirvana, as the hippie did. Communal living is not an experiment in society; it's a practical necessity.

Under the microscope the street person comes clear as the waste of an industrial age. He is poor and classless and his reintroduction into American society begs an adjustment of old definitions. Although he looks like him, he is not a hippie, for hippie meant middle class. Although he acts like him, he is not a working man because he does not work. He is déclassé. And *Down and Out in Berkeley* attempts to redefine the wandering mob by comparing it to hip. "The hippies of yesteryear were a population accurately perceived as generated by the upper middle class," it states. In contrast to that observation, the writers make another: street people are the children of working-class parents. The jobs of their fathers lack luster compared to the jobs of the hippies' fathers. Referring to an unpublished California study, *Down and Out* informs: "48 percent of their Haight-Ashbury respondents had fathers employed as administrators, managers, executives, professionals, and the like. At most only 25.6 percent of our respondents can be seen as coming from comparable backgrounds." The street person is a drone around the hive of Berkeley.

Perhaps because of their indolence, street people draw runaways to them. Doing nothing is easier than trying to fulfill the expectations of middle-class parents. On the street, for the moment, the runaway is classless. He is an adventurer, still uncommitted to street living, a child who can return home, unlike many drifters. The runaway begins as a voyeur, a tourist observing the habits of a strange minority. He may adapt to the depressed atmosphere and defect from demand. On the street he sees that nothing is expected of him except cunning in learning the craft of survival.

On the residential streets of Berkeley, the children of the intellectual elite behave as children do everywhere. They smoke dope, drink, fight with their parents, and hang out on Telegraph Avenue with the flotsam of a funky society. They may run away from home too because living in Berkeley is both blessing and curse. They are surrounded by great achievements and constant expectations. As the children of intelligent, talented parents, they are unique and at the very least many are expected to achieve a place in the arts or in the world of the mind. They are to excel academically and artistically.

I exaggerate some, but not much. My conclusions derive from a heady morning I spent at the home of novelist Carolyn

Strauss, eating homemade bread, drinking hot tea, and talking to Jenny and Donna, who had recently graduated from Berkeley High School. They were charming young women, friends of the writer, slightly precious, yet intelligent and self-confident. Wise about themselves and their parents, they understood the opportunities of Berkeley and the ordinariness of the outer world. They knew few runaways, they said, because Berkeley has a remedy for the frustrations that cause running away. Imaginative adults in Berkeley have come up with a solution: *house-switching,* an experiment in moving children into the neutral territory of another family.

Donna, a violinist, had survived her adolescence because she moved out instead of ran out. She accused her mother, a divorced artist, of ignoring her. "I couldn't stand living at home. My mother never knew how to bring up my sister and me. She wouldn't let us take music lessons. She kept the house like a pigpen. So I left and moved in with Jenny's family. I've lived there for three years."

Her friend Jenny explained how Donna's situation was repeated by several children who could not cope with divorced parents, demanding parents, indifferent parents. She described the boys who had switched from their house to hers on the invitation of her parents. One could not endure his parents' quarrels, which ended in divorce; another found his parents too restrictive; a third was having a hard time living alone with his divorced mother. To the four young people house-switching was a success in terms of affection and cooperation. They thought of each other as brothers and sisters, as they shared work and the fun that came of living together.

On its surface house-switching seemed a sensible solution to fighting families. It gave them distance and a cooling-off period, but it relied on the unselfish natures of the adults who ran the household.

"Jenny's mother deserves the credit for the idea," Donna said. "She holds that whole house together."

If California was a microcosm of the runaway world, then Berkeley was the epitome of the successful, professional middle class where ties between children and parents are pulled taut by the pressures of success. The very idea of house-switching brought up questions about ambitious parents and their children. In its pursuit of excellence, didn't Berkeley aggravate the natural friction of families? In its emphasis on achievement, didn't it allow the undecided and the untalented to feel insecure and frightened? Wasn't there the expectation that children who lived in Berkeley would be as unusual as the town itself? Was the presence of professional dedication by parents overwhelming? Did the unambitious street people appeal by contrast?

"In Berkeley everyone's into things," Jenny said. "They're so aware. But not all of the kids," she amended. "It's hard to live in Berkeley if you don't have anything."

Studying music and rehearsing with the youth orchestra as they did, Jenny and Donna were too self-assured to be drawn to the street people. Yet, one of the boys in the house spent time rapping with the drifters, they said.

"He's trying to get into something, to be accepted," Donna said. "The Ave is attractive to kids who don't have anything to do, who haven't pursued anything."

The outsider is not always a runaway, but his leaving home affirms what he already believes: he does not belong where he lives. Perhaps in another town, another city, he will find his place. The child who runs to a university town will meet other runaways who have turned the street into their home. Like them he may decide that the meanness of poverty is no worse than his failure at home. He may find fellowship on the street. If so, he will travel with his friends from one college town to another, searching for new meccas.

Across the continent in Boston I had talked to the Catholic street priest, Father Paul Shanley, who told me that he was the only diocesan priest in the country assigned full time to the street. For three years, 1967 through 1969, his ministry was, officially, to "alienated youth" in Boston, since Cardinal Cushing had appointed him to serve runaways and street people. When I met him, Father Paul had traveled out of the runaway scene of the late 1960s. He was off the street, serving in a parish in a black ghetto and counseling homosexuals, conducting mass for them in the Back Bay.

He spoke with warmth of the children who had come to Boston to find love among the street people. They had seemed to him "beautiful." Bitterly, he talked about the suburban adults who accused him of encouraging their children to defy them.

"Their parents told me to 'leave them alone and they'll go home,' but they didn't go home. One in six street people is now a heroin addict. My people are dead of drug-related causes."

Father Paul is a romantic, a cleric without a collar, a middle-aged man with long hair, famous in Boston for his sympathy to street youth. In mimeographed letters mailed to his friends and supporters, he glorified the bands of children who lived off the street. They were to him nonviolent revolutionaries, plying their way across the country, pack on back and sentiments of Herman Hesse in their hearts. Like Jim Baumohl of Berkeley, Father Paul was in love with history and with the brave young people who began a revolution.

"If any romance leaked through those letters," he said, "it's because people on the street were good. I never once saw one freak injure another. All the suffering was caused by red-neck adults and cops. What the street did to the freaks was terrible. Runaways and street people are at the mercy of predatory adults."

As Father Paul sees it, life on the street is dangerous and depraved. Children in trouble avoid city streets for halfway houses and drop-in centers in the suburbs. The street scene today is sexual, he believes.

"The street has become a horror show. It's as senseless and depraved as the straight world kids run from. The kid on the street now is the new nigger, the new freak. He's a bisexual who discovers his sexual ambivalence and runs to the city. The best-kept secret of the freak scene is its changing sexuality. New runaways are coming to the sexual ghettoes of the city."

The runaway is lost in the city. In his imagination the street is peopled with colorful men and women, exotic and kind, whose quest is pleasure and beauty. In reality the street is sordid, crowded with packs of strangers. The runaway becomes their prey.

"He's like a baby who can't survive alone," Father Paul said. "You can use a runaway for many things."

In one aspect big cities are like university towns for runaways. They protect them with the anonymity they extend to everyone. Only after several days do runaways, like many travelers, realize that the city's impersonality is destructive. It can ignore them until they become so forlorn that they willfully do anything to or with anyone to have a friend and a few dollars. Road knowledge or home-grown, the facts about sex and dope qualify them for survival. Runaways can hustle to live.

"I believe in sin and I believe in evil," the priest said. "We are all capable of becoming monsters."

8. Hustling to Live: On the Streets of New York and Houston

"Every kid is different. There are eight million stories. It's the old story: kid's story, parent's story. In between you get the truth."—Officer Arnold Dansky, New York City Police Department Runaway Unit, March, 1974.

I. New York City

By four o'clock in the morning the men, women, and children who make their living on the streets around Times Square are still working. Beautiful black girls, dressed to show, wearing high heels and tight shorts or short skirts, are strolling the avenue looking for a trick. By four o'clock they're finishing their last turn of the evening when an unmarked police car pulls up to the curb beside them. The two officers, who wear sports jackets and wide ties, may fool new girls into mistaking them for tourists, but these chicks know them. They jaw for a few minutes, then drive on, looking for Sally and Billy.

On Eighth Avenue at Forty-ninth Street the policemen spot Sally and Billy entering a restaurant. She looks down and her man looks mean. The police know what Sally earned that eve-

144

ning. They wink at each other like a pair of Broadway comics. It takes a lot of loving to keep Billy-Boy high.

Sally and Billy are black, prostitute and pimp, employee and employer, lover and beloved. Sally will do what Billy requires to hold him. She goes on the stroll for him, and he hustles for her. Together they share a life, nesting in a modern apartment and nodding sweet dreams. Billy buys to ease their life—stereo, color TV, shag carpets, plenty of clothes—and Sally pays. At twenty-five she is showing lines of wear and worry. She's losing her zest and the money isn't moving. She's getting too tired to glitter on the street.

They sit in the restaurant over a cup of coffee. She gives Billy a roll of money.

Every night Billy asks her the same question: "You holding out on me?"

Every night Sally says: "Count it, baby. It's fat tonight."

If Billy chicken-shits the roll, Sally croons him into a honey mood with stories about the tricks, the white men who pay for her loving. She tells him about the suburban daddy, who, burning rubber, drove up and down uptown streets looking for a parking place. She laughs at the bald truck driver who took her to an alley while he kept the motor running. She smiles about the old grandpa who paid for a room on East Thirteenth Street so he could take a nap later.

Tonight Billy doesn't smile. Tonight the roll is skinny as a baby's prick. When Billy asks, "You holding out on me?" he is the black-eyed devil and he will not allow her to go to the supply.

Sally begins to moan. "The Man's been hassling me, Billy. He kept a car on me all night. I couldn't hardly make a call."

The Man is after Billy, not his pros, and Billy sweats to hear it. Hard times are getting harder unless he takes Sally off the street. Off the street, they'll hit the craves, then the pain. When Billy goes the rough road, he wants to choose it, not the Man.

Sally watches Billy eye the counter. She sees him satisfy himself that the patrol car is gone. She hears him whisper like the high-time Billy-Boy: "Sugar, you know I always been a praying man."

"Billy, you a swearing man."

"Makes no difference, baby. You been praying for a vacation. You going to get a vacation. I been praying for a bundle of green. I going to get my bundle."

He moves, oh-so-smoothly, to a cigarette machine. He lights up and flashes his Fifth Avenue smile. At her? No, mama. Billy-Boy is on the prowl. When he settles on a counter stool, still looking pretty, Sally knows he's fishing.

The catch is a white girl. She is drinking a glass of water and looking scared. When Billy sits beside her, she hides behind her long brown hair.

As Billy murmurs to the girl, Sally watches his action. She sees the girl look up and listen, glance her way, then tell Billy her name.

He brings her to their booth and names them formally. "Sally, honey, this here is Carolina Cotton. Miss Cotton, Miss Jones."

He waits until Carolina slides into the seat before he sits down. He hands her a menu. "Miss Cotton has just arrived from down home and she has lost her money. I have invited her to have a meal on us."

The girl can eat and eat. She orders and wolfs steak, french fries, a green salad, a vanilla malted. Billy adds apple pie and ice cream and tells her his folks live in South Carolina.

Sally feels sorry for this little white girl. She is either real dumb or real smart. She is a shy, trampy little girl, about sixteen. Her face isn't too bad, but her hair is stringy and she's on the skinny side. Sally suspects what's on Billy's mind because he's talked before of getting a white girl to turn tricks for him.

"Tricks go for young white girls," he said. "They can do

anything with a white girl who's young and hungry."

When she stops eating and starts explaining, Miss Carolina Cotton is as fascinating as a TV show. First, she tells Billy and Sally that Carolina Cotton isn't her real name, but she don't remember her real name. Because of her horrible experiences she is a victim of amnesia. Black people, a different race from Sally and Billy, killed her whole family. Only she escaped. She ran away, crawling out the bedroom window, while a big black man was fucking her mother. Her mother was screaming. Her father was killed while he was counting his money. He was a wealthy planter, very rich. She hitchhiked to the Florida Keys and lived alone on a beach. One day a fisherman picked her up and took her home to stay with his family. After a month or so, she decided to come to New York to get a job. While she was riding the bus to New York, somebody ripped her off.

Sally wants to laugh in her lying face, but Billy sighs her quiet. He sounds sorrowful. "That is a very sad story." He wipes his hand across his eyes blotting out a tear.

He takes Carolina's hand and pats it like a down-home uncle. Troubled-sounding, he asks Sally: "How can we help this little girl?"

Sally wants to shout: "Big fool! Let the white snake go." She keeps her mouth shut and stares at him.

When the waitress comes with the check, Billy lays a hundred-dollar bill on the tray without looking at it. Carolina sees it and her eyes grow big. Sally didn't think he had a Ben Franklin left.

Turning to Carolina, Billy takes both her hands. "Carolina, honey, Sally and me want you to stay with us until you get set up in your own apartment."

Excited, Carolina rubs her ass back and forth on the seat. "Oh! You want me? You mean you really want me to stay with you? Oh, hey, that's neat, that's cool! I'll be good, I'll be so good! I'm real good around the house."

Now Billy puts his arm around her and holds her close. He lets his hand rest on her breast, and he tells Sally to go home to bed. He rocks Carolina to him.

Hopped up mad, Sally jumps up to shout. Billy won't look at her. For him it's only Carolina, and he talks to her soft and low. Carolina listens and her mouth falls open. When she starts to nod, Sally knows he's caught the dumb white trash. If Carolina nuzzles in on her and Billy, Sally will kill her.

Turning her first trick in the back seat of a cab at 5:30 in the morning, Carolina Cotton, the homeless, wandering child, earns $20. She begs Sweet Billy to take her home to sleep.

Assuring her she is going to be richer than her dead daddy, Billy stops another cab and loves Carolina all the way home.

Two years later police officers of the East Twelfth Street Runaway Unit cruise Manhattan in plain cars, searching for runaways. They're competing with the pimps to get the children first. They want to find them before hustlers like Billy grab them.

Billy himself sits in jail, sentenced on a narcotics charge. Sally, his hard-working woman, is trying to drop her habit in a drug rehabilitation program. Carolina Cotton is legend. Like a short-term government bond, Carolina paid off fast and high. Many nights she brought in more money than her father, who was actually a sergeant in the marines, earned each week.

"Her first night she made two hundred fifteen dollars," recalled Sally, relaxing over a cup of coffee not far from the restaurant where she met Carolina. "Billy told me to take her to the street, to sit in a coffee shop while she strolled looking for pickups. After a trick she'd meet me and give me the money to hold.

"I was feeling sorry for the girl. She was so young and shy. And she was picking up tricks left and right, one trick after another. They go for young white girls," she explained. "Young girls are so dumb they'll do anything."

Remembering the money Carolina handed over to her,

Sally burst out laughing. "I thought she couldn't count. I took half of everything she gave me so I'd have something for Billy. She got slick after the fourth night. Here I was sitting and waiting for her to meet me with the money like every other night, and she didn't come. I must of sat there for three hours like a fool. When I went home, this white girl is in my bed with the money laying out around her. She had beat a trick and got five hundred dollars. I was mad enough to kill her."

Carolina had robbed her customer and run home to Billy to prove how good she really was. She was as wily as Billy and was able to turn him on and depose Sally. By the end of the first year Carolina was pregnant and pushing Sally to the brink of murder.

"I saw her baby in the hospital right after it was born. It didn't look like Billy's baby to me. It looked like a Chinese baby or a Puerto Rican. I don't believe it was Billy's. I was mixed in my feelings about that trampy little bitch. When she was pregnant, Billy said to me, 'You going back out on the stroll.' I minded and I didn't. I was bored sitting in front of the television just doping. But thinking of her home alone with Billy got me jealous. One morning after she come home from the hospital, Billy left me to sit with her. I tried to kill her. I kicked her down the steps, her and the baby."

The real adventures of Carolina Cotton began to resemble the distortions of her imagination. Seduced by a pimp, sexually abused by strangers, living with two heroin addicts, one a wild woman, she was half-crazy. She warned Billy he'd find her dead one day. She wanted an apartment far away from Sally.

If Carolina would give up the baby so she could go back to the street, Billy would set her up in her own place. If she worked again, she could afford it. If she didn't, she'd have to live with Sally and Billy.

Carolina agreed to place the infant with the welfare people if Billy lived with her, not Sally. Billy said he'd give it thought. With two women working for him, he was flying high. Carolina was his baby, he assured her, and he moved her up to the Bronx.

Sally was his old lady, he promised her, and he kept his heroin cache with Sally and sailed between both apartments.

"When Billy was busted for possession, he knew I'd try to find Carolina and hurt her," Sally recalled. "He said, 'Woman, keep your hands clean. She's my retirement plan.' I found her," Sally grinned. "And I fixed her."

With Billy in jail and Carolina hustling for herself, Sally met her on the street she worked. Like Billy before her, she sweet-talked Carolina, lonely without Billy or her baby, into her bed.

"Me and her started going together. We had sex together and it was real good. I told Billy and he felt safe. He knew I wouldn't kill her," she shrugged. "I did worse. I made her start shooting dope.

"I didn't think anything about sticking a spike in her arm. I was a dope fiend and I wanted her to be one."

The affair of Carolina and Sally lasted long enough for Carolina to become addicted to heroin. As she began to crave the drug, she worked the streets around Times Square with the determination she had shown Billy in her early days. She began hustling black tricks because they would often give her heroin instead of money. Sally sympathized with her lust for dope and for Billy and herself, but she warned her to be leery of the black men she picked up.

"Black tricks get on top of you and make a home. I fear them because, usually, they want their money back. Carolina never learned. She stayed dumb to the end."

The end for the two women was Sally's being arrested for prostitution. One evening a trick turned into an arresting police officer. Before she was sentenced, Sally asked to enter a resident program for the rehabilitation of drug addicts. While she was living at Project Return, she called Carolina and heard she'd moved.

"I don't know what happened to her," Sally told me. "Probably she's on the stroll for another pimp. I don't miss her.

She was just a dumb little white girl. She should of stayed home with her mama and daddy."

In New York City many policemen believe *runaway* is synonymous with *prostitute*, male or female. Although they have picked up—and saved—hundreds of children who didn't belong there, thousands have eluded them. Like Carolina Cotton, hundreds have become salesmen in the profitable business of sex. They sell their bodies the way the Depression-era jobless sold apples and pencils—to the customer who has the cash.

The marketplace in New York embraces East Side, West Side, uptown and down. Since each neighborhood has a distinctive personality, policemen associate the peculiarities of the district with the runaways they find in them. Certain districts draw certain kids. When they arrive in New York, runaway children are attracted to Times Square and Greenwich Village, which they know as symbols of the city from television and movies. After a runaway has lived in Manhattan for a few days, according to the police, he goes to work in the area which best suits his sexual talents.

Briefly, these are the runaways of New York: in Times Square are the green kids looking for flash, or the professional hookers looking for men; in Greenwich Village, suburban kids come looking for hippies; in the East Village, abused children, the throwaways, look for contacts; on the East Side of Manhattan, experienced boys dally looking for homosexuals.

Times Square and the streets which lead to it are the centers of female prostitution. Girls work off the street or out of massage parlors. They may work independently, but usually they stroll for a pimp, like Billy. If they hook out of a massage parlor, they are usually employees of the management.

Third Avenue in the Fifties is one neighborhood that draws male prostitutes. Boys gather in front of the smart decorating shops that line the midtown section of the avenue. The shops sell antiques or paintings, but the business out front is sexual.

People who should know better say that kids with sexual problems run away to the city. Hip clergymen, graduate students with a thesis to write, supercynical policemen visualize a big city like New York or San Francisco the way Hemingway saw Paris —as a moveable feast. They have convinced themselves that the feast is sexual and that the motives for running away to the cities are perverted by biological urges. They imagine a sexual runaway, yearning for the adult diversions of an X-rated town.

In my interviews, I've observed that the children who run to the cities are naive. Their inexperience itself draws them to glamour towns like Boston, New York, Miami, New Orleans, San Francisco. Unsophisticated, they imagine that they're leaving the narrow routine and unchanging days at home behind them.

If they live in look-alike suburbs, the city is their natural destination. Their parents take the train to work or to shop and see a show. The kids may have visited the city themselves to go to a museum with their class or to attend the theater with their parents. They feel the excitement of the crowds and want to join them.

If the runaways live in the flat lands of the Midwest or the small towns of Pennsylvania or New England, their curiosity about the city is piqued by television shows. An Amish-country minister who brought his youth group to New York said: "'Kojak's the way they learn about cities. When they tour New York, these youngsters say they're glad they live where they do, but that New York's not such a bad place. Some think it's worse than they imagined, a few others better."

What prevents a runaway in New York from becoming a prostitute is a combination of luck and good sense, class and experience. If he is lucky, he is found by the police or by anxious citizens who put him in the care of a church, a social-welfare agency, or the police. If he is sensible, when he becomes hungry and frightened he will take the advice of posted notices that urge him to call a hotline, a crisis-help telephone number, sponsored by a local agency or the federal government.

The middle-class runaway has an advantage in New York or in any major city that the poor child lacks. Because of his family's income and education he is probably more adept at taking care of himself than the child of the low-income family. He may have had experiences of travel that the poor kid has not. He may be more self-assured around adults.

The child of low-income parents may have street knowledge, but this savvy is dangerous to him. As a Runaway Unit police officer explained: "We don't pick up many black kids. They speak the jive. It's hard to notice them as runaways."

The child of the ghetto and the low-income family, however, may know his way around parts of town like the Bowery or the East Village. If he keeps away from affluent streets or areas popular with tourists, which are well patrolled by police, he also avoids the people who can help him. Of necessity he may submit to prostitution.

Contrary to television documentaries and articles in Sunday supplements, most runaways the police pick up in New York are middle-class children. As policewoman Mickey Maglino, who searches for runaways, said: "The unit has detained kids from middle-class families mainly, kids who have typical growing-up problems. They fight with their parents about their boyfriends, the way they dress, their hair, their hours. Many of them come from broken homes, many of them don't. These kids head to the West Village and Times Square for the atmosphere. The kids who have real problems go to the East Village. They may have alcoholic parents and beating parents. Many of them are from lower-income brackets."

The police of the Runaway Unit discover the fleeing children as they walk along Broadway or Christopher Street. They will approach a youngster who looks out of place or speaks with an out-of-town accent, show him their badge, and tell him to identify himself. If the child refuses to answer or if his reply seems vague, the police will take him to the East Twelfth Street station.

Before they arrive at the station, the officers will probably buy the hungry child a coke and a hamburger. They'll try to talk to him as a friend. At the station they'll call his parents to check his identification if he has admitted who he is. They'll learn whether he has permission to be on the streets of New York. If they cannot verify his story, they'll send him to a private shelter like Project Yes on East Fourteenth Street, or to a city juvenile-detention center until they determine his situation. If they confirm their idea that he is a runaway, they will make arrangements for his return home.

As Lt. Neil Davino, training officer for the Youth Aid Division, told me: "In this particular section of town, the Village, many of the kids we pick up are involved with drugs and prostitution. But most of the kids I've seen are middle-class kids who went home after three or four days."

In March, before the city warmed up to summer, I rode with two officers of the New York Police Department Runaway Unit through the Manhattan neighborhoods where runaway children work. We began the drive early in the evening before the peak sexual business hours. Annoyed with pulling a public-relations duty, Officers Bill Kinsella and Arnold Dansky explained the geography of a runaway's New York reluctantly. When they sighted the first streetwalker of the evening, they perked up. Their familiarity with the territory broke down their hesitation. They were proud to reveal Sin City.

From their headquarters on East Twelfth Street, they drove to the Bowery and stopped on Delancey Street at a sandwich shop. A pretty blond was sitting at the counter sipping a coke. A streetwalker, they told me, seventeen years old, who had gone on the street as a fifteen-year-old runaway. She was a New York kid from a poor family. Her alcoholic father beat her.

"They all say their parents beat them," said Arnie. "Every kid gives you a story on how rotten their parents are, how they beat them, how much they drink. Kids don't always tell the truth."

"How do you know when kids are lying?" I asked.

"When we take them to the station, we make them call their parents and we listen in on another line," Bill explained. "If the old man says, 'I'm going to beat the hell out of you when I get you home,' then we believe the kid. If the parents don't say anything like that, then we think the kid's probably lying."

"The really abused kid goes to court," added Arnie. "If we have any doubts about city kids, we talk to the neighbors."

The blond streetwalker had told Bill and Arnie that some runaway girls were working Chinatown. But in Chinatown the streets were empty except for a few tourists who were window-shopping.

"They come here," Bill said. "Runaways, flyaways from Puerto Rico, streetwalkers like the blond."

"Why would a former runaway tell the police where other runaways are?" I asked.

"They feel sorry for them," Bill Kinsella said. "They can see themselves as they were a few years back."

"Young girls are cutting into their business," Arnold Dansky said. "The way the prostitutes look at it, it's a job. It's their body. They can do what they want with it."

From Chinatown we drove to Third Avenue. The officers explained that the rush of freaks to Second Avenue had slowed down. The dope-eating hippie freaks had been displaced by hoodlums who would kill any cop who turned his back. Second Avenue was vicious and runaways kept off it.

On the east side of Third Avenue between Fifty-third and Fifty-fourth streets male prostitutes pause in front of shops. They are fruit-hustling, playing chicken hawk. They wait for a homosexual hawk, a man who likes sex with teen-age boys. When the hawk spots a likely chicken, the willing boy, he initiates the transaction. One hawk told a *New York Times* reporter that he gave his boys $10, $15, or even $20. "We go to movies and dinners. I never force a kid and never was the first with anybody." Another said: "I fix up my apartment like a teen-ager's dream—with games and mod decorations and rock music, all the things young boys like."

The two officers pointed to a restaurant on Fifty-third Street where I saw boys, lounging in the door-length windows, peering into the street.

"They hang around in doorways, too," said Bill, gesturing toward a boy in the entrance to a store. "Usually they go with a guy to his apartment. Some of them are little boys, twelve, thirteen, fourteen years old. Some are runaways, some locals."

"These kids are rip-off artists," Arnie said.

We cut across Fifth Avenue to the West Side, to the massage parlors of Eighth Avenue, to the Minnesota Strip, a block along Eighth at Forty-ninth Street frequented by Midwestern runaways, to Ninth Avenue, another area for prostitutes, to the Port Authority Bus Terminal, where pimps scavenge for lost-looking girls. The cluster of massage parlors around Forty-second and Eighth hires runaway girls, often without knowing they are under sixteen.

"We've taken a twelve-year-old girl out of a massage parlor," Bill said. Even he sounded awed. "The girls make ten dollars for a massage, twenty-five dollars for a lay."

"On the street prostitutes make twenty-five dollars a trick or better," Arnie explained. "If they work from two in the afternoon until six in the morning, they can make two hundred to two hundred fifty dollars a day."

Driving past Washington Square Park, we completed the circuit in Greenwich Village. "In June, July, and August the park's a good-time place with lots of kids sitting around the fountain playing guitars. And lots of pimps hang out there looking for girls."

"We pick up more girls than boys in the city," Arnie said. "The ratio is about three to one."

"From September to April or May runaways get into prostitution and drugs," Bill observed. "In the warmer months, when it's easier to live, that's not necessarily so.

"Many of the kids we pick up want to go home," he continued. "If they're being sent home by the police, it's cool. They can save face."

On their way to speak to a group of out-of-town youngsters who were staying at St. John's Lutheran Church on Christopher Street in the Village, Bill and Arnie dropped me off at the unit's headquarters. The evening life of the streets was starting. The restaurant crowd and the hustlers were ready for business.

"What are you going to tell the church group about running away in New York?" I asked.

"We'll tell it to 'em just like it is!" Bill shouted. "It ain't healthy to run away like psychologists say it is."

II. Houston

In Houston I met a male prostitute, a runaway who sold himself on street corners to spite his parents. For the boy and his parents love and money were a common language. Money—theirs—communicated affection and pleasure. Love—his—meant repayment in terms of achievement. The boy who would not repay the debt of love was worthless. He had to leave, but to run was not enough. He had to run to get his own money, to show his parents that somebody found him worthwhile.

"How frank can I be?" Stephen asked, stretching his legs to admire the suede shoes with the chunky heels.

"Very frank," I assured him.

He looked me over slowly, wary of my reactions, hoping for sympathy.

"I wanted an easy way out," he admitted. "I was forced to

hustle. I made money and I ate. I've walked every inch of downtown Houston."

He rolled up his sleeve and showed me two black-and-blue
marks.

"I sold my blood too. The first time I got five dollars, the
second time seven dollars. Before I started to hustle, I slept in
the bus station. The cops left me alone."

He shrugged and buttoned his cuff.

"Nothing bothers me. If somebody craps on me, I'll get
them back."

Although Stephen Dassell had run away from home at
seventeen, he was not a legal runaway. In Texas and in Florida,
his home state, the law no longer considers him a juvenile.
Stephen needed to pass as a runaway to gain the sympathy of
the men who picked him up. It also gave him access to the runaway shelter where I talked to him.

Stephen was from Orlando. He had graduated from high
school in June and left home a few weeks later. Unlike the
Depression children who went on the road to find jobs, Stephen
was running from another economic whirlwind, the affluence
that plagues the middle-class and infects many of its children.
Stephen was running not from poverty but from disaffection.
He was running from his belief that to his family he was an
investment that was not paying off. He believed himself to be
neither a necessity nor a luxury. By leaving home he was cutting their losses.

"My parents are very tight," Stephen said. "We were either
fighting about money or my friends. Before I left, I had a big
fight with my mom because she wouldn't let me spend the night
with friends. The next morning, after breakfast, I took sixty
dollars and seventy-five cents out of her purse and called a cab.
I grabbed everything I owned and went to the bus station, where
I bought a ticket to Tampa. I got a hotel job there for thirty-two
dollars a week and met the man who brought me to Houston.

"I was working at the hotel when my friend asked me to live with him in his house in Houston. When we got here, he dropped me downtown while he made arrangements for me to move in. I was to meet him in the evening at a hotel, but he never showed up. That night it was raining and I'd spent all my money on food. I slept in the bus station and walked the streets the next day. The first time I hustled was my second night here."

"I stood on the corner of Main Street by a bus stop," Stephen said. "And I waited for the cars to pull up to the light. I walked over and asked the drivers if they wanted me to . . ."

He stopped talking and smiled. He knew I understood him and he did not choose to describe the service he offered.

He continued: "Sunday, Monday, and Tuesday nights I was able to pay for a room in the William Penn Hotel."

I reminded him that the Houston homosexual Dean Corll had killed the boys he picked up.

Stephen laughed at the idea. He savored the excitement of hustling in the city of one of the nation's worst mass murders. "I've never known anybody like Corll. There aren't a million people like him running around."

He was not ashamed of his prostitution. Sex was a commodity, a way to make a few dollars fast. Houston was a hustler's market, and he was a handsome piece of goods. His expressive almond-shaped eyes were set in a mobile face, his wiry black hair brushed into a bush. He wore a blue shirt tight across his chest and light-colored pants that clung to his hips and legs. An embroidered belt encircled his waist and a Star of David hung from his neck. He spoke vivaciously about himself and his parents.

"They had high hopes for me," he smiled. "I just threw them down the drain."

He held out his slender hands with their clean, tapered nails.

"I have a grand piano at home. I've taken music lessons for years. My grades were good and I expected to go to college. My parents wanted me to stay home to attend college, but I wanted to go away, get my independence, see my friends, travel when I pleased.

"I changed during my senior year. I was edgy. I couldn't look at my parents. I couldn't say anything nice."

He was silent, puzzling over his transformation.

During his last year in high school Stephen began to believe that his parents didn't want him. He tried to explain his feelings, but he hesitated. It was another indecency he had difficulty putting into words.

"You know when you're wanted," he began. "And you know when you're not wanted. You can't compromise with my parents. They never sat down and talked with me. They just yelled."

His mother had plans for Stephen that she feared he would spoil. She and his father had gotten him a piano, a baby grand that symbolized their expectations for him. He practiced every day for years. He played beautifully but lost interest when he started running around in high school.

His father said Stephen needed to learn the value of money and they encouraged him to find a job for the summer. But first, as a graduation gift, they sent him to New York to visit his sister. From New York he hitchhiked south to the Carolinas, to Atlanta. He made friends on the road and wanted to keep traveling. When he telephoned his parents for money, they refused to pay for his wanderings. He returned to Orlando and took a job as a waiter in a hotel in Disney World. When the management ordered him to cut his hair, he quit.

He was tired of taking orders, from his mother, his father, his boss. He wanted to make it on his own.

"I have my independence now," he grinned wryly. "And it's not feeling too good."

That evening he was to begin a cashier's job at the Burger Factory, a hamburger joint in the Montrose area of Houston, a neighborhood south of Houston Heights frequented by homosexuals. Stephen Dassell wanted to believe his quest for the easy dollar was over. He was going to work for his money and get his own place, then return to Orlando to live, alone or with a friend. Not with his family.

"I'm even going to try temple again," Stephen said.

The flight from home becomes a search for love. For Stephen and for Carolina, for runaways to religious sects or college towns, for children who do not return, running away ends a lie about love: the radical runaway does not love his parents as he thinks he must. He feels, right or wrong, that neither do they love him. He considers himself less important to his parents than he should be. He may feel guilty about disappointing them, but aren't they supposed to love him whatever he does? He accuses them, verbally or tacitly, of being more in love with their possessions and their reputation than they are with him. Everything they have revolves around money: attractive homes, cars, vacations, clothes, even him. They buy him toys, then stereos, clothes, schools, music lessons, trips. In exchange he is expected to produce a return on their investment.

Money and love become the same coin. Since his parents show their affection and approval with what the dollar can buy, they register their disapproval by snapping shut the wallet. They expect their children to repay them with self-control, success in school, a decent appearance.

Their emphasis on cost convinces the child that he is an undesirable expense. His apparent indifference to their anxiety mocks them. Depression families had hard times feeding and clothing their children; inflation families seem anxious about receiving no immediate value for money spent. Many feel that by raising children they are buying stock in the future, but they're anticipating solid dividends on the investment.

"I'm not living up to my potential," is an expression I have heard often from kids ordered to perform well in school. Their parents insist to them, and to me, that their children have the potential ability to excel and they expect better grades than they're getting. The student realizes more thoroughly than his parents that money cannot buy them a plastic child who can be molded to specification. He is trapped by their belief in money. The orthodontist can improve his teeth, the private school can improve his education, the psychologist can improve his attitude. If there is failure, the fault is his. His parents have provided everything money can buy.

The bewildered child has meager resources to refute the logic of his parents. How can he, less successful than they are, convince them of their ignorance? He finds fault with their demands and restrictions of him: his clothes, hair, friends, schoolwork. These are squabbles without a victor. Hair, clothes, grades are aspects of personality that have little to do with money. They illustrate his difference from them and his allegiance to other youngsters. The adolescent's denim jeans, long hair, illicit social pleasures make a point: he is not an imitation of his parents. He cannot repeat their childhood or create the one they have imagined for him.

9. A Family Affair

"I'm not an emancipated woman, but I've changed many of my ideas because I have a runaway daughter."—Jean Zinner, McLean, Virginia, August, 1974.

What makes one child run away and another stay home? Except in extreme cases where parents beat a child or berate him constantly or where the child is mentally ill, it has been my experience that between runaways and nonrunaways there is no apparent difference. No certain pattern of behavior to cause parents or teachers to say: "There's a possible runaway." All teen-age children are possible runaways, and the one we might pick out of a class as *least likely to run away from home* will surprise us by admitting that yes, she has run away several times.

As I prepared my manuscript for publication, I asked the seventeen-year-old students in my twelfth-grade literature course to answer a few questions for me. I wanted them to write their ideas about school, their friends, the adults they knew. I asked them to become anonymous so that they would be frank. Because of the increasing numbers of runaway girls I did ask them to state their sex. I wanted to know if the girls, more than the boys, were resentful toward their parents. Were they more placid or passive, more frustrated or disenchanted with home or school than the boys? The answer in all cases was *no*. Both boys and girls responded like young people ready for a change, eager to graduate from high school and strike out on their own.

One question was: "Have you ever considered running away from home? Why? Why not?" In the sheaf of answers I found a runaway girl. She wrote: "I've gone many times." After explaining that at first running away was her method of waking up her parents to the importance of her ideas and experiences, she denied that running was only a way to get attention. She said: "Running was necessary to experience something real and not preplanned. It gave me a feeling of self-confidence to hold my own in the outside world."

A boy wrote of running away as a test of his capabilities. "I've considered running away, not from home, but to enjoy independence, to assert myself, to prove that I'm capable of taking care of myself."

Two dozen other seemingly satisfied, college-bound seniors from professional, affluent, middle-class homes admitted thinking about running away. They showed their kinship with runaway children as they talked of the warfare at home. Here are the replies of youngsters who were born privileged:

"Life at home is usually unbearable, and academics seem useless. I'm a protected, isolated little rich brat, essentially, and I'd like to experience more of the world."

"I have fantasized about running away from home and considered it in less drastic ways, like going to boarding school, but that would be a superficial escape. I would still be in academics and under the economic supervision of my parents. In moments of fury I have left the house, but my anger has never been sustained enough for me to run away. I have a strong sense of the future which makes running away less attractive."

"When I was in a lot of trouble once," a boy confessed, "I considered running away, but I decided against it because it was financially impractical and much easier to weather out the storm ahead."

"I don't run away because I'm incapable of supporting myself. But I can't wait to get out of the house. I can't really talk to my parents and I'd rather not see them."

"I have considered running away because my parents were always arguing, especially when they were drunk. I really couldn't take it. The only thing holding me back was lack of money. I had no place to go."

"When my parents seemed set on making me miserable, I've thought of running away. They fight and go through hard periods and I've thought that if I run away, it might provide an impetus to resolve their problems."

"I have everything to lose if I run away. I will let my parents run the show because they support me, but when I leave home, I will run the show. Now I will try to benefit as much as I can from my youthful captivity."

From my inquiry in the classroom I found a few naysayers, children who lived in peaceful homes. Their self-assurance was based on solid security. A boy commented: "There is nothing that I can't cope with at home and there is nothing drawing me away from home."

"I have never considered running away from home. There is an assurance of love and stability at home which I may not find elsewhere," a girl decided.

The most confident wrote about love. To my question about the possibilities of his running, a boy asked another: "Have you ever considered blinding yourself or cutting off an arm?" He addressed me when he wrote: "I wouldn't expect you to ask if I loved my parents, but on the question of runaways I think it's pertinent. My parents instill in me the ambition and desire that make life great. I love them and they love me."

A few would run for adventure because life at home restricts them; they want to see the world. They would run after freedom to assert themselves or because their parents drink and fight and make them miserable. They would run because their parents issue orders without explaining them, or punish them for minor offenses. Some would leave because they feel they are not taken seriously, some because their parents insist on their standards and values and ignore the feelings of their children.

They have *not* run away from home because they are practical youngsters with an eye to the future. Their escape comes legitimately when they leave for college in the fall. Having reached senior year in high school, they realize that freedom is close at hand. They can continue to humor parents and teachers for a few more months, receive the benefits of security, gather strength for their own entry into life outside home and school. They can nurse their individuality in private, knowing that soon they will leap into a new world.

One of my students who knows two boys who ran away admires their spunk. As he wrote, "I think kids who run away are not particularly different in values or goals from others their age, but they have more courage and independent spirit than most of us. They are also more impulsive and short-sighted. Still, they are willing to give up the material security of home. That takes courage."

Although my students mention many of the same reasons for wanting to leave as the runaways gave me, they do not know abuse and deprivation. They do not possess the sense of being unwanted. They do not share with radical runaways the fear that their parents do not love them. Most like or respect or love their parents. They do fight with them, defy them, lie to them, and hurt them, but few are so cruel as to condemn them by leaving home suddenly.

"When my parents punished me for something I felt was not wrong, I thought of running away from home," a student told me. "Other times I considered it because I got sick of school and restrictions. I didn't go because for some weird reason I respect my parents. As much as I hate them as parents, I love them as people and I wouldn't want to hurt them."

What differences do exist between runaways and nonrunaways transcend economics, sex, intelligence. I searched for three years to locate the causes of running away in America and I am still surprised when I hear of a certain child's running. Unlike Bill Treanor, the former director of Runaway House in Washington, D.C., I cannot construct a formula for detecting a runaway or determining who will stay at home. In 1972 before Senator Bayh's investigating committee, Bill described the kind of child who would probably not run from home. He said: "That is a young person who has at least one other sibling, who is living with both of his natural parents, who has not moved during the period that he has been in school—his family has not changed houses, or at least neighborhoods—and whose family has some kind of value system that they are trying to transmit to the child and are consistent about it. The reason I say that . . . is because I do not recall ever seeing a runaway that was raised that way."

I have met children like those Bill Treanor describes. They were runaways whom I knew from school. A child defies his parents—and all predictions.

Recognizing the parents of runaway children is easier than pointing to a potential runaway. It is they who bear the mark of Cain, the telltale signs of long nights and days of anxiety. They share nervous habits which set them apart from other parents. They answer the telephone after the first ring. They are afraid to see a police car drive slowly past the house. They rush to the mailbox to look for a letter. They look gaunt and they are stern. They show their unhappiness in irritability, in not being able to smile, in tense conversations. They are angry, like the father who asked a Boulder runaway-house counselor: "Is that son-of-a-bitch there? I want him home now. He ripped his mother off. How much did he come there with?" They may assume indifference, like the mother who said: "That's all right. I don't mind. Tell her she can stay away until September." Like other parents, they will wonder: "Where is she? What is she doing?"

With a child missing, whereabouts unknown, they may drink too much and smoke too much. "It's a hell of a way for a kid to take a stand against his parents," a distraught father complained.

In the eyes of the community the parents of a runaway are child abusers, psychologically if not physically. In fact, they are victims, as the child is, of believing that there is only one way to rear children. Until they are shocked by a child's running, they may have put faith in old-fashioned rules, or acted like judges whose decisions are final.

The parent as judge and jury is a role that men and women may not believe in, according to Carolyn Maietta, clinical director of Huckleberry's for Runaways in San Francisco. Defensive about their strictness, parents have told her: "That's how a father's supposed to be. My son's not old enough to decide. I feel it's my duty to decide for him."

"It's foolish," Carolyn said. "Haven't we learned yet that there aren't any absolutes, things aren't final?"

When their child runs away from home, parents may begin to understand the folly of finality, to realize the frustration he may have known in trying to please them. Not knowing where the runaway is, like his not knowing how to appease omnipotent parents, introduces them to the futility of being unable to control the most intimate aspect of life, the family.

The parents of a runaway may feel singled out by their child as different from other parents—stricter, harsher, meaner than the parents of children who stay home. Parents may berate themselves for being too strict and too lenient. They have niggled over the child's irresponsible behavior, they will admit to themselves, but they have overlooked his dismay at their arrogance. They may come to understand running away as retaliation. Their child is getting back at them for underestimating his capacity for being responsible for himself. He is also shouting out for the hundredth time that he is different from his parents.

A harsh truth which parents do not accept easily is that children are different today from the children of their generation.

Today's youngsters are conscious of themselves as their parents never were. Honed by television and progressive education, they have matured earlier, socially, than their parents did. They are prodigies of education and electronics and have absorbed the spirit of protest and dissent prevalent during the final years of the 1960s. Without understanding them, many became enamored of the passions incited by the fights for civil liberty. They saw themselves as participants in the cause, any cause which supported an underdog. Consequently, they exhibit a self-righteousness unusual in children.

Between them and their parents a moral distinction prevails. Those who know both generations well see it as an ethics gap, not simply an age difference. Marty Frick, a counselor at Gemini House, Boulder County's home for runaways, said to me: "I take everything the kids say with a grain of salt. I don't believe that they are right and their parents wrong, but they are different. No better, no worse, only different."

A Connecticut boy told her: "I'm not immoral. I'm amoral." She recalled a sixteen-year-old girl from Clearwater, Florida, who said: "Everybody is provincial. Everybody is out to justify the way he lives. Including me." A sixteen-year-old boy who had run west from Cape Cod told me: "It's what I've always wanted to do."

All children, runaways or not, expect attention. All adolescents are self-conscious, but today's teen-age children are conscious of self the way pregnant women are sensitive to daily changes in their bodies. They are living in an historic and emotional period of heightened awareness. They see themselves as the final cause in the fight for human rights.

They present themselves as finished products, beings whose personalities have been completed by their fifteenth or sixteenth year, persons who have already been formed by the experiences of the past. Many youngsters seem to imagine no room for change, no possibility of ever altering habits or tastes. "That's the way I am," they'll say about what they choose to do or not to do. They believe they are—and will be—what they seem today. It's as if adolescence is the climax of life for them.

To parents, many children seem without ambition. School is a bore and a job only a way to earn money. Parents imagine that children are indifferent to the future, yet when the youngster reaches fifteen or sixteen the future has arrived. Parents do not understand that for many a youngster adolescence is a political state, the arrival at maturity with its privileges and power. At home he may insist on his rights: on privacy above all. He may object to childish restrictions, and wants nobody's will, parents or teachers, imposed on him. He wants acceptance with no strings attached.

Unfortunately, many parents do not remember what it was like to be fourteen or fifteen. They treat the adolescent like a young child, insulting his growth by ignoring it.

If he feels insulted, a child may affect a pose of sullen silence and grating self-indulgence. It protects him from the chilling idea that he is suspended in infancy, that all he can do is obey. He may never fulfill what is expected of him, nor what he expects of himself.

Frustration frightens him. Conveyed by the tone or words of impatient elders is the thought that he may be doomed to eternal stupidity and everlasting impotence. The possibility of such slavery is a mind-fuck, as Danny of Huckleberry's said. Whether they run or stay, these children cover their resentment with anger, their fear with feigned superiority. They are in danger of never growing up because they believe they are grown up.

The isolation of such runaway children is a sad omen for their future. "Somehow these kids never learn to connect on a real gut level," Marty said. "Their ego doesn't get involved with other people and they don't learn to stand in another person's shoes."

The child who runs away stands in his parents' shoes once

or twice: when he is planning to leave or when he considers telephoning them. In spite of what his parents did or did not do, he knows that they will feel shame and loss at his running away from home.

Acknowledging a runaway becomes an admission of failure. Many parents pretend to outsiders that the runaway is off visiting someplace. They are humiliated by the blatant accusation that they are inadequate. They suffer from the guilt of remembering too well what they did and what they said to cause the child to leave. They endure uncertainty like a terminal cancer as days pass and the runaway does not call, does not write. Is he dead or alive? Is he being drugged and raped somewhere? Can he call? For if he could, he would surely telephone or send a postcard.

"I knew my son would not do this to me," said the mother of a boy, supposedly a runaway, who was murdered in Houston.

"I go through agony," Jean Zinner, mother of a runaway Virginia girl, said. "Waiting to hear just one word. All I want to hear is one word. If she is sick or dead, I want to hear of it. Sometimes you wish even for that. Knowing something is better than not knowing anything."

When I talked to Jean and Charles Zinner, they had been hoping for word of their daughter for six months. Beth had run away in March for the second time, climbing out her bedroom window, taking her flute and $20. After calling the police immediately, her parents began uneasy weeks of telephoning their daughter's friends, placing notices in the personal columns of the newspapers, writing letters that went unanswered.

The frustration of not knowing where she was nagged at them. Although he did not inform the Zinners, a police detective heard she was living in the neighborhood. Later the Zinners found out that Beth had attended school for a week after she left home. They had called her friends, but, loyal to Beth, they denied seeing her. The Zinners were too strict, they thought. Beth did not have the freedom they did to go to parties, or cruise the suburb, unquestioned. Beth could take care of herself, they believed, because she had lived on her own in California for five months.

As a runaway, Beth Zinner was a repeater. She ran the first time in May, 1973, when she was fourteen. School-guidance counselors had told her parents that Beth had cut certain classes for two months. The Zinners were shocked and surprised as the advisers insisted she get psychological counseling. Something must be wrong at home, they inferred, for Beth, intelligent, should do well in school. Were the Zinners too restrictive or too demanding, the school wondered. Whatever the reason for Beth's indifference, a psychologist might help.

"They blame the parents for everything," Jean Zinner complained of the school counselors. "We're no good and she's good.

"I used to ask her, 'Why don't you go to school like a nice, normal girl?' 'Are you smoking pot?' Beth kept saying, 'Everything's fine, Mommy. Don't worry!' Everything wasn't fine and I was worried sick. Beth was a rational girl before she went to senior high. She was a lovely, bright, creative, musical child. Everything changed for her in the tenth grade. She became restless, then secretive. She ran away a few days before our appointment with the psychiatrist."

When Beth left, she hitchhiked to California, where she worked up and down the coast from San Diego to Berkeley for five months, playing her flute, earning $10 and $15 a night in clubs that didn't question her age. She made leather belts and bags which she was able to sell to shops catering to tourists. She joined a commune in the mountains and pooled her money with the other campers. She kept a journal of her experiences, writing descriptions and sketching what she had seen, where she had been. She did not write to her parents.

One day Jean Zinner received a call from Alameda Hall, the juvenile-detention center where Beth was placed after her arrest in Berkeley for being in the university's Student Union Building after hours. Jean was astounded because it was five months after Beth had run. In August, horrified, Jean and

Charles Zinner had watched on television the revelation of the Houston murders. Privately, each believed that Beth was dead.

"When I got the call from California," Jean said, "I realized that they don't die that easily.

"We sent Beth's plane fare and went to meet her, expecting, oh, I don't know what. That she'd look thin or be sick, that she'd be scared of seeing us after so long. She came off the plane and she looked wonderful! We had a lovely reunion. I didn't try to pry, but my husband asked her: 'Are you going to be honest with us?' 'You don't have to worry about me, Daddy. I'm going to finish school,' she said. She wanted to return to California after high school and enroll in a junior college. Everything was fine. At first."

As I listened to Jean and Charles Zinner, I saw two people who proved the futility of being only loving parents. Loving her was not enough to convince Beth to accept their standards of behavior. Now, after her second flight from home, they were beaten, worn down by worry and despair. Although I had not known them long, I knew they were not child beaters. They were two decent human beings who had tried, and failed, to change a child with their love.

The mother was thin, wiry, about fifty years old. She was a very good tennis player, she admitted. Playing every day, she had taken Beth to the courts with her and taught her the game.

"She's a better player today than I am and thirty years ago I could have given Billie Jean King a run for the money."

Her daughter had said she was too old, and the remark rankled. "Too old for what?" she asked me. "To be the mother of a teen-age child? Then everybody's too old."

Her husband was silent. He let his wife talk and he added only a few words, a clarification, or a comment on how poor the schools were. His job as a printer for a metropolitan newspaper was incidental to his commitment as father to a recalcitrant daughter. Once, during his wife's long lament, he muttered: "We have a life of our own to live."

They gave me Beth's poems and showed me her drawings: her poetry exposed in metaphors her tragic sense of life. Life was a mirror that stared at her, framing and limiting what she saw. It was a forest where the borders were terrifyingly near her and the clearing absurdly empty. Life was a dream that she woke from screaming because she could not reach the end of it. Beth's vision of the world was not her parents', nor would it be.

The Zinners were traditional parents, conservative in their rearing of a child, not allowing their pride in her precocity to divert them from their purpose. "I wanted to bring her up as a normal child," Jean Zinner said. She had told me about teachers who said Beth was gifted. When she was two and a half, she began to read. She could pick out tunes on the piano at three. The Zinners cherished her distinction. While they did not accept her talent as an indication that she was unique, they developed her artistry with piano lessons and flute lessons. The creativity was a blessing from God, the child was separate from the gift.

Compared to other children, her friends or kids Jean met on the tennis court, Beth was different, however. Before she moved into adolescence, she was an entertaining, delightful girl. As she grew to be a teen-ager, when the music lessons and the tennis lessons and schoolwork did not ease her restlessness, she became explosive, contradictory, secretive. Of course she tried marijuana and beer, cutting classes and hitchhiking. Her nature demanded to know the limits, to see for herself what was so dangerous about the forbidden. She thought they were inconsequential escapades, but when the school urged psychological counseling and her parents concurred, she felt shamed. In her eyes, and theirs, something was wrong with her.

I thought of the clinical psychologist who, sympathizing with parents and runaways, had explained to me: "People don't have to be sick to have problems with their kids, or their parents. Often the interaction of two different personalities, that of the child and the parents, creates a problem. Quiet parents may have an active child, or a quiet child may have active, outgoing parents, and their personalities clash. Since an essential character difference between a parent and child is impossible to overcome, the child may react by running away from home."

Running away was Beth's first response to the fear of going to a psychiatrist, more proof to her of not being quite normal. What she was actually running from was her knowledge of being apart from her parents, and her classmates, of not belonging to them, emotionally or intellectually. Like every child, she was afraid of being different.

Being adolescent means being different from one's parents in behavior and attitudes. Being adolescent usually means demonstrating that difference by defying them. However, if the nature of the child separates her from parents who have devised the structure of her existence, then it is she who is at fault. She carries the burden of conforming to their idea of child.

They tried to control her by their determination to succeed as parents by following the rules. She did not accept the rules as other children do when they bargain with their parents for privileges. Her control, and it was so powerful that she may have been unconscious of its strength, was running away from home.

As Jean Zinner told the story of her daughter's return to the household, she sounded like the mother of many returned runaways. The prodigal was embraced and reinstated in the family by parents who decide their child is a human being who wants respect for his uniqueness, not love for his helplessness. Beth had the will, the stubbornness her mother called it, to forge her independence.

"When she came home, everything was fine for a while until she met a spoiled boy, another runaway, whose mother lets him smoke marijuana at home. She asked me if she could smoke marijuana at home. I said no, it's my house too and it's against the law. She accepted that, I think, but she kept her door locked all the time. I hate closed doors and I had to knock at her door and ask to be allowed in. That hurt me."

Beth fell in love with the boy, or so Jean thought. They

went to parties together. To the movies. Bowling. She was having a normal American girlhood, the Zinners believed, although there were fights about smoking marijuana and her late hours.

"I allowed her to go out Friday, Saturday, and Sunday evenings, until eleven thirty or twelve. Isn't that enough for a fifteen-year-old girl? How bad a mother can I be?

"I was even glad the boy was around. It kept her home. I can understand young love, but I don't approve of birth-control pills at age fifteen. I talked to Beth very bluntly and told her so."

Beth had asked her mother for permission to get a prescription for the pills. In love, she and her boyfriend wanted to have sex.

"She tells me what's on her mind. Sometimes I wish they wouldn't tell," Jean Zinner sighed, glancing at her husband. "I'm not an emancipated woman, but I've changed many of my ideas because I have a runaway daughter."

When Jean took Beth to a gynecologist because she was bleeding heavily during her periods, the doctor prescribed birth-control pills without asking Jean. She raged at him, threatening to sue him. He tried to pacify her by saying the girl was not a virgin, that it was a wise procedure since the pills would also control her menstrual bleeding.

"What am I going to do?" Jean begged her taciturn husband. "I let her have the birth-control pills. She had them anyway."

When Beth returned from California, the Zinners sold their home and rented a house in Virginia near a high school with a strong academic reputation. Adjusting quickly to the new school, Beth earned good grades that allowed her to accelerate and combine her junior and senior years. By planning to take an English course during the coming summer, Beth could graduate in June and begin college the following fall. But by the second semester the tedium of daily classes and constant expectations had worn her down. After she began skipping classes again, the school counselors telephoned Jean to report her.

"What do I do?" Jean asked another high school adviser in the new school.

"Take her privileges away," he suggested.

"I can't do that!" Jean wailed. "She'll run away from home."

Beth held the ultimate weapon and with it had won much: her mother's grudging consent to use the pill, her mother's tacit consent to smoke dope outside of her home, and, primarily, her mother's fear of crossing her. Beth was punishing her parents for making her feel different, different but not special, odd but not unique.

To the Zinners, who believed in the sanctity of the family, a child's running away from home was an indictment of their parenthood. They had been tested and found wanting. Given a second chance, they were rejected a second time.

Jean was distraught as she defined the threat. "It is the most frightening thing in the world for parents to feel if they say or do the wrong thing the child will run away. Beth held running away over us like a weapon."

After a quarrel with her mother about friends coming over late one evening to play their guitars, Beth left again. The next night after dinner while she was in the bedroom playing with her dog, she climbed out the window. Minutes later Jean entered Beth's room to see only the dog wagging his tail.

Clearing his throat in order to control his voice, Charles said: "I'm disgusted with her and I'm mad at myself. We brought her dog back from California for fifty-five dollars. Now we have the dog, not the girl. I sold my home with its four and a half percent mortgage to rent this house so she could go to school in McLean. I'm paying more in rent than I did with a mortgage. If she comes back willingly, we'll discuss the problem and work it out. Otherwise, if she's sent back by the police, I'm placing her in a Catholic boarding school for girls. They hold 'em tight there!"

Patting Charles's hand, Jean tried to soothe him. "Maybe she'll send us a little letter, something.

"After she left I searched her room for clues to her whereabouts. I found some letters she wrote to people in California, but she never mailed them. They were filled with half-truths and truths. She signed a made-up name and bragged about her beautiful baby grand piano, which she has, her expensive flute, which she has, and a special guitar which she doesn't. She said she worked in a music store, which she didn't, and lived in a trailer on a mountain in Maryland which she does not. She wanted to make herself an independent person. Why couldn't she wait until she grew up?"

Finding the runaway is possible if the parents are willing to swallow pride and make inquiries. Searching requires time and tact, patience and dedication. Like the Zinners, many parents are ashamed to say that their child has run away from home. The Zinners explained Beth's second absence by telling friends that she was visiting in California. This time they have curtailed their search. They informed the police of her leaving and they wrote letters to California addresses which she had mentioned. They also telephoned the junior college which she was interested in attending, asking to be called if Beth applies for admission.

During Beth's first runaway episode the Zinners appeared on a local television show to discuss runaway children and to announce that they were the parents of a runaway daughter. Already in California when the show was produced, Beth never knew about the publicity, but the neighbors did. According to Jean, she was mocked on the street or in the grocery store by caustic remarks.

"I would do anything to find my child," Jean said. But the results of the television appearance were damning because it distorted the Zinners' anguish into self-righteousness. Because they were tense and worried, they came across as stern and harsh. When they discussed their daughter, they sounded patronizing. They gathered no sympathy from the television audience, but the absent Beth did.

If parents insist on keeping the child's running a family

affair, they can hire the services of a detective agency. For a high daily fee a private detective will look for the child with discretion. Private detectives investigate runaway cases on the theory that somebody knows where the missing youngster is. A boyfriend or a girlfriend, a psychiatrist or a minister, an acquaintance at school—detectives believe someone is privy to his whereabouts. Detectives try to find that person and inform him of his responsibility toward the child who is loose in a dangerous world.

If parents cannot afford to hire a detective, perhaps the police will locate him or perhaps he will return by himself. The 1972 national survey of youth, which was conducted by the University of Michigan Institute for Social Research, produced figures on the duration of runaway absences, which give hope to nervous parents. Of the youngsters interviewed who admitted to running away from home, 70 percent went to the home of a friend or relative. Thirteen percent of the runaways went on the road. Seventy-two percent were absent from home no longer than three nights; 15 percent were gone from four nights to two weeks; 13 percent stayed away from home from two weeks to more than one month.

Questioned about their return, 53 percent said they returned by themselves. Twenty-nine percent were brought back by their parents, by the parents of friends, or by relatives; 13 percent were returned by authorities; and, according to the study, 6 percent never went back.

I asked adults who are experienced in searching for runaways for suggestions on locating missing children. Police and ministers differ on the importance of parents' joining the search. For the busy police, parents may interrupt their schedules; but at least one minister, the Reverend Fred P. Eckhardt, pastor of St. John's Lutheran Church in New York City's Greenwich Village, urges parents to search actively for the runaway. Dr. Eckhardt is the originator and director of Operation Eye Opener, the Greenwich Village program which warns possible runaways of the dangers of surviving in New York. Begun in 1964 in the pastor's church at 83 Christopher Street, the prevention program runs weekend institutes to inform out-of-town youngsters what life in the city is like for the homeless. In 1968 the church initiated a recovery program when it agreed to help find a runaway girl. With luck and the assistance of young volunteers from the Village, Dr. Eckhardt found the girl within half an hour. Since 1968 Operation Eye Opener has sought and turned up hundreds of runaway children, using members of the church staff and youngsters from the Village.

One Saturday afternoon after Dr. Eckhardt had sent a group of Pennsylvania teen-agers sightseeing with their leaders and his volunteers, he talked to me in his study. Halfway through the weekend, he was bone-tired, yet he spoke of running away as continuing to be a severe problem. During the week he had found three Connecticut girls, thirteen- and fourteen-year-olds, at Saint Patrick's Cathedral. The father of one of the girls had asked him for help in his search.

"When the parents come, we recover ninety percent of the runaways. I invite parents who think their child is in New York to come to the city to look for him," he said.

The minister understands that many children believe that their parents do not want them at home. If the youngsters know that they are looking for them, they may return home willingly.

Parents who want to find a runaway must make an active search. If they do not admit his leaving home, they will limit their resources. If they hope to locate him, they must talk to people who may have seen him. Calling the police to file a missing-persons report is not enough, but the police station is the place to start if they are certain the child has run away. If the family lives in a heavily populated city or county, the chances are that the juvenile bureau or missing-persons division will do nothing but ask the parents to come to the station. There they will record pertinent information about he missing child. They will also add the youngster's name to those broadcast over the police radio. Usually the police are so inundated by calls from frantic parents that they must ignore them. They do not have the time or the manpower to carry out a thorough investigation.

Next, parents should call their child's friends or the parents of his friends to ask for information and to tell them how worried they are about the missing youngster. Perhaps the friends will advise them on where to look for the runaway, but parents should not expect it. Their loyalty is to their friend, not to his parents.

Parents should call the child's school and speak to the principal and the homeroom teacher. Like Beth Zinner, the youngster may attend classes if she remains in the neighborhood. The principal can alert the teachers to tell him if the runaway comes to school. If the school has a guidance counselor, parents should speak to him. If the runaway has talked to him, the parents can try to determine whether the child is in trouble outside the home.

Parents can look for the runaway in places which he has mentioned like waffle shops and hamburger restaurants. They can go to spots that attract teen-agers, like shopping plazas, bowling alleys, pinball parlors. They can drive around the section of town noted for its appeal to college students.

If there is a runaway house in the area, parents should telephone and ask the counselors to put a note from them to the child on their bulletin board. Runaway-house workers may not tell parents whether the child is staying in the house or whether he has visited, but they will tell the runaway if they see him that his parents have called.

For $3 parents can order a copy of the *National Directory of Runaway Centers* from the National Youth Alternatives Project, 1830 Connecticut Avenue, N.W., Washington, D.C. 20009. The directory lists shelters available to the runaway child throughout the country.

"The more places a runaway can go, the longer he can stay away," said a representative in the Washington, D.C., office of Pinkerton's, the international detective organization. On this assumption the detectives conduct their case, investigating every aspect of the child's life.

"We want to know who his friends are, where he goes to school, where he hangs out," two Pinkerton men told me. "We need current pictures to show people in the area where he may have gone. We try to find an address book to check out the names. We go to the people the child has associated with. We check the gin mills and pizza joints and follow the trail of phone calls and letters the runaway sometimes leaves. When we pick a kid up, he seems satisfied to go home with us. He can brag to his friends that he was tracked down and caught by a private dick."

A local Washington detective, C. T. "Jimmie" James of the National Detective Agencies, advises the parents of a runaway to check appointments the child may have had with a dentist or doctor to learn if he kept them. He suggests they get a copy of their long-distance calls to see whom the child has called.

"If we get into the case," he continued, "we go to our informants who have drug contacts to get leads. We check the drive-ins where teen-agers work. If there's a boyfriend, he can be a very good source of information. If there's a rock group in town, we determine whether the child is interested in rock and we look for her in the next city where the group will appear."

Some families will advertise for their runaway through notices in newspapers of the city where the child may be. Local radio stations, usually the university stations, may accept personal messages to broadcast. Although these methods may succeed in contacting the child, I have never heard that they did. They do allow parents to feel that they are trying all possibilities of reaching the runaway.

Playing on the emotions—and drawing out the money—of families distraught about a missing child are several outfits that claim to be youth locators. Entrepreneurs will print photographs and information about a missing person in bulletins or cheap magazines which they mail to police departments. For the advertisement they charge parents $50 to $500 depending on the size of the picture and page.

The police call advertising in these publications "a rip-off" for the parents. They do not use the bulletins to find runaways and they may not receive them. Sgt. Edward A. Smith of the District of Columbia Police Department's Missing Persons Division suggests that parents make up their own missing-person circular to send to police. He advises them to reprint a clear, recent photograph of the runaway on plain bond paper and include a description of the child. If they mail this to police stations in the area where the runaway may be, the police will post it on their bulletin board and look out for the child.

For parents who want to hear how others have dealt with the runaway problem there is the very legitimate Families Anonymous. Families Anonymous describes itself as a national "self-help program for relatives and friends concerned about drug use or related behavioral problems." Operating like Alcoholics Anonymous, FA meets regularly with parents whose children are drug abusers. Although the emphasis falls on parents of the drug-taking child, parents of runaway children attend meetings also. They share their experiences with other parents who have endured similar situations. Groups of Families Anonymous are beginning throughout the country, meeting in churches and city and suburban offices. The national headquarters will supply information through Post Office Box 344, Torrance, California. The telephone number is 213-775-3211.

For runaways who want to call home without telling their parents where they are, there are two national hotlines which will accept their calls in confidence. Operation Peace of Mind, funded by the Texas Criminal Justice Council, was set up to relieve the anxiety of parents who thought their runaway might have been murdered in Houston. Governor Dolph Briscoe of Texas began the nationwide, toll-free hotline as an attempt to open communication between runaway children and their families. By the fall of 1974, Operation Peace of Mind had answered more than four thousand telephone calls from runaways who wanted either to send a message to their parents or needed to know where they could get help in the city to which they had run. According to a news story in *The New York Times* in October, 1974, more than two thousand runaways had sent messages to their parents that they were alive. Runaway children anyplace in the country can dial 1-800-231-6946 for advice, suggestions, or the volunteer's promise that he will relay the runaway's message without telling the family where he is. Children who make contact through a third party may be encouraged to return home.

In August, 1974, the Department of Health, Education, and Welfare funded a national hotline based in Chicago. Like the Houston line, the operators of the free telephone service will not ask the runaway where he is. They will send a message to parents or to anyone the runaway asks for. Also toll-free, the number is 800-621-4000. The number, which is advertised on posters printed by the government, was established as an experiment but will probably continue after the trial period.

The selling point for runaways to use the hotlines is the confidential nature of the conversation between child and operator. Parents cannot call the line demanding information about a youngster. If the runaway makes contact through the lines, the parents will be informed.

Sponsored by state and federal governments, the two hotlines indicate that the lawmakers are aroused by the runaway issue. The public weal has been threatened. As the authorities are recognizing, the runaway issue goes beyond the distress of individual families. Running away in America is the revolution of children who refuse to remain silent.

Part II

The Runaway Revolution

When I talked to Father Paul, the Boston priest nostalgic for the old days on the street, he spoke of youngsters as revolutionaries. Runaways, in particular, had created a revolution in the 1960s, he said. They had left home and swarmed to the cities to live as they imagined the free and independent did. The revolution then was idealistic. It broke the pattern for young people throughout the country. The expectations of parents shifted as they confronted children who refused to attend college, join the army, be safe and respectable. They were the first wedge, those boys and girls, the radical front, the avant garde that shocked the older generation awake to a new image of children.

The first runaways had their own ideas about the future. Depressed about the prefabricated life their parents spread out before them, oppressed by the middle-class values they had shared with their families, they wanted a change, at least for the moment. They trooped to the streets of cities like Boston and San Francisco to band together with war protestors, hippie communes euphoric on dope and freedom, dropouts from schools, colleges, and nine-to-five jobs. They believed they could escape authority for a never-never land where responsibility was duty to oneself and love meant sharing what there was until it ran out. They learned that the extreme of freedom was license and the other side of love was abuse. Most went home, choosing to be neither prey nor parasite, to try again to make it, to get their head together in the straight world. The early runaway passed on an idea of equality and an image of freedom. He became the flag of revolution.

"Runaways are nonviolent revolutionaries," Father Paul told me. "Everything starts with them because they're free and unencumbered."

As the equal rights promises of the last decade failed to include the children, the runaway revolution continued as proof of the grim facts: children were neither free nor unencumbered. They were the last human chattel, the property of their parents or the state. They were at the whim of institutions which claimed to work in their behalf: the law, the police, the courts, the government, psychiatry, the schools. They were saying to all of us that many children must endure what other people rejected long ago: Love only if one proves worthy of it. Respect only if one earns it through the traditional means designated by adults for children. Justice only if one is lucky enough to be born middle class and affluent.

I see running away from home as the strongest force for children's rights because it is the spontaneous rebellion of hundreds of thousands of youngsters. The problems of all American children, those who leave and those who stay home, have come of age. Because they have remained a steady exodus of unhappy children, America's runaways are creating a political revolution for all children. The efforts to classify the runaway child as delinquent or mentally ill have faltered. Because the runaway does not fit naturally into any category except American Adolescent Final Quarter Twentieth Century, he has impressed the public with the importance of his cause. Within the past three years I have seen institutions which subordinate children's issues turn about.

Since running away from home is a fact of growing up for
so many children, psychiatry is revising its definitions on the nature of childhood. In 1968 many doctors believed running away
was a mental disorder. Today there is uncertainty about the pru-
dence of slipping the runaway child into a category that does not
fit the majority.

The law as it is delivered by the police and the juvenile
court is altering its opinions of runaway children. The police no
longer call running away from home a crime. Some juvenile
courts are willing to yield their control of runaways to social
agencies. State legislatures like Michigan's are revising the juvenile code to eliminate court jurisdiction over runaways.

The United States Government itself is considering children as individuals separate from their families as it has provided
money for runaway shelters and national telephone hotlines.

The predicament of the runaway and his family became a
national issue when the Houston murders of young boys were
tied to running away from home. Although the murdered boys
were not runaways, the sensational case instructed the public
about the thousands of running children whose return is left to
chance.

If institutions can adjust their thinking, so can the family,
where the conflicts begin. Idealistically, it will be in the family
where the child's sorrows end first. If it changes from an autocracy into a loving democracy, children may stay home and grow
up safely. If it does not, runaways will continue to rebel against
the indifference and disrespect from which they suffer.

10. The Case of a Million Runaways: The Houston Murders

Part I. The Parents and the Police

"I know David. I don't care what the authorities say. David is not a runaway."—Mrs. Fred Hilligiest, in the Houston *Tribune*, August 12, 1971.

In May, 1971, thirteen-year-old David Hilligiest told his mother he was going swimming. He planned to walk to a pool not far from home in Houston Heights, stopping first for a friend. Neither David nor his friend, Malley Winkle, ever returned home.

More than two years later another thirteen-year-old, Stanton Dreymala, left his home in a suburb of Houston to ride his bike. Stanton had spent the early evening with his family visiting a sick relative in a hospital. When the family returned home, his father let him go out for a while. He never came back.

When the Hilligiests and the Dreymalas notified the police that their sons had disappeared, the Houston Police Department automatically labeled the boys *runaways*. Their names were filed among the thousands of Houston runaways, and forgotten.

In August, 1973, the police announced to the horrified

189

citizens of Houston and to the rest of America that they were digging up bodies of two dozen boys killed during the past three years. The nation was sickened as it watched men dig into the earth and expose the bones of nameless boys, boys who had vanished from their neighborhoods like David and Malley and Stanton. The three youths were victims of homosexual killer Dean Corll and his two accomplices, Elmer Wayne Henley and David Owen Brooks.

After that discovery in Houston, Texans asked the same questions again and again. How could Corll have killed so many boys over three years without being found out? How could so many boys disappear without alarming their parents? How could those boys from a single neighborhood vanish without the police detecting a pattern? What was wrong with the Houston Police Department?

The police tried to deflect the criticism against them by opening a counterattack. They called the parents irresponsible and the boys wayward. Furthermore, they announced, they all came from a bad neighborhood, Houston Heights. According to the police and reported by the press, the Heights, an old neighborhood northwest of the city, was a shabby section of town, run-down and deteriorating, attractive to transients and one-parent families who couldn't afford to live elsewhere. In August, 1973, because of police publicity, the Heights became notorious as a crucible that produced the killers and provided the neglected children who were victims first of their families, later of homosexual murderers. The children of Houston Heights were prey to pushers and perverts, it was implied. Unsupervised by parents, neglected by school and church, they roamed at will, so the stories went, a danger to themselves and others.

Like every parent, I was appalled by the murders. I went to Houston in 1973 to investigate the details and accusations of the police against the parents. I wanted to know what kind of people lived in the Heights and why the police did not search for their missing children.

In Houston I learned soon enough what the police were afraid to admit: they could not handle the runaway problem because there were too many children leaving home. They were incapable of searching for missing children because the police department did not have enough men and women to go looking for them. If they were teen-agers, missing children, like the Hilligiest boy, were ignored. They were written off as runaways.

In Houston and in major cities across the country, the problem for the police on runaway children, or children believed to be runaways, was one of increasing size, of uncontrollable numbers, of immeasurable proportions. It was impossible for an understaffed police department to investigate the annual exodus of thousands of children.

All over Texas, youngsters were leaving home. Over five thousand a year ran away in Houston. Dallas police reported four thousand children on the runaway list each year, San Antonio six thousand. The Houston police had assumed that all their missing teen-agers were runaways because hundreds of thousands of children were running away in America.

During 1971, when David Hilligiest and Malley Winkle disappeared from Houston Heights, the police department recorded 5,652 juveniles as missing persons. During 1972, when other parents from the Heights filed reports on their absent sons, the Juvenile Division recorded 5,228 cases of missing children. In Police District 6, which is the Houston Heights area, 415 juveniles were listed as missing for 1971. In 1972, 446 juveniles were recorded as running away from the Heights. In May, 1973, the report for the first five months of the year showed 2,243 juveniles reported to the police as missing, an increase of 3 percent over the citywide figures for the previous year.

Nine of the murdered boys were identified as coming from the Houston Heights neighborhood, but they had vanished over a three-year period. They could hardly have set a pattern to unsettle the Houston police. Of those nine boys only one sixteen-year-old from the Heights was a recurrent runaway. His parents acknowledged that he left home often, but the sixteen-year-old and his older, stay-at-home brother were both killed by Dean Corll.

As the public criticized the police department for not doing its duty, the police hid behind the decisions of the courts. They insisted that Corll's victims were runaways who were not affected by the laws which they enforced. They said running away from home was not a crime in Texas; it was not even a misdemeanor. They were performing a public service by taking runaway reports when parents called. They emphasized that Texas courts had interpreted the laws so broadly that their hands were tied in the case of the runaway juvenile.

When I arrived in Houston, I called Dorothy Hilligiest, the woman who insisted her son was not a runaway. She invited me to her home in the Heights to talk about David and the efforts she and her husband undertook to find him.

As my cab left the freeway, it turned into a street of small frame homes dwarfed by beautiful old trees. West Twenty-seventh, home to the Hilligiests and Corll's convicted accomplice Wayne Henley, was a wide thoroughfare with houses set well back from the street. At the end of the first long block was the Hilligiest home, a bright yellow house surrounded by a trim green yard. Although other houses on the block were not so spruce as that one, the street was far from the crumbling ghetto of my imagination.

Dorothy Hilligiest opened the door of her home, and I stepped out of the muggy September morning into her comfortable air-conditioned living room. Mrs. Hilligiest was a pleasant woman, effusive and kind. She made me feel at home with cups of coffee and snapshots of her six children. Their portraits hung on the walls and their photographs decorated the desk and the dining room buffet. Five of the Hilligiest children survived, the oldest a married daughter of thirty-one, the youngest, an eleven-year-old boy. The dead child, David, she talked about as if he were alive but still missing.

"Here," she said, pointing to a boy in his first communion

class, "is David." She showed me snapshots of the child with his dog on the front porch, another one of David holding his older sister's first baby. He was a slender boy with sandy-colored hair and a gentle smile.

"When David didn't come home from swimming, Fred and I called the police to report him missing," she told me.

A police officer answered the call perfunctorily, telling her he would connect her with the runaway desk. She insisted that her son was not a runaway. The policeman replied that in David's age group all missing children were classified as runaways. He was too young to be a missing person and too old to be a missing child.

"Fred and I were indignant about the runaway status," Dorothy Hilligiest said. "It was a stigma on David and on us. The police are lax when they think a child is a runaway. They shouldn't classify a child a runaway until they know for certain he is one."

Although the Hilligiests asked for a police search, the policemen told the parents that unless they had evidence of a crime they could not enter the case. The parents were surprised.

"We didn't know you couldn't just call the police to say, 'My child is missing.' We thought they'd get out and look until they found him.

"We always assumed that the police department was our representative. They had the tools to find a missing child, but their attitude was very casual. They said they couldn't make a report out for twenty-four hours. They never came to the house. They didn't ask for a snapshot of David. This is the way we learned how the law works."

Dorothy and Fred Hilligiest searched for their son for two years. At first, before their money ran out, they used the services of a private detective. He charged $20 an hour for his investigation and turned up nothing but rumors.

"He was getting close," Dorothy Hilligiest recalled. "The last thing he asked me was whether I knew anything about homosexuals operating in the neighborhood."

"I played my hunches," Dorothy Hilligiest said as she discussed her efforts to find David. "I talked to other boys who ran away from home and came back after a week. None of them knew anything about David. I talked to Wayne in May. He and David were not close friends, but the Henleys lived down the block. Wayne asked me if I'd heard anything about David. He said he wished he could help. He did distribute some circulars for us."

Going through the scraps of paper and articles that she had accumulated during the two years of their search, Mrs. Hilligiest found the circular she and her husband and Malley Winkle's mother tacked up in neighborhood stores and distributed in Chicago, California, New Orleans. Reprinted on it were photographs of David and Malley, and it offered a $1,000 reward for information, to be treated confidentially, about the two boys. David's hair was slicked back wet, Malley's hung in his face. Both boys were smiling, probably at a school photographer, the shy thirteen-year-old David and his venturesome sixteen-year-old friend.

"David was a timid boy," his mother said. "Malley was game for anything. Malley's father was ill, bedridden in a veteran's hospital. The Winkle boy had too much freedom, but he wasn't a neglected child. He wouldn't stay put. 'Boys will be boys,' Mrs. Winkle said to me. I told David, 'That boy is going to get you in trouble one of these days, trouble you can't get out of.'"

So Mr. and Mrs. Hilligiest began a routine that is becoming familiar to parents of runaway children. The private detective and Mr. Hilligiest had combed the beaches around Freeport. The Hilligiests drove their car into the countryside looking for David in Children of God colonies. They called runaway houses in Houston and Dallas. They talked to ministers who operated programs in churches for runaway kids. They called every hotline or crisis-center number they could discover. They wrote messages to David through underground papers as far north as Toronto. They paid for advertisements in a national missing-youth bulletin.

"I wanted to put an announcement about David on television, but that was against the laws of the Federal Communications Commission."

Exasperated, Mrs. Hilligiest recounted her attempts to involve the federal government in their plight. She wrote to the Social Security Administration in Washington and sent the bureau a stamped envelope that included a letter to her son. If David used his Social-Security number in applying for a job, she hoped the officials would forward the letter.

She called the Federal Bureau of Investigation and asked what help it could give her to find her son. The FBI men replied that they were unable to do anything. It was out of their jurisdiction.

"If my son were draft age and missing, you'd find him," she scolded the FBI.

"They sound stupid for men in high office," she complained. "As citizens we put people at the head of our government who are smarter than we are, but when there comes a need, they won't do anything for us."

Fred Hilligiest walked into the house through the kitchen. Home for lunch from his job with the city traffic department, he looked tired. His strong face had deep lines, his eyes were sad. He had tried everything he knew to find his son and he had still failed.

"We had to take everything on our own," he murmured.

"We were grasping at every straw," his wife added. "We were doing things we normally never believed in."

Mrs. Hilligiest told of writing to clairvoyant Jeane L. Dixon in the fall of 1972. She begged her to use her powers to help them find David.

By letter the seer replied: "Regrettably, from the information given in your letter I have not been able to pick up any vibrations which means it is not possible to get anything psychically. However I shall keep trying, and should anything come to me later which may seem helpful, I shall certainly be in touch with you."

From the day David disappeared his mother was certain

that he was dead or kidnapped. He had no reason to run from home. School was almost over for the year and the family was going on vacation to a lake in Kerrville, Texas.

On the day David and Malley walked to the swimming pool, Dorothy Hilligiest was busy packing food and clothes for the trip. When she saw David last, he was going out the door, heading for Malley's house.

"He was wearing a shirt and corded blue bell-bottoms—dress jeans—and a pair of shoes. He had his bathing suit on. Usually, I drove the boys to the pool, but that day I was too busy so they said they'd walk."

Walking to the pool, David and Malley accepted a ride in a white van, according to Malley's eleven-year-old brother. He saw them climb into it when the driver stopped. Dean Corll drove a white van and often gave boys a lift.

Two years and three months later in August, 1973, Wayne Henley killed thirty-three-year-old Dean Corll and led the Houston police to David's burial ground. Wayne Henley was fourteen years old when he met Corll through his friend, David Owen Brooks. Corll befriended both boys, spending so much time with Wayne that Mrs. Henley said: "He was like a father to Wayne." According to their written confessions, Henley and Brooks procured boys for Dean because he promised to pay them $200 for each boy they brought him. Although he often paid them only $5 or $10, they would invite their friends or neighbors to parties at Dean's apartment. They picked up hitchhikers and took them home to meet Dean.

Nobody talked about the beginning of Corll's killing the boys he raped. Yet at some point he became afraid that they would expose his homosexuality. Henley stated that Dean committed sodomy with the boys Henley and Brooks procured for him, then tortured them. Brooks stated to the police that he interceded once to save a boy's life. The police found an eight-foot-long board equipped with straps for binding the boys by their wrists. Whatever these details suggest, Corll also committed the ultimate violence. According to Henley and Brooks, he strangled the boys to death or shot them in the head. Having admitted helping Corll bury the bodies, Elmer Wayne Henley was indicted and convicted in six killings; David Brooks was indicted in four and convicted of one murder.

The depravity that bound the three began to dissolve when Corll threatened to kill Wayne Henley. Henley had passed out from sniffing spray paint after a party at Corll's house in Pasadena, a suburb in South Houston. He awoke in the morning to find himself handcuffed. Corll was talking about killing him and a boy and girl Henley had brought to the party. They were already tied to the torture board. Henley begged to be released and promised to help Dean murder the couple. When Corll freed him, Henley grabbed his gun and shot him to death.

Then Wayne Henley called the police, who found Corll's body in the hallway of his home. He told the police the grisly details of his association with the homosexual. By evening the Houston police were uncovering bodies buried in a boat-storage yard. The remains of one boy, said Wayne Henley, belonged to a neighbor who lived on his block in Houston Heights. David Hilligiest.

On Wednesday evening, August 8, the Hilligiests had gone to the funeral of a relative. When they returned, Fred went to bed and the two younger boys watched television.

Dorothy Hilligiest answered the telephone. "A friend phoned and told us that the Henley boy had named David as one of the victims. I was numb. 'Freddy, wake up, wake up!' I shouted. We were like crazy people, screaming and crying. 'I'll kill him. I'll kill him,' Freddy said."

While she relived the terrible discovery of her son's death, Dorothy Hilligiest maintained her composure. For over two years she had lived with fear. Now that she knew what had happened to David, she accepted it. The certainty was a release for her.

"Never in our wildest imagination had we thought anything this terrible had happened to the boys."

By September 7, 1973, David Hilligiest was identified officially as one of the boys buried in a boat shed in Southwest

Houston. By then the number of bodies totaled twenty-seven; the identifications possible through fingerprints, dental records, and x-rays were seventeen, maybe eighteen. Because of the heat, the shallow graves, the length of time in lime-filled plastic sacks, the bodies were as distorted as the facts of the murder. One fact was accepted: twenty-six or twenty-seven boys from ages thirteen to twenty had died in a crime that nobody believed possible.

Dorothy Hilligiest had met Dean Corll when he worked in the Heights for his mother at her candy factory. He had invited David and other neighborhood kids to play pool and have some candy in the rear of the praline shop. Remembering her disapproval, Dorothy Hilligiest told me: "I went to the factory one day and knocked on the door. A slight-built fellow, on the blondish side, who must have been in his mid-to-late twenties then, came to the door. He was very polite. I asked him if David was there and he was. I told him not to let David in anymore because it was a place of business and I didn't think the kids should be playing inside."

As she recalled the episode with a younger Corll and a smaller David, she sighed. "I always insisted on knowing their whereabouts and on keeping discipline. I was told that I was overprotective. Raising children in the city, not knowing everybody, made me that way. But in this case David and Malley weren't getting in a car with a stranger. They knew Dean. They were doing what any normal child would be doing in his neighborhood. They were going swimming. Some of the other boys were going to school or to the movies. They were not runaways."

As I told her about the dismay in Washington over the Houston case and the federal legislation to help runaway children and their parents, she looked weary.

"We need to change the laws to give the children more protection, but we don't want to suppress them or we'll raise a bunch of neurotics. We want to raise them normal."

Then she added, "Why do they wait for a crisis to do anything about our children?"

*   *   *

Out in Meadow Creek, a suburb of South Houston not far from Dean Corll's Pasadena house, live James and Elaine Dreymala, the parents of Stanton, the final victim of Corll's sadism. I drove to Meadow Creek on a September evening to meet the Dreymalas. Brick ramblers were lined up on green lawns behind tall pine trees. Wide windows faced the street, a narrow road where kids on bikes circle the neighborhood in the deepening twilight.

Elaine Dreymala led me to the family room, where eleven-year-old Michelle was turning off the television set. When her mother introduced us, she chatted about starting school again and having a new teacher and harder work. Excited about the year, she left us to do her homework.

As James Dreymala entered the room, he reminded me of Fred Hilligiest, a man worn down by hopelessness. He settled into his chair and his wife sat beside me on the couch.

"We feel we're the most fortunate parents," he said. "We knew so soon about our son. Other parents waited over two years to learn the truth."

He had agreed to talk to me, he explained, because no one else, not the police or the newspapers, had asked him to explain how Stanton became a victim. When he called the police to report the boy's absence, they quizzed him about reasons for Stanton's possibly running away.

Are you sure he had no reason to leave? they asked. When was the last time you saw him? What was he wearing? How did he leave? Did he have money with him?

Stanton had threatened to run away from home once when his father was angry. It was nothing serious. Every young boy contemplates running away, his father thought. James and Elaine Dreymala were also convinced that Stanton was not a runaway. He had not taken with him what he valued, his hairbrush and his identification bracelet.

"Society may brand these particular youngsters as being

runaways," James Dreymala said. "My wife and I could not care less. We are satisfied that we know how Stanton got involved."

Stanton was a lanky, blond boy, thirteen years old, a month away from becoming fourteen and entering the eighth grade. He had made himself a bicycle from bits and pieces and he rode it everywhere. He rode a motorbike too, but he kept it on the dirt trail up the road from the Seven-Eleven store. He was on the track team at school and he played cornet in the band. He played baseball, right field in the Pony League. During the summer he went to a church camp and met a girl he liked. He enjoyed being with his friends, but he scorned schoolteachers and homework.

His father was teaching Stanton how to drive. The boy had taught his father how to play chess. He called his mother "Shorty" because at five feet, nine inches, he towered over her. He was proud of his height and proud of his pale blond hair. His folks gave in and let him wear his hair long. His share of the bargain was to brush it regularly. He mowed lawns during the summer and made good money. One summer day he spent $15 at Astroworld, the amusement park. He liked to sing and talk at the rap sessions his church sponsored on weekends.

"Our major comfort lies in our religion," Dreymala said. "Our son was baptized three years ago. He rededicated himself at camp this summer. After camp he gave me a marijuana cigarette that he got from a kid at school. I asked him if he smoked marijuana. He said no. His teachers felt certain he wasn't involved in drugs."

James and Elaine Dreymala are Seventh-Day Adventists, a couple in their midthirties, a handsome pair: he, dark-haired with short trim sideburns and pained brown eyes; she, fair, very pale, her blond hair carefully arranged. Elaine seems composed, but her eyes seem to strain from her head in wonder.

As James talked about the boy and the case, Elaine agreed with him or corrected him on details. He spoke precisely, anxious to examine the facts of his son's disappearance and the police department's inefficiency. His deliberate examination of what happened and when it occurred, in careful sequence, was his effort to understand, to seem in control of the knowledge that his son was strangled to death by a maniac who tortured and abused him.

"We believe they took him off the street, off his bike. He was abducted physically, but he gave them one hell of a fight. When the police showed Stanton's photo to Henley and Brooks, they said, 'Corll picked up that boy and took care of him.' Still," he acknowledged, "we go through all kinds of speculation as to what really did happen."

Stanton left his house Friday evening, August 3, to ride his bike. Although it was 9:30 P.M., his father permitted him to go out because the family had spent the evening in the hospital visiting the boy's aunt. At 11:30 P.M. Stanton phoned his parents. He told them he was at a party with some friends, that he wanted to stay all night. His father told him to be home in twenty-five minutes. He was not to stay. The boy had never attended a party, nor left home before that night.

By Saturday morning he was still not home. In the afternoon Stanton called the neighbors to ask for advice. He was afraid of something, maybe of staying out all night after his father had ordered him home, but he did not explain. He had called the girl he'd met at camp, to tell her he was "across town, off Montrose, at the party of a guy named Gary." Montrose, a Houston neighborhood several miles from Meadow Creek, is known as a homosexual district.

On Sunday morning, August 5, Stanton was still missing. His parents began driving—to the swimming pool, to the bowling alley at the shopping center, following the suggestions of children who said they'd seen him here or there. By this time the boy was dead, according to the medical examiner who determined that he was killed either late Saturday night or early Sunday morning.

James Dreymala did not report Stanton's absence to the

police until Monday morning. He explained to me that he wanted to give his son the chance to come home without police interference. When he called the police, he talked to a friend in the Detective Division. His friend told him they received fifty or sixty calls a day about missing children.

On Wednesday evening, August 8, while James Dreymala was teaching an evening class at the college, Elaine heard the ten o'clock news. She did not connect her son's disappearance with the story of torture slayings and the police discovery of bodies. Earlier that evening the police had called to get a description of Stanton's bicycle. Elaine told them it was an odd bike made out of the pieces of old bicycles.

On Thursday morning while Dreymala was at work, a young reporter arrived in Meadow Creek to ask Elaine for Stanton's picture. Her son was a victim in the sex crime, the reporter told her. Stunned, Elaine Dreymala tried to call her husband.

James Dreymala had left for police headquarters to identify his son's bike. Police had found it in the boat shed, inside a wrecked, abandoned car. No body had been identified yet as Stanton Dreymala. The most recent victim was a tall redhead, not a tall blond, said the police. Later, the police and Dreymala realized that the lime had changed the color of the boy's hair.

By Friday evening seventeen bodies had been exhumed from the boat shed. Police had come to the house to pick up Stanton's fingerprints and inquire about his dental records. On Monday, August 13, they said the prints they took from the boy's room did not match those from the bodies. On Tuesday, August 14, eleven days after he disappeared, the police identified Stanton Dreymala positively from fingerprints on his schoolbooks and from his dental records.

"We went through five days of torture," said James Dreymala. "We would have been spared three of those days if the police had tried to identify Stanton first. I don't hold their labeling him a runaway against them. How could they know? But, he was Corll's last victim. Why didn't they work on him first?

"I feel anger still at Corll and Henley and Brooks. In my mind Corll's the guilty one and he's dead. Death's too easy for Henley and Brooks. They should suffer as we are suffering."

He told his wife to get the picture of their son. As she returned to the room, he said he wouldn't do a thing differently if he had another son to raise. "If I had to label a regret, it would be the amount of time I spent away from my family. I was away from home two or three nights a week, sometimes four, teaching night classes. Others work longer hours," he added.

The boy grinned out of his snapshots. Dressed in a coat and tie, his pale blond hair brushed neatly, he smiled, pleased to be dressed up, going someplace.

For a minute the father fumbled for a reason for his son's death. He thought there were more vices in a city than in a small town because there were more people.

"In a small town everybody knows what everybody is doing. You go the same distance in a big city and you have no idea who people are or what they're doing."

He stopped, exhausted by his efforts. Mrs. Dreymala wanted to cry again. The snapshots of their son lay on the couch beside her.

Their search for a reason, for an explanation for the inexplicable, delayed the pain of acceptance. So the Dreymalas blamed the city and the Hilligiests blamed the indifference of the police force. The police blamed the laxity of parents and the permissiveness of the courts. Junior high school principals and ministers blamed broken homes. Observers of the social scene blamed street life and drugs. They pointed to the wanderlust of today's children, to restless youth who hitchhike for kicks. The newspapers accused society in general and parents and police in particular. The Vatican blamed the devil.

"We are in the domain of sadism and demonism," said an editorial in the Vatican's daily *Osservatore Romano*. "This is beyond the borderline of crime because it is beyond the borderline of reason."

The murdered runaway children of Houston Heights and the suburbs were not runaways at all. They were only children who were trying to grow up in a bedeviled society. Their parents were not cruel or indifferent or ignorant of the dangers around them. They were busy men and women who were trying to lead a reasonable life in an irrational world. Like the parents and the boys, the police were overwhelmed and powerless. They could not have saved the children from the devil if they had tried.

Part II. The Police and the Runaway

"I want to set the record straight on our authority as it relates to runaway juveniles. First, the Civil Guardianship Act of the State of Texas governs the handling of juvenile offenders in the State of Texas. According to the Honorable Robert Lowery, Juvenile Court Judge for Harris County, there exists no statute or interpretation of the law that classifies runaway per se as a violation of the Juvenile laws or Penal Code of this State. The Juvenile Courts have repeatedly advised the Department that runaways per se must be handled as a public service, and does not constitute grounds for the initiation of any investigation keyed to the procedural laws governing the investigation of criminal offenses."—Herman Short, Chief of Police, at a press conference in Houston, August 13, 1973.

When I telephoned the Chief of the Juvenile Division for an appointment, he agreed to see me, but he imposed one restriction. Captain Horton refused to talk about the case.

"I'll talk to you about our procedure with runaways, lady," he conceded, "but I'm not going to discuss the murders."

I asked him why not, and he said because he didn't want to. I promised him my questions would be pertinent only to police procedure in runaway cases. He said to come right over.

Capt. Robert L. Horton was fifty-nine years old and angry. He had worked for the police department for thirty-two years and not once in those thirty-two years had he read an accurate acount of anything he'd said. Or so he told me.

Throughout our interview he was defensive. The news-papers had accused the police of incompetence in handling the murders of twenty-seven boys. Captain Horton answered questions I did not ask him because he was replying to charges made by parents or reporters that the police were indifferent to investigating the reports of missing children. Reporters who interviewed parents of the dead boys sympathized with them and criticized the Houston Police Department harshly.

Smarting from the attack, Chief Herman Short had called a press conference to explain the law to reporters. He called their criticism of his department a "disgusting attempt at scapegoating." He told the press that runaways were not breaking any Texas law, that the police were performing a public service in dealing with runaway children. According to writer Arthur Bell in an *Esquire* article, he hedged about the responsibility of city police.

"This ghastly business is not Houston's responsibility. Many of these murders didn't happen here at all. Some were committed near Galveston and Beaumont."

At the end of the session, Bell reported, Chief Short struck out at the parents. "Obviously," he began, "parents could do better raising their children. Some of these families were not exactly discharging their own responsibilities in disciplining their youngsters. Though it isn't this department's official concern, many times out of fear, parents will not report their children as missing to the proper authorities. One of the juveniles, Malley Winkle, was never reported as a runaway."

Chief Short was not the only Houston police officer who pointed a finger at the public. "We can't raise people's children for them," a Houston police lieutenant said. "We're not baby-sitters!"

Police seemed to have done little to ease the tragedy of those involved or the shock of the general public. A police spokesman quipped: "We got wall-to-wall bodies." Police officers first showed reporters David Brooks's statement, then complained bitterly when it appeared in newspapers.

In spite of tactless words and thoughtless behavior, the insensitivity of the police was irrelevant to the real problem. As Captain Horton was taking pains to make me realize, the problem was one of too many runaways, so many runaways that nobody could keep count.

"The figures on runaways are not accurate," admitted Captain Horton, "because many runaways go unreported. Parents report girls with greater frequency than they report boys so there seem to be more girls running than boys."

"Houston is a typical *city*," he said, stressing the word *city*. "In small communities it's different."

He implied that in small towns the police have time to look for missing children. In cities they are busy coping with crime and criminals and not with undisciplined children.

The Houston parent who reports a child missing from home must have evidence of a crime before the police will investigate the disappearance. The police procedure regarding missing children is like Catch-22: If parents know where the child is, the police will pick him up. If parents don't know, the police won't know either so they do what they can: take information from the parents, list the missing children as runaways if they are under seventeen, and broadcast their names and descriptions on police radio. If the missing child has reached seventeen, the legal age for adult status in Texas, the police will file a report with the missing-persons division.

"We take the report on missing children instantly," Captain Horton declared. "We do not delay in taking the report when a parent or a guardian chooses to report that child as a runaway. There is no waiting period.

"After taking the report instantly," repeated the captain, "we issue a police radio broadcast in the form of a teletype which goes out locally. Or, we send out an APB—an All Points Broadcast—if the parents believe the kid is going out of state or somewhere specific like Dallas. In smaller communities the police don't sit on the teletype so they may not pick up the APB. They may be out looking for Mrs. Brown's cow."

Captain Horton was talking fast, explaining point by point the police procedure in runaway cases. He made the operation sound reasonable, but the luck of the police had run out in August. Relying on the theory that the youngsters would return by themselves was no longer good enough. Of the 2,243 Houston runaways reported by the end of May, 1,299 had gone home; 944 had not.

"If there is reason to believe that the kid has met with foul play, we keep broadcasting," he insisted.

Each case is kept active for thirty days, he emphasized. In that time a police officer telephones the child's family to learn if he has come home. At the end of the thirty days the Juvenile desk tries to determine again if the child has returned. An officer calls the parents or sends them a form letter asking for further information. If the runaway is not home, his report enters an active folder.

The police departments of other big cities follow a procedure similar to Houston's. Scrupulous about paper work, they ask parents to come to the juvenile bureau to file their report. They may enter the information on a computer rather than air a radio description. But for too many cities, finding a runaway is accidental, not intentional. Writing up a runaway report is not the same as turning up a runaway child. In Houston a detective in the Juvenile Division told me: "If officers stop a car with a juvenile in it, they may ask for identification. If the name is on the missing list, they will bring him in, but we don't have the manpower to look for him.

"Parents seldom notify the police when the child comes home," the exasperated captain said.

Police did not notify the parents of the missing and murdered boys when Wayne Henley led them to the boat shed graveyard and told them the names of the boys he had buried there. Like the Hilligiests, several families learned of the deaths of their sons from a television news show.

"If a kid is sixteen or under," Captain Horton continued, "and he runs from his home state to Texas, we need authorization from his local police agency to pick him up. We don't take it from the parents who write or call. We work through the police departments."

The out-of-state runaway who is seventeen years old has little trouble with Texas police, Captain Horton admitted.

"As long as a seventeen-year-old kid wants to remain in Texas, he's home-free. He's all right until his own local authority issues a legal pickup order for him. The police department will also execute a court order on a kid."

Then, following the technique of his chief in dealing with inquisitors, he produced the explanation about runaways that, theoretically, removed them from his jurisdiction. "Remember," he warned me. "In the State of Texas a child who runs away from home is not violating the law. The runaway is a child apparently in need of supervision, but he is not committing an unlawful act.

"The new family code of the State of Texas," the captain enunciated, "says a runaway is a child who has voluntarily absented himself from his parent or guardian for a substantial length of time without parental permission."

In his determination to impress me with the noncriminal, nondelinquent nature of running away from home in Texas, the captain shoved the code toward me across the desk. I read it.

He pointed to the title and to the words: "Effective September 1, 1973."

I could hardly believe it. The bodies were exhumed in August; the murders took place during 1971 through 1973; and the law had not become effective until September, 1973. I looked at him, amazed, and he jumped up. He grabbed his jacket and strapped on his holster.

"Lady, I'm not going to answer any more of your questions," he shouted. "It's four o'clock and I'm going home."

Earl Kirkland had worked with Captain Horton in the Juvenile Division for nineteen years. Now as Lieutenant of Police in the Community Relations Division—the public relations man—he agreed with the captain on the inaccuracy of reporters. Still, he was willing to help me understand how the murders could have happened in Texas.

He knew I was going to ask him about Captain Horton's mistake in showing me the law, but he was expansive and full of goodwill. Smiling broadly, he handed me a copy of the old juvenile law, the law that was applicable when the Houston police uncovered the bodies of the murdered children. In effect since 1943, the civil statute dealt with juvenile delinquency and defined a delinquent child as one who violates the penal code. Seven clauses defining delinquency followed the age limitations that defined childhood.

"Where do you see the term *runaway* in that definition?" he prodded me.

I did not see the word *runaway*, but I read the clause other police departments use to label the runaway child delinquent or in need of supervision. A delinquent child "so deports himself as to injure or endanger the morals or health of himself or others."

"That clause on health and morals killed us," Lieutenant Kirkland said. "How were we supposed to interpret it? After the Gault Decision in 1967, it became invalid. The judges would not accept it. No runaway law has been operative in Texas since Gault. As a police officer, I'm not supposed to enforce anything that is not an offense against criminal law."

In May, 1967, the United States Supreme Court ordered a boy released from an Arizona industrial school where he was committed for using obscene language to a housewife. When he was fifteen, Gerald Gault allegedly talked indecently to a woman over the telephone. Since she had received several obscene phone calls, she wanted to end them. She thought she recognized Gerald Gault's voice and she knew the boy was on probation to an Arizona juvenile court for being with a youngster who snatched a purse. She called Gerald's probation officer, who picked the boy up and took him to a juvenile-detention home.

At his first hearing the next day, Gerald was denied the legal rights an adult would have had. Neither he nor his parents had received any written notice of the charges against him. He was not represented by a lawyer. The woman who was accusing him of obscenity did not appear at the hearing to charge him or to be cross-examined. He was not informed of his privilege against self-incrimination. Indeed, no one was even taking notes on what did occur at the hearing. Did he admit using obscenities or did he admit only holding the telephone while a friend called the neighbor?

While the judge reviewed Gerald's record, he was returned to the detention home and held for two or three days. At the conclusion of his second hearing, the judge sentenced Gerald Gault to the state industrial school until he became twenty-one years old in six years. If Gerald had been convicted of obscenity as an adult, he would have received a maximum sentence of two months in jail or a fine of $5 to $50.

When his mother told the court that she would appeal the decision, the court told her there was no appeal possible in juvenile-court rulings. With a lawyer she tried to correct the injustice done her son in Arizona courts, but she failed. Finally, the lawyer and the American Civil Liberties Union asked the Supreme Court to hear them. On May 15, 1967, three years after Gerald Gault entered the state school, the Supreme Court decided in his favor.

The landmark Gault Decision began to establish procedural rights for juvenile offenders who might be placed in detention. These rights included what Gerald had been denied: the right to receive notice of the charges, the right to have a lawyer, the right to confront and cross-examine witnesses, the right to avoid incriminating oneself. The decision declared that "neither the Fourteenth Amendment nor the Bill of Rights is for adults alone." According to Lisa Richette, in her book *The Throwaway Children,* "the inclusion of children within the meaning of "persons" under the Fourteenth Amendment is perhaps the most important thing in the Gault decision."

According to the Houston Police Department, the Texas courts interpreted the Gault Decision as a warning to leave the kids alone. Their truancy or their running away was the responsibility of their parents, not of the police. When the police revealed the Houston murders, the public, outraged by the lack of police supervision, found no comfort in court decisions.

In spite of his false heartiness, Lieutenant Kirkland was a man in a dilemma. He did feel responsible for the welfare of the citizens of Houston, but the dual job of enforcing the law and keeping order in the state was too big for the police to handle.

"We're damned if we do and damned if we don't," the lieutenant groaned. "We're up against a lack of acceptance on the part of the citizens. As a police force, we have one-half of the people we need. We have twenty-two hundred people in the department including radio dispatchers and jailers. We can't get men to join the force because the pay is low and public acceptance is low."

The lieutenant was dredging up replies to all the accusations he had heard since August. He had his own pet peeves: the interpretation of juvenile law by the courts; the meager salaries of policemen and the antagonism of the public toward the police department, the erosion of the family, the basic immaturity of children.

"We protect children from everything but themselves. The runaway youngster has either a school problem or a problem within the family. If running away can be cured, the cure lies in the family, not in the courts. Since the Gault case more and more court decisions have said that kids and adults be treated similarly. Such decisions are not good enough. Treating a child like an adult won't protect the child."

He sounded like a judge who was quoted in an excellent paper, "Children's Rights," by Nora Klapmuts of the National

Council on Crime and Delinquency. She reported Judge Lindsay G. Arthur as saying that children "should not have equal liberty; they should have less. Neither should they have equal protection—they should have more."

Lieutenant Kirkland decided: "The states should pass a law stating that any child who absents himself from his home or his legal guardian is guilty of a misdemeanor. This would give the police at least the legal right to take the runaway into custody. Then, it would also be against the law for anyone to harbor a runaway. We could get the adults on the harboring charge."

He listened to me describe Stanton Dreymala, Corll's final victim. The boy had told his father he was in Montrose, a homosexual neighborhood, at a party. I wondered why the police had not followed up that information after the boy was reported missing.

The lieutenant shrugged. How could they? By questioning every homosexual in Houston?

"A runaway is a sitting duck for a homosexual," he said.

The boy was not a runaway, I reminded him. With his father's permission he'd gone out to ride his bike. During the ride he accepted an invitation to a party.

"Maybe he was in a jam he couldn't face," the lieutenant suggested.

A misery of uncertainty continues to mark the Houston case. According to Lt. Joseph Navarro in the police department's Juvenile Division, the remains of seven or eight bodies are still unidentified. They may never be claimed.

One Houston Heights father whose son has been missing since 1972 is almost certain his boy was a victim. Because the boy has not been identified from the remains, his father digs in the beach at High Island on the Gulf of Mexico where other victims were buried. By finding his son's bones he hopes to end the single doubt that plagues him and his wife.

Former Chief of Police Herman Short is selling real estate

because his friend the mayor lost the election in November and the new mayor chose not to reappoint him.

Captain Horton remains as head of the Juvenile Division, but Lt. Earl Kirkland was transferred from public relations to the property room, where lost articles wait to be claimed.

As the Houston police buckled under bad publicity, other police departments protested that the gruesome case could not happen in their cities. Their bravado is wishful thinking as figures on runaways reported to the police remain steady or rise and police continue to follow the procedures of Houston, taking information from worried parents and hoping youngsters will return home.

For example, in Denver for the years 1971, 1972, 1973, the number of reported runaways averages 3,500, the number of those who returned home averages 1,950, the number arrested averages 1,750. Chief of Delinquency Control W. E. Hallman explained the discrepancy to me. "The number of reported cases may not accurately reflect the actual number of incidents. There are more actual runaways than are reported."

A policewoman in the Juvenile Missing-Persons Office described procedure on runaways, defined in Denver as missing children from ten to eighteen. "We wait," she said. "Unless we get some word that a child is in a particular location, we wait. We don't send out a detective unless there is indication of foul play. Running away is not a crime." Echoing the police in Houston, she assured me: "We perform a service."

After two years I had learned that the police play with words as every institution does. Running away is not a crime like stealing or shooting, but in most states the runaway is considered delinquent, incorrigible, or a person in need of supervision. He has committed an offense against a local or a state statute. As Chief Hallman said, "Running away is a violation of the Colorado Children's Code. It's enough to place a child in the custody of the police."

Like Denver, San Francisco admits to a steady number of

reported runaways. "There has been no significant change in the last five years," Chief of Juvenile Operations Don Murphy said, commenting on the yearly 2,500–3,000 reported local runaways, in June, 1974.

The 2,500–3,000 figure is based on reports from local parents and guardians who telephone the police to tell of a missing child. The San Francisco police told me that 90 percent of these children return home on their own; 8 percent are returned by the police; 2 percent are not returned. These general statistics seem faulty. While I believe that most runaway children do go home, the 90 percent figure is high and unsubstantiated by facts. It seems a prefabricated defense, a protection against the public anger if another mass murder happens here.

At San Francisco police headquarters on Bryant Street, I talked to two sensible young inspectors one afternoon about the problem of the police with runaways. One of them spoke honestly: "To be frank with you, we can't look for every runaway reported to us. There are too many of them. We take a report on them, but we can't search for each individual."

As Lieutenant Kirkland complained, police departments everywhere are damned if they do and damned if they don't pick up wandering children. If the police don't apprehend possible runaways, the children may be treated brutally on the street. If the police do pick up and detain children they suspect of being runaways, they may be upbraided by irritated parents and civil libertarians.

In June, 1971, the Berkeley City Council restricted the Berkeley Police Department in their handling of underage street people and runaways. In the three summer months of 1970, the Berkeley police had arrested 1,000 runaways and sent them home. According to the police officers who told me the story, the parents of arrested local youngsters were angry. They talked about police pressure and said the department was infringing on the civil rights of their children. They demanded that police stop combing the streets for runaways. They urged the City Council to curtail the police in the matter of juvenile arrests. The City Council established guidelines for the police department to follow in detaining children and youths.

Consequently, police arrests of runaway children in Berkeley have dropped from the high figure of 1,198 during 1970 to a low of 258 in 1973. The low figure does not accurately reflect the number of runaways there. Juvenile Bureau officers said that they could pick up 100 runaways in two weeks if they put their minds to it.

"We used to look at runaways as an extremely serious problem," said Lt. Henry C. Sanders of the Berkeley Juvenile Bureau. "Kids are an easy mark for deranged people in this community. We brought kids into the station to establish their identity. However, since 1970, we haven't really concentrated on them. Since the City Council's action, the police officers feel so what, who cares."

In New York City, on the entrance desk at the East Twelfth Street station in Greenwich Village is a sign that reads: "If you don't like the police, call a hippie for help." The sentiment is a souvenir from the days of confrontation when long-haired youngsters bad-mouthed stick-swinging policemen. To the harried parents who enter the station looking for the Runaway Unit, the sign is a deliberate reminder that citizens depend on police to protect them and their children.

In 1972, when the New York City Police Department's Youth Aid Division established the special Runaway Unit, New York police handled 13,207 cases involving local runaways between ages twelve and fifteen and about 10,000 out-of-town fugitives, according to *The New York Times*. After the Houston killings the New York police counted 20,000 runaways in the city. Of that number the Runaway Unit may rescue 30 to 35 children each month, Officers Dansky and Kinsella said. From June, 1972, when the Runaway Unit began its operation, through March, 1974, the unit recovered 592 children.

As Capt. Francis J. Daly, commanding officer of New York's

Youth Aid Division, testified before the House of Representatives in May, 1974: "We feel that the recovery of runaways is a legitimate police function. Each runaway recovered minimizes their exposure to the streets and the possibility of their becoming crime victims or engaging in delinquent or antisocial behavior. We also see it as a positive aspect of police work, in that we are out on the streets, seeking out runaways and returning them, in many cases, to distressed but grateful parents."

Captain Daly appeared before the House committee which heard witnesses on proposed legislation to aid runaways and their families. He supported the provision in the bill which allowed for well-managed shelters. He also agreed with the idea of a national registry of runaways, an aid, he believed, in reporting, identifying, and recovering interstate runaways.

The strength of the captain's appearance before the committee lay in the fact of the Runaway Unit itself. As a special corps within the police department, it serves as a model to other cities disturbed by children whose only crime may be leaving home without permission. Those cities and university towns troubled by an influx of traveling youngsters would be wise to establish a police department runaway unit. With their knowledge of the city, special police, trained to detect runaways, would be invaluable on the streets where children are in danger.

In every American police station there is a permanent fixture of the runaway era—the bulletin board of missing children. The board hangs as a reminder to police of their responsibility. Faces of lost children stare from circulars and snapshots. Assumed to be runaways, known to be missing, they look like the youngsters at home. The photographs focus on one fact which the Houston case only exaggerated: in a time of violence like our own, a humane police department, educated to understand children and their parents, is a necessity for life.

II. "In Need of Supervision": The Law and the Runaway

Part I. The Law

"I do not believe that any child who is sixteen years of age has the right to disregard her parents' control and supervision."—the judge in the case of the pregnant runaway, Maryland, September 26, 1972.

I went to the Eastern Shore of Maryland one hot summer afternoon during 1973 to follow up a runaway case that had appalled me. The "Matter of Mary Susan Parker," as court transcripts would title it, seemed a clear case of the injustice in law toward runaway children. I learned soon enough that the case was far from clear; it was muddied by the ambiguity that surrounds juvenile law and its belief that children are the property of their parents.

A girl who ran away from home because she was pregnant was caught, jailed, and sent to court. At the hearing the judge decreed that she obey her mother and submit to an abortion. I wanted to know the background of this unusual decision. I was going to ferret the story out of the town itself. I discovered that a story, like justice, depends upon the nature of the person who gives it out.

The case seemed simple: a sixteen-year-old girl had run away from home with her boyfriend. She was pregnant and wanted to marry him. Since the boy was sixteen too, the law said that he needed his parent's permission to marry. Because the girl was pregnant, she did not. The boy's mother refused him. The girl's mother insisted she have an abortion. The girl said no, abortion was murder. The high school lovers tried unsuccessfully to get married in a town where nobody knew them. Then they headed for a beach where the boy's family had a cottage. Their plan was to hide away from parents and doctors until Mary Susan could no longer safely undergo an abortion. She was about ten weeks pregnant then and the doctor had advised her mother "the sooner the better" for a suction abortion. After a week, however, someone in Brad's family thought to have the police go to the cottage.

The young couple returned to town with the police and were held in jail until their parents came. Brad's parents took him home. Mary Susan's mother had filed a petition with the court declaring that her daughter was *beyond her control.* The girl was to stay in jail until the hearing in juvenile court decided her future. Since Mary Susan had run away with Brad a year ago, her mother believed that if she were released, she would leave again. She was locked into the county jail on a floor separate from the adult prisoners, in a room apart from anyone else. Forlorn, looking like Orphan Annie, as the high school principal described her, Mary Susan was alone. She was isolated for five days before the hearing.

Her court-appointed lawyer came to speak to her in the jailhouse and found her very depressed. She insisted to him that she wanted her baby.

Because of the conflict between Mary Susan and her mother over the abortion the hearing would be dramatic. The juvenile court was to decide whether, as a runaway, she was *a child in need of supervision.* Most important to Mary Susan was the judge's decision: was she to be allowed to give birth to the child?

Mary Susan told her lawyer that she loved Brad and wanted to marry him. He tried to explain the difficulties of young marriages and the problems that developed when the couple had an infant. She was adamant. Convinced by her persistence, the lawyer prepared to support her in court.

I was not in the courtroom that fall morning, but I have a copy of the transcript which appeared in the state's newspaper of court proceedings. The newspaper used the names of the girl, the boy, her mother, but I have changed the girl's name to Mary Susan Parker and the boy's to Brad Johnson.

Mary Susan's mother explained her daughter's relationship with Brad: "I really didn't think they were seeing one another. Mary Susan was punished for a whole month and she wasn't allowed out even on weekends, and that's because of Brad," the mother stated.

Brad was trouble to Mary Susan's mother. He came from rough people. The Johnsons were a hard-headed bunch, said the folks who knew them. His older brother was serving two terms of life imprisonment for murder. Brad and Mary Susan had run away together once before. They used to sneak around to see each other in spite of Mary Susan's mother.

Mary Susan's mother learned of her daughter's pregnancy from her sister-in-law. The girl had confided in the woman telling her she had an appointment with the doctor because she had missed two periods. The mother went to the doctor's office and saw her daughter there. Mary Susan told her she was pregnant and said Brad was the father. She refused an abortion.

"We discussed this with her, the doctor and I, and we didn't seem to be getting anywhere," the mother recalled. "I made an appointment for her at the Health Center and asked the nurse to talk to her. Even then Mary Susan said she didn't want to have an abortion. Later I had to do some shopping at the county plaza and I asked her to sit in the car and think. I was gone about forty-five minutes and when I came back and started to go home, she told me to call the doctor, that she had decided to have an abortion."

Sitting in the car, waiting for her mother, waiting for the harangue to resume, Mary Susan must have understood her situation perfectly. No one except Brad was on her side. If she continued to say no to the abortion, her mother would take her to court as she had last year when she ran away. The court would make her give up her baby one way or another.

She looked out over the parking lot to the Tastee-Freeze where all the kids went when they got their driver's license. They would meet at the Freeze, buy something to eat, and discuss their plans for the evening. All the good parties started at the Freeze. Boys and girls began to get acquainted there. On the day they married, they drove their wedding car around and around the Freeze to the shouts and waves of the customers.

She would marry Brad and have his child. She would lie and tell her mother that she had changed her mind.

The subterfuge worked. Her mother believed her. She could return to school until her mother had made arrangements with the hospital for the abortion.

The next morning Mary Susan signed herself out of school for a doctor's appointment. Outside she met Brad and two of his friends drove them to Center City, where they tried to get married.

When Brad appeared in court for Mary Susan's hearing, he told the court why they had run away. "We figured that if we stayed away long enough so that she couldn't get an abortion, then her mother couldn't make her get one."

Brad said he wanted to marry Mary Susan, but his parents would not give him permission. He told the judge he thought he could get a job and support his family. The judge disagreed.

Summarizing the hearing, the judge said: "I am well aware of the romance and unreasonable response, particularly on the part of young people in this type of situation, which is completely unrealistic as to who is going to support them, how they are going to live, where they will find a job. Because again, I have been on the bench long enough in this county to see these cases end up right back in court."

Certainly his experience as a judge formed his decision when he listened to the mother's plea in court: "I don't want to force Mary Susan. I am here for help." Certainly he believed the unborn child was as important as the two waiting before him. Yet, his decision was surprising and shocking.

"I have no hesitancy at all," he explained, "in supporting the mother in this case, and directing that Mary Susan obey her mother, and that she submit herself to the medical procedure of abortion. I feel this is indeed a practical way to deal with this problem."

Expedience governed the ruling that day in court. As another practical measure, Mary Susan was to be held in the county jail until the day of the abortion. To make sure that she not run away again, the sheriff himself was to deliver her to the hospital.

"Is the sheriff going to sit on her stomach too?" her lawyer asked the judge in dismay.

The judge also supported her mother's petition that Mary Susan was beyond her control. He agreed that she had run away from home because she did not want an abortion. Still, he found her to be a *person* or a *child in need of supervision,* a classification which she shares with thousands of other runaways.

The phrase *in need of supervision* is used by the court to gain control of unruly or unwanted children. (The law refers to the brief intials CINS or PINS to identify such a child.) Classifying a youngster as a CINS separates him from the harsher epithet *juvenile delinquent.* The term *juvenile delinquency* refers to an act that would be a crime if it were committed by an adult. In Mary Susan's case being a CINS meant that she had broken the state code defining proper conduct for children. In the Maryland juvenile code, she was: first, truant from school "without justification," and then, "disobedient, ungovernable," and beyond the control of parents, guardian, or custodian.

She had also deported herself so as to "injure or endanger"

herself. Finally, she had committed an "offense applicable only
to children," and she required "guidance, treatment, or rehabilitation."

The offense applicable only to children was her running
away from home, an act which violates the juvenile code in every
state of the union. As previously noted, the age at which a child
ceases to be classified as a *child* or as a *minor* differs from state to
state. In Mary Susan's state "a child is a person who has not at-
tained eighteen years of age." For the minor, leaving home without parental permission is one of a series of offenses the law uses
to define the *child in need of supervision.*

Other offenses may include: the habitual use of vulgar language in a public place, wandering the streets at night, smoking
cigarettes or using tobacco in any form, begging, drinking liquor,
loitering, attempting to marry without consent. The antiquity of
some of these descriptions is exposed by their language. A child
may be adjudged delinquent if he "wanders about railroad yards
or tracks, jumps a train, patronizes saloon or dramhouse, public
poolroom or bucket shop," visits a "house of ill repute." The catchall of legal definitions describing the child in need of supervision
is that he "associates with thieves, vicious or immoral persons."

Such restrictions were introduced by state legislatures to
protect children. Yet, juvenile courts and police departments
throughout the nation use them to establish standards of conduct
for people under age eighteen. When sixteen-year-old Mary
Susan ran away from home pregnant, she had failed to attain the
behavior required of her by family and state.

As the hearing ended, the judge sent her back to jail to
await transfer to the hospital. On the same day Mary Susan
instructed her lawyer to take the case to the Court of Special
Appeals. The juvenile court would take no action until the higher
court heard the case.

The lawyer drove to the capital city that afternoon and by
evening he had presented the "Matter of Mary Susan Parker" to
the Court of Special Appeals. The six-man court met the next
day to judge the appeal. Its decision was to reverse the juvenile

court's support of Mary Susan's mother and to release the girl from jail immediately. The judges were repelled by the idea of forcing a sixteen-year-old into a hospital for an abortion.

In overturning the juvenile court's ruling, the Court of Special Appeals referred to Maryland's abortion code, which states that no person is required to have an abortion. A 1971 statute concludes "a minor shall have the same capacity to consent to medical treatment as an adult." The court determined that if a minor is able to *consent* to such medical treatment, she is also able to *dissent*. On that basis the law granted freedom of choice to the sixteen-year-old minor Mary Susan Parker. If she was able to consent to abortion, she was able to refuse it.

Mary Susan herself could now decide whether the embryo would survive. The six-man court believed, however, that her own life needed supervision. A runaway was dangerous. A pregnant runaway was a double danger. She was a threat to society and herself. Others might emulate her lack of self-control. The Court of Appeals concurred with the juvenile court. Mary Susan Parker was a *child in need of supervision*.

Freed from jail, Mary Susan chose to live not with her mother but with an older aunt and uncle who had stood by her in court. They offered her a home and promised the court to help her fulfill the terms of her probation. She was responsible to the Juvenile Services Division of the Circuit Court for a year.

Several days after leaving jail, Mary Susan Parker entered a hospital to abort her child. Perhaps she came to believe she could not care for it properly. Maybe she realized Brad would not marry at sixteen. Perhaps her aunt said she could not live with them unless she had an abortion.

Although I tried to find out, I never did learn why Mary Susan changed her mind.

Part II. The Runaway

"In a town this small everybody knows everything about everybody else."—a high school girl at the Tastee-Freeze, in Mary Susan Parker's town, July, 1973.

To the outsider the town is an anachronism. As I walked along the main street looking for the courthouse, strangers nodded and smiled in passing. They took the time to point the direction and to say good day. Then, they turned to their companions to talk about the plans for another shopping center.

Set back from the street on trim lawns, the red-brick courthouse rose grander than the buildings around it. The post office was taller and the bank more ornate, but the courthouse was stately. It was the pride of the town, the seat of county government.

To one side of the courthouse was a collection of small buildings, former slave shacks, now a row of offices for the lawyers. Behind the courthouse was a squat brick building, the county jail. It housed prisoners on two floors, the sheriff on the third.

On the main street there was a moviehouse open only on the weekend and a craft shop selling the work of local potters. McCrory's department store was having its summer clearance and the windows of shoe shops were piled high with sandals and sneakers for sale.

At the end of the main street, down at the river, ducks pursued each other and gulls dipped for food on this summer afternoon. A couple of boys were throwing a stick into the water for their dog to fetch and the dog fetched, then shook himself dry over the boys.

A fisherman tied his boat to the dock and watched the scene. He sucked on a can of beer and smiled. "The wife and I are from Philadelphia. We moved down here a couple of years ago. We tried living out West too. We ended up right back here. It's the last bastion of the old civilization."

He pointed to the handsome federal houses that line the streets on either side of the dock. Green lawns, tended by black gardeners, slant to the edge of the water. He gestured toward a brick building close to the river and said it was a customhouse built early in the eighteenth century.

"A friend of mine bought it. It still has its original slave dungeons. He's going to keep it that way. He likes the old way of life."

He grimaced when he heard I was from Washington.

"That's a mean city. The cities aren't strict enough on the lawbreakers."

I told him it wasn't all that bad, and he asked how a senator could be robbed and shot in front of his own home.

I shrugged and began a long walk back through the town out toward the county shopping plaza. I stayed in a motel near the shopping center because the town had no hotel. The motel was air-conditioned and empty and its restaurant served home fries with breakfast every morning and hot rolls every evening.

The dinner waitress was blond and plump and she wore her fair hair pulled off her neck with a rubber band. She looked young enough to know Mary Susan so I asked her if she went to the high school. No, she had graduated from a local college in June and decided to stay around.

"I didn't want to go home to get a job. I like it here. I've spent the best four years of my life in this town," she told me.

I questioned her about the Mary Susan Parker case, and she remembered that her political science professor had taken his class to see the judge who decided the case.

"He didn't look like a judge to me. He looked like somebody's father. I think we made him nervous asking questions. He didn't want to talk about the case. Said it was still in litigation.

"You should talk to the townies," she advised me. "They hang out at the Tastee-Freeze. Especially the kids."

Across the plaza on the western tip of the shopping center the Tastee-Freeze faces two highways, U.S. 213 and Route 291. As the courthouse is the focus of the town, so the plaza is the gathering point for the county. All highways lead to the shopping center, where every day is a party.

As I watched teen-agers order ice cream, I thought about living in the country, where children can run free. Perhaps my fearful idea that every American adolescent is a possible runaway was germane only to the city. Maybe carefree youngsters who worried only about football and dances thrived in this rural place. I recalled my husband's story of his riding a blind plug horse out into the country to pick peaches when he was fifteen and I remembered summers at my grandmother's cottage picking apples and saving money for a trip to New York. Maybe this town like that era provided a sentimental childhood for its young. I expected a freak explanation for the runaway behavior of Mary Susan Parker and I thought the Tastee-Freeze would begin to give it to me.

When I reached the Freeze, it was eight o'clock and the cars were beginning to drive into the lot. Girls in jeans and halter tops ran from car to car saying "Hey!" to their friends. The boys gathered behind the Freeze in groups of four or five and talked about their summer jobs and their cars and how much they had to drink last night. Drinking age is twenty-one, driving age is sixteen, but sometimes the kids spike their Sprites.

Inside the Freeze the girls were filling orders, but Marsha wasn't too busy to talk. She invited me to a storage room at the rear of the shop.

"Our specialty is the parfait," Marsha giggled. "After we eat the ice cream out of the parfait cups, we fill them with Sprite and gin and call them Parfareeze. We drink beer most of the time. I don't get drunk except for special occasions. Grass is around if you want it. I tried it once and that was it."

She stared at me when I asked her about sex. She answered slowly and seriously. "If I loved a guy and I couldn't get married, I'd live with him. In college though. Not around here. My parents would be hurt. They downgrade the morals of the day. They don't get anxious about drinking, but doing drugs and having sex shock them. The difference between my mother's time and mine is that everybody did it then, but they kept it a secret. Today everybody does it, but we're open about it."

She hesitated and admitted: "Girls do have sex with a boy

they date steadily. It's just accepted by the young. Oh, we're careful and the boys use, you know, protection. Yes, there are several pregnancies a year, a lot of marriages, and a few abortions. I know of only one girl who's given the baby up for adoption. The black girls usually have their baby and keep it."

When I asked her what she thought about Mary Susan Parker's running away from home pregnant, she said: "All the kids were for her when she ran away. We were furious that her mother wanted her to have an abortion. The news got around and everybody was talking about it. In a town this small everybody knows everything about everybody else. Most kids can't wait to get out of high school and out of town. Another couple ran away this year too. Her parents wouldn't let them date so they left together. They ran to the beach and came back when their money ran out!"

Cindy came to tell Marsha that Roger was out front waiting for her.

"Oh, he'll wait." She was confident.

Marsha had said that her friends couldn't wait to leave town. They thought some other place would give them the chance to live without accounting to the townspeople. These children, like youngsters in other towns and cities, lived out their childhood fulfilling somebody else's expectations of them. Marsha for her parents, the kids at the Tastee-Freeze for each other, were doing what was approved and expected during their special place in time.

Mary Susan Parker was never one of them. She was a hanger-on, only hoping to belong. Hapless from birth, she was daughter to a woman who had made mistakes with men and marriage. The mother tried to prevent her daughter from repeating them. She wanted to give her child a new start, but Mary Susan defied her in public and won.

When I called Mary Susan Parker's uncle, he was willing to let me come to the farm to talk to them. To her uncle, the idea that a schoolteacher wanted to interview them was acceptable.

They had refused to do a television show, but they might be able to make a teacher understand.

His wife, however, said no. She and Mary Susan did not want to talk about the case. They wanted to forget. Her husband supported her, she added. They were giving the girl a second chance to be part of the gang at the Tastee-Freeze.

I knew Mary Susan only through interviews I had with the people involved in her case—the probation officer and the principal of her high school, her lawyer and the judge. To them Mary Susan was a legal problem and a social problem. She was also a child who was in need of supervision.

The metamorphosis of Mary Susan Parker began when she decided to run away from home the first time at fifteen. Until that decision to act for herself, she lived haphazardly, dependent upon somebody else's luck. Her mother and father separated, then divorced. Mary Susan and her sister and brother moved in with grandparents while their mother tried to make her way alone.

Mrs. Parker met a man who wanted to marry her. She told him about her children and he agreed to take the girls. The boy would stay with his grandparents. Mary Susan and her sister came to live in her stepfather's house.

The girl felt displaced, shifted from one house to another. She felt awkward and unwanted. To her mother the new husband came first; the girl was living in his home on his terms.

When she met Brad, she met herself. He was like her. His family gave him a hard time too. He couldn't figure out what they'd do or say to him next. He learned how to fend for himself as Mary Susan had. He distrusted adults and shied away from the kids at school. He made friends with a couple of guys and their girls and soon Mary Susan was one of them.

They tried everything the others did: beer and gin and wine, dope when they could get their hands on it, sex. School was a drag, another place where they failed to do what others wanted, another group of people who didn't really give a damn about children like them.

When Mary Susan asked Brad to run away with her, they were both freshmen in high school, both fifteen years old. They returned when the police picked them up hitchhiking.

Her mother filed her first petition with the court, stating that Mary Susan was disobedient, and she was placed on probation with the Juvenile Services Division of the Circuit Court. A year later when she ran away again, her situation at home had not changed, but this time Mary Susan was pregnant.

In the mind of the law her regeneration began when she agreed to end the pregnancy. When I talked to her court probation officer, he was proud of her. He told me: "She has grown from a confused, scared, unconfident adolescent to someone who can make decisions. She'll finish school, marry Brad Johnson, set up a home, be a housewife, work to help out. She has the normal aspirations."

Marrying, setting up a home, being a housewife and mother —Mary Susan believed in these dreams before she went to court, but she ignored the system and its schedule of normality. Consequently, Mary Susan was to synchronize her desires with the court's ideas of acceptable behavior for children. If the judicial system was to function, children must conform to laws which defined them by age and conduct.

Schools operate by schedule also, but their product is education, not justice. They realize that education is an indefinable process. Educators don't know whether it's more important to teach birth control or biology. They may try both or stick with earth science and hygiene. Being uncertain keeps them human. They make allowances for children whose schedules don't coincide with theirs. They may even try to understand why a child may suffer.

The first person to report Mary Susan Parker as a runaway was the principal of the county high school. A sympathetic young man, he viewed children as extensions of their families.

"She's little Orphan Annie, a sandy-haired, freckle-faced kid. Ninety percent of her life she's been left to fend for herself. The runaway syndrome is still there. She and Brad are often late to school. They'll come in together or spend free periods sitting together out in a car. They've isolated themselves because they were isolated as children. They belong to the dropout culture. They may make it. They probably won't."

Losers and loners belonged to the dropout culture, according to the principal. He saw a runaway syndrome in children who played truant, indifferent students without the will to achieve. They lacked the self-assurance of the boys and girls at the Tastee-Freeze because their parents ignored them until they made trouble. To their parents these youngsters were another burden piled onto many, another example of their own failure.

By running away from home Mary Susan fought against her mother's control, trying to define herself as an independent being.

"A juvenile is not a person legally," her lawyer was to tell me. "Someone adult has to speak for her."

Mary Susan tried, and failed, to find an adult to defend her. She had asked an aunt in confidence for advice about her pregnancy and the aunt told her mother; the doctor and nurse agreed with her mother about the abortion; the high school principal reported her truancy immediately; a justice of the peace refused to let her marry Brad; the sheriff held her in jail while he released the boy; the judge ordered Mary Susan to obey her mother. Except for one man, her court-appointed lawyer, she bucked a conspiracy of adults who insisted she defer to them. Her attorney believed she had the right to decide for herself whether her unborn child was to live. He considered Mary Susan Parker a person who, in the eyes of the law, had the right to refuse medical treatment. A state statute gave minors the right to consent to abortion. Why couldn't they also refuse abortion?

When I telephoned him from Washington, Mary Susan's attorney sounded like an informal country lawyer, easygoing and chatty. He had practiced law in the county for three years when he was appointed to represent Mary Susan.

When I asked him what the girl was like, he said: "She's a cute little blond, a typical, immature, sixteen-year-old. She was mild, meek, and scared during the days of the case. But I saw her at the Tastee-Freeze a month ago with a guy. She didn't speak to me. Maybe she didn't see me or maybe she didn't want to see me.

"She went to live with her aunt and uncle. Her mother paid the legal fees and lost her child."

It seemed to me that Mary Susan's mother had lost her child long before the case came to court. I asked the lawyer to explain why Mary Susan was judged by both courts to be a *child in need of supervision*.

"She didn't play it cool," he said. "She lived for a week with Johnson instead of seeking legal help. She would never have been adjudicated in need of supervision if she hadn't run off into the boondocks with him."

His argument went like this: if Mary Susan had gone to a policeman or juvenile services officer of the court to deal with her mother's demand for abortion, she would have displayed maturity. If she had asked a person in authority, like the high school principal, to help her, she would have shown the court that she was behaving in a responsible manner. Instead, she chose to run away from school. She was a truant and a runaway.

"At what point does a child have the right in law to run away?" I asked the lawyer when I talked to him in his office.

"The area is wide open for litigation," he said. "If her life's in danger, she has the right to run away," he explained. "If she's only running because her folks make her go to school, she hasn't the right. There's a gray area in between these two extremes."

"What rights does a child over sixteen have?" he asked rhetorically.

His question implied that children *under* sixteen have few rights within the law.

"The Mary Susan Parker case clarified children's rights in

this state in one area: by statute juveniles had the right to obtain medical treatment or advice for pregnancy, contraception, and venereal disease without parental consent. Because of the Court of Appeals decision they now have the right to disregard parental wishes in these areas. The case is not a landmark decision, not a common law right. It's a statutory decision, and one the judge disapproves of.

"The judge is not a villain by any means," he added. "He's an expert in juvenile law. He wrote most of it in this state. Although I didn't think he'd order an abortion, he was upholding the girl's mother. She had turned to the legal system for help in controlling her child."

The lawyer believed, as the judge did, that the law was a force for civilization, necessary to bring order out of confusion. He accepted its vagueness toward children but foresaw that their legal rights would be established case by case.

When I saw the judge for the first time, he was giving instructions to a jury, speaking of reasonable doubt and the impossibility of mathematical certainty. He was cautioning the jury in a manslaughter case to weigh and sift the evidence.

"Use the same kind of common sense that you use in the ordinary affairs of life," he advised them.

At fifty-six, the judge looked like somebody's father. He was a father who had endured whatever fears his own children gave him, a father whose solidness and security came from his service to the state, from the honor of a family that had established itself in America in the eighteenth century and helped to govern the colony.

The man himself became a judge in 1960 at a time when the court officer in juvenile affairs sold fertilizer for a living. Instructed by the governor in 1967 after the Supreme Court's Gault Decision, the judge worked to create laws equitable for children. He initiated a department of juvenile services within the court system. As the only judge of the Circuit Court in the county, he also assumed responsibility for the disposition of juvenile cases. He was a practical man whose pragmatism outweighed his sensibility.

When I questioned him about his decision in the Mary Susan Parker case, he said: "I understood that time was of the essence for the suction method of abortion, which both mother and doctor preferred to the surgical procedure."

The judge supported his decision by claiming that Mary Susan's baby had a right not to be born. He scoffed at the men and women who cried shame at him.

"They revere the right to life, but they're unconcerned about what happens to that life after it is born. Children born to children under these circumstances have many difficult days. Usually a social agency or the grandparents take care of them."

He called the statutory decision permitting a minor to disregard the parents in sexual matters "a vicious thing."

"I do not believe that any child who is sixteen years of age has the right to disregard her parents' control. The court can certainly support parents in doing what they think is best for the child."

By supporting Mary Susan's mother, he unleashed a storm of protest in magazines and newspapers throughout the country. One afternoon at his son's apartment he read about himself in *Playboy*.

"The newspapers and magazines made me out to be an ogre, the villain of the piece," he said wryly. "The headlines condemned me for putting the girl in jail. I had no choice but to detain her, to assure her being in court for the hearing. Her mother could not guarantee her not running away a third time and the county has no facilities for juveniles."

Perhaps as his reaction to the unfavorable publicity, he had made another decision: "I told the juvenile services that never again would I put a child in jail. I'm going to let them provide the custody."

A new Maryland law upholds the judge's conclusion about

juvenile detention. In effect since January, 1974, the law forbids committing a *child in need of supervision* to an adult institution. Other states like New York have ruled that noncriminal children, those neglected, abused, or forgotten, who are judged in need of supervision, must not be placed in reform schools with young criminals. The State of Massachusetts has closed its juvenile-detention centers. The District of Columbia has shut down Junior Village, a catchall institution for children who committed crimes as well as for abandoned or runaway children. The theory behind the practice is benevolent; children who are victims should not be locked up with those who are burglars, rapists, and murderers.

The judge explained the purpose of the juvenile court. "It is not meant to punish or try crimes," he said. "It's an informal court, not a criminal court. Yet the juvenile court does make legal determinations. The historical idea of the juvenile court as a loving parent is outdated. Children like runaways, truants, those judged incorrigible, need the threat of the court to make them conform. We have to use compulsion. The basic theory of the court is to treat children as people who need correction because of their youth."

As the judge explained—reasonably, outrageously—the power of the law over children, I remembered three novels about totalitarianism: *Brave New World*, *1984*, *A Clockwork Orange*. In these books, which are set in a frightening future, children and their parents are controlled by the state. Through propaganda and brainwashing, by division into class, by fear of punishment, they exist as automatons.

Mary Susan had tried to take charge of her life, to bypass convention and live for love, but she had failed. As a runaway, she was entangled in the law that gave power to people because they were older, because they had given birth to her, because by tradition they knew best.

When the judge said, "The court is the only institution that has authority," I knew Mary Susan would have disagreed. She performed now as everyone expected her to. She blended, chameleonlike, into the background of home, school, court system. She fulfilled, finally, the requirements set up for children by law. She became less than a victim of society. She was its creation.

As a runaway, Mary Susan Parker was a juvenile-status offender. She did not break a criminal law; she violated a state code of behavior for children. Because she was pregnant and a two-time runaway, she had been locked into jail for the convenience of the court. This custom of the juvenile court is known as *preventive detention,* which the law employs to restrain runaways and truants and to keep children on hand for their hearings.

Like a runaway slave, Mary Susan was to be returned to her mother until the Court of Special Appeals forbade the abortion decision. At this point she was free to decide the fate of her unborn child, but not her own. The juvenile court placed her with relatives and under its supervision until she became eighteen.

The laws concerning children reek of ambiguity. It is impossible for the law to be clear; it is not always practical for the law to be kind. The law reasons like a Puritan minister to contain the behavior of unruly children. A state's juvenile code is based on the suppression of children, supposedly for their own good, actually for the convenience of the adults. These statutes differ from state to state as they define which youngsters need the supervision of the court. Children whose parents did not want them in the first place are its worst victims; children whose parents find adolescence a trial suffer from the juvenile court's alliance with adults.

The law, which is founded on control, lacks control. The discretion of the juvenile court in family matters is too broad. It allies itself with parents and schools and police and traffics in petty illegalities like running away and truancy, which should be

left to social agencies. The court accepts too easily the petitions of
parents who want to lose their children in the penal system; it
uses preventive detention too quickly.

I am not the first to cry foul at the juvenile-justice system.
Experienced lawyers and judges like Lisa Aversa Richette of
Philadelphia are working to change the laws as they apply to
children. They want to limit the children who must appear in
juvenile court, according to their offense.

The runaway child's appearance before the juvenile court,
not his running, is the crime. "The threat of the court," as Mary
Susan's judge called it, turns the law into a bully-boy and convinces the child that adults rule by force. The law can help the
runaway in other ways. It can refer him to a runaway house or to
a group home for adolescents where trained staff understand his
running. It can advise him and his family to ask for counseling at
a mental-health clinic or through the school guidance counselor.
It can suggest private agencies which will help him.

While the process of revising the law takes place, children
and their parents should be taught about the juvenile code of the
community, instructed on their rights and responsibilities within
the law. The consequences of the law as it pertains to the child
who runs away from home, plays truant, or becomes pregnant
should be publicized. By state edict students are required to learn
the history of state and country; so boards of education can add a
unit on the juvenile code of the state to the curriculum. Beginning in junior high school, children today read and respond to
sophisticated literature. They can also learn of their place in the
law.

12. "The Runaway Reaction": Psychiatry and the Runaway

308.3 *Runaway reaction of childhood (or adolescence)*

"Individuals with this disorder characteristically escape from threatening situations by running away from home for a day or more without permission. Typically they are immature and timid, and feel rejected at home, inadequate, and friendless. They often steal furtively."—from the *Diagnostic and Statistical Manual of Mental Disorders,* published by the American Psychiatric Association, 1968.

In 1967 six psychiatrists in Washington, D.C., decided that running away from home signified a mental disorder. They believed that the child who ran was delinquent and sick. They included the "runaway reaction of childhood" in the second edition of the American Psychiatric Association's manual of the terms and phrases defining mental illness. DSM-II, as the doctors call the handbook, is the American dictionary of pathology.

The six doctors and two statisticians who were the committee on nomenclature for the manual added the "runaway reaction" to the major behavior disorders of childhood. While the police and the law were beginning to realize that runaways were not necessarily juvenile delinquents, these doctors asserted the delinquency of runaways when they accepted the new category, which is based on the behavior of reform-school boys. With the addition of a medical diagnosis to the legal classification *runaways,* the psychiatrists implied that millions of American parents were rejecting their children.

The nomenclature committee worked in a vacuum, oblivious to the social and cultural changes of the decade. They were ignorant of the research going on at the National Institute of Mental Health, where a group of scientists were preparing a major survey of suburban runaways, the Shellow Report. Since the nomenclature committee met during 1963 and 1964 to revise the manual, its work preceded the youth rebellion of the late sixties. Perhaps no one could have predicted the future mass migration of the young when being a runaway would symbolize idealism. However, the psychiatrists were hasty to include the runaway reaction as a major disorder on the narrow evidence which Dr. Richard L. Jenkins provided them. Dr. Jenkins, professor of child psychiatry at the University of Iowa and Chief of the Child Psychiatry Services, served on the committee of eight which revised the manual.

Including his diagnosis in the handbook, the committee relied on his analysis of three hundred inmates of the New York State Training School for Boys. Today psychiatrists will admit a disagreement among them over the diagnosis. They talk about the dangers of defining a mental disorder in terms of a symptom like running away from home. The words identify a reaction, but they are not limited to the particular group of delinquent children within the runaway population. The ambiguity of the phrase *runaway reaction* is damning to all runaways.

An editor of the revised manual, Dr. Paul T. Wilson, a Washington, D.C., area psychiatrist, told me that the *runaway reaction* was not useful as a diagnosis because it does not convey an accurate description of all runaways.

"There are eighteen thousand reasons why a child might run," he said. "Why he ran is not covered by the term *runaway reaction*. There was a lot of controversy about that particular category."

Since psychiatrists were dissatisfied with the special category, the next edition of the manual will eliminate it as a major classification. However, the *runaway reaction* will still be included as a subdivision under the "hyperkinetic syndrome," a major childhood disorder. Since it denotes excessive motion, *hyperkinetic* comes close to describing running away, but a hyperkinetic disorder is also a mental disorder. The runaway child will remain a case.

With its inclusion in the manual as a category of mental imbalance, the medical decision contradicted the conclusion of the Shellow Report that the majority of runaway children show no signs of personal or family pathology. However, probing a child's runaway reaction creates more patients for more psychiatrists since the sick, rejected child comes from the sick, rejecting family. The proper person to handle the runaway becomes the doctor, displacing the disputed police officer or judge; the proper place for treatment becomes the doctor's office, rather than the overcrowded juvenile court. Then in 1968, as noted above, the psychiatric profession became officially involved in diagnosing running away as a malady.

Psychiatry splits into several theories to explain running away from home. Two major explanations have appeared: one, that a child's running away is pathological, the basis of Dr. Jenkins's description; the other, that running away from home is a forthright reaction to an unsatisfactory situation, as the Shellow study sees it. The common denominator of both ideas is the assumption that the family has frustrated the runaway.

The doctors who call running away from home a personality

disorder have based their conclusions on studies conducted in a clinic like Jenkins's reform-school setting, or from the files of a social-service agency. The children these doctors examine have already been judged delinquent or deprived or disturbed. They may represent a certain economic class or a particular condition; but they are guinea pigs for a doctor who wants to prove a pet theory.

Dr. Jenkins's reform-school boys were delinquents who also ran away from "a rejecting or disturbing home situation." They were not sent to the training school because they had only run away. Running repeatedly was only one aspect of their delinquency. They were sneak thieves and, feeling unwanted at home, they often stole from their families, then ran. In a 1971 essay for the *American Journal of Psychiatry*, Dr. Jenkins described the runaway reaction as "the frustration response of a hurt child to the conviction that he is not wanted in his home. Such a conviction is typically emotionally overwhelming and devastating."

The doctor listed traits of the runaway that he observed at the training school. He is emotionally immature, apathetic, seclusive, according to the doctor. Because he wants to win favor and perhaps make friends with an older, stronger boy for protection, he reveals a penchant for "passive homosexuality." He feels worthless and afraid, easily discouraged, and is, as the doctor concludes, "difficult to treat."

Dr. Jenkins's analysis may be sound, but to apply his studies of delinquent boys to the entire runaway population is far-fetched. The doctor did not consider girls, who compose at least half of all runaways, nor did he include the suburban, middle-class child. Like any clinical analysis, the focus is too narrow for the conclusion that runaways are unbalanced or mentally ill.

By 1973 Dr. Jenkins, today Professor Emeritus of Child Psychiatry at the State Psychopathic Hospital of the University of Iowa in Iowa City, expanded the description of the runaway reaction for his book *Behavior Disorders of Childhood and Adolescence*. By then he was aware of the Shellow Report, and he admitted the difficulty of classifying running away "as a mal-adaptive response." He conceded the variety of reasons for a child's leaving home and, in spite of his research with reform-school boys, he softened his early theory that tied running away to delinquent behavior. In another article on the runaway reaction written with Dr. Galen Stahle for *The Journal of the American Academy of Child Psychiatry,* Dr. Jenkins wrote: "Although no particular pattern of delinquency seemed to be peculiar to runaways, stealing and truancy from school were quite prominent."

By 1975 Dr. Jenkins was trying to convince the psychiatrists of the new committee on nomenclature to broaden the descriptions of the behavior of different types of runaway children for a revision of the manual of mental disorders. In a letter to me in June 1975, Dr. Jenkins said: "The chronic runaway child is typically, but not always, an example of an unsocialized child who is timid, furtive, and grossly lacking confidence in himself. I picked the title 'Runaway reaction' because this is the only delinquent action which is highly characteristic of these children. However, there are other children who have the same personality structure who have not (at least as yet) run away and there are runaway children who do run away repeatedly who do not fit the description of the *Runaway reaction.* Of course, of the children who run away only once, most do not deserve a psychiatric diagnosis."

A fellow psychiatrist with a different viewpoint is Dr. Helm Stierlin, former Acting Chief of Family Studies, Adult Psychiatry Branch of the National Institute of Mental Health. When I talked to him, he was completing his book *Separating Parents and Adolescents: A Perspective on Running Away, Schizophrenia, and Waywardness.* He calls the separation process a test of growing up. In his work he asks himself whether running away reflects pathology or a legitimate attempt at separation. Like a careful scientist, he answers yes and no.

Yes, running away from home is a legitimate effort to grow

up and yes, depending on the situation of the family, it may signify abnormality. No, not all runaways are delinquents.

"The runaway is opening himself up to new experiences, new values. He may be stronger and healthier than the troubled child who does not run. He may have the skills to survive, to relate to his peers, to fight." The German-born analyst explained his ideas to me slowly and carefully one day in his office.

"From my experience running away from home is an immense problem," the doctor emphasized. For five years Dr. Stierlin and his associates at the National Institute of Mental Health studied thirty-six families of adolescents in a treatment program for academic underachievers. The children were referred to the program by schools and private psychiatrists for having severe problems related to their schoolwork. Doctors at the mental-health institute investigated the possibility that these children might develop schizophrenia.

The boys and girls in the study group were between fourteen and sixteen years old. Not all had run away from home. From the one out of three who did run, Dr. Stierlin delineated three types of runaways: the crisis runaway, the casual runaway, and the abortive runaway.

The *crisis runaway* leaves home because of a dramatic change in him or in his family. The crisis may be the onset of the conflicts of growing up: an awakening sexual drive, experimentation with drugs, truancy from school, the guilt that comes from exploring sex or drugs. The crisis may center on parents who disregard the child. At the time of the flight the crisis may lie hidden, yet it is important enough to cause the child to leave home. Although the parents may slight their child, there is an involvement between them. The parents may be disappointed in him, but not indifferent. He is meaningful to them. With help the crisis runaway may master his situation and return to school and home.

The *casual runaway* runs easily. He just takes off. He's

adept at making it outside the home. A girl finds it easy to exploit her sexual attractiveness; a boy can always find girlfriends. These children are the offshoots of neglectful families, of parents pre-occupied with themselves, who think that the children interfere with their lives. The youngsters run away from hatred and in-difference.

The *abortive runaway* belongs to a special group, Dr. Stierlin believes. He is a lonely child who shows signs of a split person-ality. The runaway attempt he makes is unsuccessful.

"The abortive runaways," he said, "exemplify crucial family dynamics. The runaway attempt cannot succeed because of the binding force of the family. The runaway is usually back within one day."

Dr. Stierlin's clinic was his office. He saw children who were ill and he saw children whose behavior worried their parents. He treated children whose parents wanted a rationale for their ac-tions. He talked with children whose schools believed they might adjust to classes and schoolwork with counseling.

As Dr. Stierlin explained the types of runaways, I recalled a mother who told me her daughter had left home because the school was insisting she see a psychiatrist. Transferred to a new school because of a busing order, the girl disliked the change. She showed her insecurity by cutting classes and skipping school, by ignoring her homework.

"School scared the life out of her when they talked about counseling," the mother said. "I told them not to pressure her, that I would arrange a private visit."

The girl ran away the day before her appointment with a psychiatrist. She left her parents a note saying since she was treated like a criminal, she might as well act like one. Her parents were anxious for her happiness, but at the same time they were determined to obey the state in its decisions about the education of children. Since the state had ordered transferring children from one school to another to accomplish integration, the parents supported that order. They also complied with the girl's new school by agreeing to a psychiatric interview for her.

"Children may cope with their environment by running away," Dr. Stierlin had said.

The separation of child from parents occurs naturally as he grows up, according to the doctor. But, the normal conflict of the adolescent who is separating himself from his family is aggravated by demands from his parents.

"The separation process starts from the moment of birth," Dr. Stierlin continued.

The five-year-old who leaves home for kindergarten resembles the teen-ager who hitchhikes to the beach. They are both testing their independence and new strength. Leaving the safety of home for school is a major development for the young child; exploring alternatives with his mind is a major development for the adolescent.

"Separation is a test of adolescence. It's not a total separation but a kind of changing. Loyalties continue to exist and in some respects become deeper," the doctor said.

"Around age thirteen or fourteen the adolescent becomes able to use his mind in a more free-wheeling fashion. Mentally, he has a final spurt of growth. His intellectual capacities mature. He recognizes a pull from society that he is to take a responsible role in line with the adult image. Interweaving with this pull from adult society is the alternative culture of the peer group with its different values. The peer group's values have a delinquent touch to them: taking dope, drinking, having intercourse. Yet they provide another proof of his maturation."

If the adolescent cannot manage both adult and youth cultures, he may feel guilty about his behavior. He may be caught by lies to parents, teachers, friends. If he cannot explain to his parents what is bothering him, if his friends can't help him, he may become depressed and feel discomfort. He may run away to relieve his depression. In this sense, flight is a substitute for suicide.

As Dr. Stierlin said of his study: "We came to view the running away of several of these patients as desperate attempts to get away from their depression."

Although Dr. Stierlin began our interview by mentioning his disagreement with the runaway-reaction definition, his conclusion seemed to support Dr. Jenkins. In his paper "Characteristics of Suburban Adolescent Runaways," based on the study of underachievers at the National Institute of Mental Health, Dr. Stierlin observed:

"Running away fits into a syndrome which encompasses delinquency, low tolerance of frustration, and poor impulse control. Nonrunaway underachievers, in contrast, tend to fit into more typical neurotic and borderline syndromes. They tend to contain conflicts within themselves. They suffer from these conflicts instead of trying to cope with them through action and interpersonal agitation. Our overview establishes therefore the average runaway as a type that seems set apart from other types of disturbed adolescents."

Four years before the psychiatrists added the "runaway reaction" to diagnostic vocabulary, the federal government sponsored a research project on the runaway explosion. The government wanted to know why so many children were leaving home during one of the most affluent periods of history, the early 1960s. Through the National Institute of Mental Health a team of men and women conducted a thorough investigation into the lives of almost one thousand runaway children. The Shellow Report, identified by the name of its director Robert Shellow, concentrated on children who were reported missing during the year 1963–1964 to the police of Prince George's County, Maryland.

Prince George's lies on the northeastern border of the District of Columbia. Since 1950 the county has altered dramatically. Its change from a pasture to a tract-filled suburb typifies the instantaneous growth of suburbs throughout the country. Prince George's represents the mixture of affluence and poverty, black and white, blue- and white-collar, more typical of the city than the suburb. With the expansion of the county came social and political anxieties. Among these was the problem of children running away from home.

Robert Shellow and his colleagues used the suburb as their clinic to make sense of the phenomenon of teen-age runaways. They began their job with the police missing-persons report as the necessary preliminary to an interview with the parents. They stated that talks with parents were their primary sources of data while interviews with children were used to interpret their findings. They went to schools, police department, and juvenile court for records on the teen-agers. Finally, to obtain a point of comparison, they administered a questionnaire to thirteen hundred students in grades seven through twelve in eleven schools in the county.

The researchers located two separate populations of runaways: a minority of deeply troubled youngsters for whom flight was closely connected to the pathological history of their families; and the majority, who showed no evidence of severe personal or family problems. Although the act of leaving was the same for both groups, the intention and meaning of it differed.

The writers explained: "Had we considered only the seriously disturbed minority, we would have arrived at essentially the same conclusion as these previous studies which attacked the problem through clinical and agency populations, that is, that runaways are damaged children badly in need of individual and expert care. Such a conclusion would be entirely inappropriate for children in the other and larger group, however. These, too, are troubled children, but they are troubled in much the same way as other adolescents are troubled. Unlike the pathologically driven frequent repeater, the others need no custodial care and have no special need for individualized professional services."

Searching for proof that fleeing youngsters were not delinquents, contrary to the runaway-reaction theory, the Shellow research team read police and court records of children who had run away and examined the number formally charged. They discovered that "five out of six runaways had *never* been charged," and "most runaways did *not* have a history of delinquency before their reported absence." After the runaway episode, one out of four had formal charges against them.

One explanation is apparent: after running away a child is more apt to be charged as a *runaway*, as *beyond control*, as *incorrigible* than he was before he left home. He is more likely to appear before a judge after he has been charged with a delinquent act. Before their runaway episode one out of six children had appeared in court; after it, one out of three. As the report announced: "But the most striking feature to emerge from these findings is that the great majority did not get into trouble at all either before or after running away."

Police and court records gave the researchers data on the repeating runaway. He turned out to be the stereotype, the child who might fit Dr. Jenkins's description. He was consistently involved with police and courts, he experienced serious problems in school, his family background was chaotic, and his own personality showed signs of individual pathology. But as one of the thousand runaways the government team was examining, he was in the minority.

Then as now, the majority of runaways were children having a tough time growing up. The basic issue in running away was conflict at home. As the researchers concluded, youngsters were compelled to leave by difficulties outside of themselves, by problems that lay "in the different social systems in which they move, in their relations with their parents, with the school system, and with their peers." They found that the suburban runaways of the early sixties, like their 1976 counterparts, were not pathologically disturbed; they found them to be children whose parents had played a part in their running.

Relieved to talk to sympathetic researchers, parents of runaways told them what they thought had caused the child to leave. An argument, a punishment, a demand for better grades, each might have spurred the child to run, and the parents knew it. As the report stated:

"More than three out of four of the parents of runaways reported conflict within the family, mainly over issues such as the child's school performance, his choice of friends, his rejection of family rules and values. . . . From the child's point of view, however, whether runaway or not, it would appear that trouble at home is the rule. Over 80 percent of the adolescent comparison group and an even larger majority of those in our intensive interview sample, which included nonrunaways, reported trouble at home. What we have then, is the great majority of children claiming to live in family settings characterized by conflict."

Some adolescents flee as a political ploy. As the report stated, it is a "calculated maneuver in dealings with parents, ultimately designed to change the relationship rather than deny it." An example of their campaign for control is the fact that three-fourths of the suburban youngsters stayed near home. Like the children who run away today, anticipating reconciliation, they did not leave the metropolitan area. The report also showed that they returned soon. "Almost two-thirds of the runaways were home again within 48 hours; one-half decided to return on their own, while the others were either located by friends or family or returned through the help of the police."

Families of these runaways represented a wide range of incomes in the suburb. The majority came from the middle-income group, 15 percent came from wealthy homes, 28 percent from poorer families. Their families moved from one home to another more often than families whose children did not run. Over a five-year period more than two-thirds of the runaways had moved at least once, displacing them from their accustomed schools, friends, and neighborhoods.

While it skims the surface of family relationships, the Shellow Report is generous enough to admit the contradictions inherent in the runaway problem. For example, the report states that the runaway is likely to come from a broken home or a family with a stepparent; only half the suburban runaways lived with their natural parents. Then, however, it observes that half came from intact families.

Shellow's researchers discovered that the boy-girl ratio was sixty-forty, according to police records. However, 60 percent of the runaways who were reported to the local juvenile court were girls. Fearful of being unable to restrain a runaway daughter, parents used the courts to support them. Popular prejudice forgave wild sons, but disapproved of rebellious daughters. This kind of sexual prejudice of the sixties remains unchanged today.

Because "Suburban Runaways of the 1960s" was compiled before 1967, the report could not imagine the lure for discontented youngsters of the hippies, the drug culture, or the political movements of the late 1960s. When the Shellow study reported on the impulsive quality of running away, it evoked nothing more vivid of the times than the beehive hairdo: "Girls frequently took no more than a set of curlers and a can of hair spray."

Were those suburban runaways unmoved by the events of the period? Were they aroused only by their own misery? The answer seemed to be *yes*. I wondered why the report contained no references to the assassination of President Kennedy or to the fight for civil rights or the war in Vietnam.

I asked researcher Juliana Schamp why the interviewers had ignored the influence of current events on runaway children. Since television brought the outside world home, I thought perhaps its immediacy had stimulated their leaving.

"We wanted to see what the children would tell us rather than ask them questions like that," she explained. "The striking thing was that they were uninterested in such events."

Today many runaways claim an interest in the abused, neglected, rejected peoples of the country. They identify casually with fellow sufferers like the American Indian and the black man. While their compassion may be superficial and actually self-centered, they are aware of discrimination. Their own cause fascinates them as they speak of the injustice they have known from parents, police, the courts, school. After years of national dissent, today's runaway is often an untutored student of social protest.

Mrs. Schamp spoke of the Shellow-study youngsters as early emigrants. She said: "We had picked up the initial wave of the movement that was to take place at the end of the decade. Then we saw running away as part of a growing-up process, as a demand for greater recognition and control of their lives. We weren't prepared for the mass migration."

Perhaps because it was the first wave of a force that is altering the conception of childhood, the researchers saw the runaway as a folk hero. He was not mentally unbalanced, they contended, nor was he only a defiant youngster who left home tired of routine and expectation. He was a contemporary of us all, a latter-day Holden Caulfield, who wanted a respite from demand, who, in running, showed "a desire to step back, take stock, and rest before engaging again one's parents, teachers, or friends." As the researchers concluded, his "running away came to appear as a reaction to the ambiguities . . . of the adolescent in the modern world. Runaways are frequently among those adolescents who are too shrewd, too questioning to accept comfortably the mere promise of adulthood in the indefinite future while pacified with privilege in the present."

The runaway was kin to all adolescents, the report affirmed, but he chose to disappear as his method of facing trouble. He was an aggressive politician who dramatized himself by running rather than by passive resistance. Runaways have the same problems as young people who do not run, the report concluded, and "other adolescents deal with these problems differently but not necessarily in ways that are better either for themselves or for the community."

Ten years after the survey of suburban runaways in Prince George's County, Maryland, the study is important for the scope of its research and for the perspective it gives to the clinical theories that runaway children are psychiatric cases. The report stresses, as Mrs. Schamp did when we talked, that the majority of runaways are healthy youngsters who want change.

"We were not seeing a selected bunch of kids as the psychiatrists did," she insisted. "Running away is not limited to severe pathology as they felt."

School psychologist Kevin Dwyer refines the Shellow description of runaways who fall into the major group of healthy adolescents. He calls them the "socially active," while, like the Shellow researchers, he describes the minority group as "emotionally disturbed." These are depressed, suicidal youngsters. They are vulnerable, because they are disorganized, Dwyer explained. They get hurt easily. They become depressed when they accept the judgment of adults at home or in school that they cannot take care of themselves. They are, in Dwyer's words, "hypersensitive to their inadequacy."

The majority of runaways—the "socially active"—are boys and girls who are self-assured. They have friends and they enjoy themselves with them, in school and out. They belie Dr. Jenkins's description of runaways as timid and friendless. According to Dwyer, they are also bold and sociable. They get into trouble because they are involved. Gregarious, they too are vulnerable—to the pressures of the group.

"They may be taking drugs because they want to be liked," Dwyer said. "Because they don't want to lose somebody's friendship, they'll try the drugs he offers. They all have an unbelievable fear of rejection. They wonder what they did wrong if their friends pass them in the hall without speaking."

Dwyer's clinic was Montgomery Blair High School in Montgomery County, Maryland. He has worked as a psychologist for fifteen years; for eleven years he has counseled students. When I spoke to him at Montgomery Blair during a recent school year, he told me that one hundred students out of nineteen hundred in the high school had run away that year.

Their running could not be explained simply, he said. It was complex behavior, a maze of cause and effect.

"Young people do not run away for a single reason," he told me. "For some kids it's simply the thing to do. For others it's the better choice over suicide or becoming psychotic. Kids run away because they're bored or frustrated, because they want sexual freedom or because they want an abortion. They may be in a power struggle with their parents so they run away to hurt them and to reduce the hassle and the limits on them."

Like Kevin Dwyer and Juliana Schamp, I learned that runaways are heterogeneous. When I began to seek them out, I went to the runaway shelters where they gather. I chose the houses purposely to find clusters of children who had left home. Many of the children I met had been beaten or neglected by their families. They were the ones who had to run for their lives and, for a little kindness, would tell their sad stories without hesitation. Their parents could not, or would not, support them, and they ran from foster homes or group homes. Speaking about brutality, they showed me their wounds. They were children who were often involved with the law either as escapees from reform school or probationers from juvenile court. The runaway house was my clinic, and I began to believe that every runaway child ran from a vicious home. When I met other runaways in other places, I realized that it was impossible to apply a single reason to a complex emotion like a child's leaving home.

Later, when I began to travel, I saw a new runaway, a self-assured, cunning youngster who was proud of himself for making it outside of his family, for being accepted as he was, not for what they wanted him to be. Many of these travelers bore no resemblance to the pathetic children of the runaway house. The runaways I knew through school were different still, jaded with the fatigue that comes of meeting the endless demands of parents and teachers.

The psychiatric descriptions can apply to many runaways. Many are running from a particular crisis, as Dr. Stierlin suggested. None can manage easily the conflicting expectations of parents and friends. Many are leaving a threatening situation or running because they feel rejected at home. Some do have neglectful, insensitive parents. Most have parents who worry about them constantly because they are frightened by their adolescence.

We have misjudged adolescence and our teen-age children must struggle with an outmoded concept. Mrs. Schamp and the Shellow researchers discovered how archaic our understanding was ten years ago. "To us the running away indicated a major social change in the definition of adolescent," she told me.

The years from twelve to eighteen are no longer the tail end of childhood. Adolescence has become a premature condition of adulthood. Adolescents from healthy families who run away are telling us that the introduction to maturity has been faster and more complicated than their parents can remember. Far from pathological, most runaways are strong-willed youngsters who are forcing us to accept the seriousness of their lives.

To me the runaway child is not a romantic, but he is daring, even courageous. He is also impulsive and reckless. He has not thought things through, nor has he asked for advice outside the family. The running suggests that he may be imitating the way in which his parents face problems. Many parents of runaways will overlook an unpleasant or difficult issue. Their reasoning may be that if they do not admit to them, the problems will vanish. A child absorbs, then acts on, their mode of reasoning. If he runs, the problem disappears, or he forces his parents to contend with it. Runaways and their parents may be equally inexperienced in living together as changing individuals.

I refuse to accept the medical opinion that the runaway is a peculiar kind of adolescent, one who is unbalanced and delinquent. If he fits into a variety of pathological categories, then all adolescents are patients, ripe for clinical analysis. The biological connotations of maturing and the sociological connotations of growing up, straddling two cultures, create the diagnosis: the adolescent is an invalid. If the diagnosis is true, his prospects of recovery are gloomy. The prognosis for growing up in America may continue to include running away in America.

13. Youth Advocacy: Runaways a National Issue

"Fiscal year 1975 is the year of the runaway."—James Hart, Commissioner of the Office of Youth Development, the Department of Health, Education, and Welfare, August, 1974.

"How many runaways are there in America? One million every year as the Senate Subcommittee on Juvenile Delinquency has announced? Or, between 1,475,200 and 2,364,800 over three years as the University of Michigan's Institute for Social Research estimated?"

"Who are the runaways?"

"How do we classify runaway children? As delinquent or mentally ill?"

"Who is responsible for the runaway? The police? Social-welfare agencies? Traveler's Aid?"

"How do we handle children who can't, or won't, stay home?"

"Where do runaways go?"

"Does the government fund a program that suggests how

parents should raise their children? How much is it going to cost?"

"What is the constituency of runaways? Is the runaway issue a political asset?"

"Will runaway shelters give children an incentive to run? Will they become federal flophouses?"

"Who gets the credit for legislation assisting runaways and their families?"

"Who will be responsible for a runaway program? The Department of Health, Education, and Welfare or the Justice Department?"

These questions and their uncertain answers delayed the federal government's acceptance of runaways as a national problem. Lawmakers seemed to dally with one question in particular: "Should we intervene in a family matter like a runaway child?" The answer came suddenly in August, 1973, when the murders of twenty-seven boys in Texas were tied to running away from home.

Slowly the government has answered the questions, often haphazardly and incorrectly. Reluctantly it has decided that running away from home in America is not only a family affair. Runaways have become a national issue, a perplexing social problem. Because of the deaths in Houston, families with a missing child urged congressmen to take action on behalf of their runaways. Until then, local governments had asked Congress to help them pay for the drain on county, city, and state resources which runaways depleted. Public and private agencies had applied for grants from the Department of Health, Education, and Welfare or from the Law Enforcement Assistance Administration to fund runaway houses, but the government was apathetic. Sometimes it gave a little money; usually it did not.

For three years, while running away continued as part of growing up in America, I watched a little activity and heard much talk about runaways, but until 1974 I saw no money moving. Those modern prophets of disaster, the statisticians and poll takers, had warned that thousands of children were leaving home and foretold that thousands more would run, yet only a few citizens did anything. In spite of prediction and fact, the government neglected youngsters who ran. They would, it thought, either grow up and go home, or stay away, forgotten.

The Houston murder case was the catalyst that caused Congress to stop shuffling papers and decide on legislation. Earlier the Senate had heard about runaways when Senator Birch Bayh of Indiana introduced a bill to aid them. In 1972, he interested the senators, mildly, by relating running away from home to juvenile delinquency. After all, he noted, nearly half the serious crimes in America were committed by people under eighteen. So Congress began to notice an issue, as runaways became the scapegoats for juvenile crime. Today's runaways are tomorrow's juvenile delinquents, Senator Bayh warned when he opened hearings on the Runaway Youth Act in January, 1972. As Chairman of the Juvenile Delinquency Subcommittee, he announced his bill melodramatically with two days of television and the macabre stories of runaway children. Senator Bayh had invited runaways to the Senate to testify. Abused, neglected, ignored, the children talked about their mothers' not wanting them, their fathers' beating them, the bizarre behavior of people they met on the road, their use of drugs for pleasure and sex to repay favors. They represented children from middle- and low-income families, children whose parents had separated and children whose parents lived together. When articulate adults described the increasing runaway population, their rhetoric was redundant after the embarrassed, halting words of the youngsters.

Bayh's bill asked for federal funds to finance runaway houses in cities where runaways gather. Besides shelter, the houses would be able to give the children medical aid and psychological counseling and would work to bring families together. They would serve as an alternate solution to the traditional handling of runaways through police departments or courts. Modeled on

shelter programs like Project Place in Boston or Runaway House
in the District of Columbia, they would continue their counseling of families after they were reunited, to follow up the home
situation which caused the running away. Bayh also asked for
money for research into the statistics of the runaway population.
Each aspect of his bill would be fulfilled through the Department of Health, Education, and Welfare. The Runaway Youth
Act required $10 million a year for three years. Admitting that
the bill was not a panacea, Senator Bayh considered it a beginning toward a comprehensive program to help prevent juvenile
delinquency.

Through his work on delinquency Senator Bayh became
convinced that runaways were an issue at least two years before
the Houston murders shocked the nation. Perhaps he saw himself as the champion of children who had no advocate in government. A lawyer on his staff had told me: "Runaways have a
built-in constituency because so many families have had the
problem." Certainly the senator was aware of the voter appeal
of forlorn children.

For whatever reason, Senator Bayh listened to the lawyers
on his staff and told them to write a bill. They, in turn, had
heard the men and women who had counseled runaways for
years, often without enough money to pay the salaries of fellow
workers. Bill Treanor, former director of Runaway House in
Washington, D.C. Brian Slattery of Huckleberry's for Runaways
in San Francisco. Jim Butler of The Bridge in Grand Rapids.
Gerda Flanigan of Metro Help in Chicago. They had hammered
on the conscience of the government. They asked how one million American children could run from home without evoking
an official reaction. They insisted that the government owed the
dissenting children of the United States the attention it showed
to organized protestors like blacks, women, Indians, the elderly.
They came together to draw up legislation.

During the summer of 1971, John M. Rector, then deputy
chief counsel of the senator's staff, and Michael A. Nemeroff,

assistant counsel, were collaborating with Bill Treanor of Runaway House. They were constructing the program of government aid to runaways and their families that would result in the bill that bounced back and forth between the Senate and the House for three years.

When the Juvenile Justice and Delinquency Prevention Act, which included the runaway measure, was before Congress in August, 1974, I interviewed Bill Treanor at his office in Washington. He talked about the history of the legislation and his role in making it. He was the original youth advocate, the Ralph Nader of the children's crusade. He initiated and coordinated projects for youth into being; he persuaded men and women of the importance of the cause of children's rights and they were eager to serve.

After Washington's Resurrection City was abandoned in 1968, Bill Treanor, who had worked for the Poor People's Campaign, observed dozens of youngsters wandering around the city homeless. With a local minister he began Runaway House, one of the first shelters for runaway children in the country. As Treanor realized the scope of the problem, he agitated for the national recognition of runaways through federal money and law.

Treanor is now the director of the National Youth Alternatives Project in Washington, a private, nonprofit agency dedicated to the rights of young people. When he was the director of Runaway House, advising Senator Bayh's subcommittee, he and the committee staff used FBI arrest statistics to determine the number of runaways throughout the country. They estimated that 1,000,000 were leaving home each year. Recently the Institute for Social Research at the University of Michigan developed figures much lower than those the juvenile delinquency subcommittee had produced. Social scientists in Ann Arbor said that for a three-year period the number of children who ran away was between 1,475,200 and 2,364,800.

Treanor scoffed at the university's low estimate, but he admitted that neither set of figures had spurred the government to act for runaways and their families. The irony was that it was not the estimated 1,000,000 children annually that moved those in power, but an insignificant number: 27. That 27 boys had died in Texas was the single fact, the solitary statistic, to rouse the United States Government.

Besides Birch Bayh, William Keating, former Republican representative from Ohio, had understood the problem before the Houston case exposed the size of the runaway population. Representative Keating of Cincinnati drew up a runaway measure in 1971. Although it was similar to Bayh's later bill, it cost less. The Keating version included financing runaway shelters through the Department of Health, Education, and Welfare and buying computer equipment for the police to use in reporting runaways nationally. Several advocates of government aid to runaways acted shocked with his provision to the Justice Department's Law Enforcement Assistance Administration for police equipment. Men like Treanor believed that bringing in the police smelled of fascism. According to them, it was essential to remove the stigma of delinquency from runaways. In the early days their cry was: "Decriminalize the runaway!" Ironically, many police departments agree that the runaway is not a juvenile delinquent. In Houston the police dismissed five thousand yearly as nuisances. The final irony in the issue is that the passage of the legislation came about only because of a compromise which included the Runaway Youth Act in a comprehensive juvenile-delinquency prevention bill.

In 1971, Keating's bill was ignored by the House of Representatives. In January, 1973, the representative reintroduced the Runaway Youth Act in the House with Minority Leader Gerald Ford as a cosponsor. Even the former Minority Leader's interest was not strong enough to carry the bill. It died in committee.

The Keating bill is a good example, however, of how the runaway problem became a national issue. When I interviewed the representative, he told me that Cincinnati Juvenile Court

Judge Benjamin Schwartz had asked Keating to take legislative action on behalf of runaway children and their parents. In the five years from 1966–1971, the judge had seen the numbers of children who ran away from home in Cincinnati increase 100 percent.

In 1973 Representative Keating said: "The problem has grown in magnitude since I became interested in 1971. Children are leaving Cincinnati, not running to it."

Another sign that the problem had become an issue was the jealousy that developed between the staffs of the two congressmen. One of Representative Keating's assistants told me that Bayh's staff was only looking for a popular issue when it seized on their measure. They had, I was told, based the senator's proposal on the Keating bill. The difference between the two was that the Bayh bill omitted the grant to the Justice Department for computer equipment while it increased the money requested from Congress from $4 million to $10 million annually for three years.

The senator's staff denied the story.

"Senator Bayh didn't need to grab at anything Keating was doing. The story is simply not true," John Rector, chief counsel of the Senate subcommittee, said.

When I asked Senator Bayh himself whether his Runaway Youth Act was a revision of Congressman Keating's bill, he bristled: "I haven't heard that before! If Keating's interested, have him show it. Let him pump up support in the House. We need all the help we can get!"

When I interviewed Birch Bayh in his office on Capitol Hill, almost two years had passed since he had explained his Runaway Youth Act to the Senate. During the spring and summer of 1973, he was directing his energies toward a juvenile-delinquency bill that would develop programs to prevent crime. At hearings on the Juvenile Justice and Delinquency Prevention Act, the senator talked of the tragedy of children trapped by a

shameful system. Remembering the sad runaways who had testified for his early bill, he said: "The failure of our juvenile justice
system is even more tragic when we realize that more than half
of our incarcerated juveniles are initially locked up for such noncriminal offenses as running away from home or being truant
from school."

The runaway house replaced jail for wandering children in
the original runaway bill. But, an opponent in the Senate had
argued that the passing of the Runaway Youth Act would create
"federal flophouses," and give children an incentive to leave
home. Many parents I met feared the same thing. If the kids
knew they had a place to sleep, running away would be easy
for them. Did Senator Bayh agree?

"Ridiculous!" he sputtered. "The pressures that cause kids
to run away are so great that they leave without any thought of
where they'll go."

What were those pressures, I asked him.

He rattled off: "Physical abuse, sexual abuse, broken
homes." He hesitated and added: "Immaturity. It exists in every
home."

Birch and Marvella Bayh have a son who was entering his
final year in one of Washington's toughest college preparatory
schools. I asked him quickly: "Has your son ever run away from
home?"

The senator smiled: "Not to my knowledge, but he's been
mad enough to."

Another senator with teen-age children, Walter F. Mondale
of Minnesota had supported Senator Bayh's Runaway Youth Act.
He acknowledged:

"Perhaps what has kept us from acting sooner on the runaway problem is its closeness to home. Most of us have a friend,
a relative or a neighbor whose child has run away. Maybe ours
will be next. A parent cannot help blaming himself, wondering
what other people think, when his child leaves home." Then he
added: "We will only increase our guilt if we fail to recognize

the existence of the problem and provide assistance to the children and families who need it."

Suddenly it was August, 1973, and the Houston police were digging into the sand around a South Houston boatyard where the bodies of several boys were buried. Twice the dead boys were identified as runaways by the police: the first time when their parents reported them missing, and again when they were exhumed. In fact, they were not runaways, but missing children, boys captured and murdered by a madman. The horror was that while the legislators and bureaucrats were musing on the perils of runaways, children loved and protected by their families were being killed in their own neighborhoods because the police counted them as runaways—and there were too many to look for.

Congressmen heard the wail of agony out of Houston and around the country. They heard the lamentation of parents who wondered whether their missing child lay among the piles of unidentified bones in Houston. They read telegrams from parents whose sons were missing, urging them to act, to help, to acknowledge running away from home as a national tragedy. Invoking the traditional chorus of shock, anguish, and fear, those in power vowed to search for a solution.

Congress acted on the assumption that the dead boys had been runaways. The deference to federal money disappeared along with their willingness to let local governments fumble with the problem. They assumed, at last, that running away was a national dilemma as congressmen from coast to coast began to agitate for legislation to aid runaways and their parents. They started by supporting the current proposal before the House of Representatives, Senator Bayh's runaway bill. Congressman Augustus Hawkins of California and Congressman Spark M. Matsunaga of Hawaii sponsored the Bayh bill in the House. From its beginning, former Senator Marlow Cook of Kentucky was a proponent of the legislation. Congressman William Ford of Michigan supported a bill similar to Bayh's Runaway Youth Act except that it amended the Juvenile Justice and Delinquency Prevention Act to account for runaways.

During the political year 1973-1974, from the summer of Houston to the grim August of 1974, senators and congressmen quibbled over a Runaway Youth Act. Men and women from both political parties agreed that something should be done. They were uncertain what it was to be. In June, 1974, the House Subcommittee on Equal Opportunity combined the Bayh runaway measure with the juvenile justice act. The original bill became one section in a multimillion-dollar, four-year anticrime program for delinquent children.

During the early winter of 1973, I had walked through the long halls of the Department of Health, Education, and Welfare and the National Institute of Mental Health trying to discover programs aimed specifically at runaway children. I had found very few. By January, 1972, HEW was financing only four shelters because the Department had not accepted running away from home as a national problem. A year later a runaway house in Las Vegas and the *National Directory of Runaway Centers* were two more of HEW's projects. The National Institute of Mental Health gave $5,000 once to a runaway center on Second Avenue in New York, but when I visited the storefront room in August, 1973, the place was boarded up, deserted. When the money ran out, the project had died.

Youth specialists at HEW had said they weren't doing anything about runaways. They had no money to work with. However, they told me jealously, the Justice Department's Law Enforcement Assistance Administration, LEAA, was using monies from its enormous budget to fund several programs. Many of the HEW people disdained the LEAA's money. Using it for runaways would place them in the criminal-justice system, they argued. Putting the runaway child under the care of Justice returned him to his old slot, that of *juvenile delinquent,* instead of *social problem.*

They chatted with me about *youth advocacy,* a phrase they'd heard from the men and women who worked in runaway houses. Youth advocacy meant defending the defenseless, supporting children who relied out of necessity on the benevolence of parents, schools, police, courts. Youth advocacy meant pleading for the rights of children who had no rights, taking the youngster's side when all of society deferred to the parent. The term implied a change in the traditional order of relegating children to the juvenile-justice system. The professionals at HEW considered themselves youth advocates, but without money they were without power to advocate.

After Houston, Secretary of HEW Caspar Weinberger gave his youth advocates the power to spend money to assist existing runaway programs. Horrified by the Houston murders, he had met in the fall of 1973 with the men and women who understood the runaway situation in their localities. As they explained running away from several viewpoints, they spoke about the usual problems: so many kids, too few facilities, unnecessary police action in most cases, unwarranted court attention in others. They described the child's fear of going to a runaway house where counselors might call his parents or the police, yet they sympathized with parents who wanted that call to know their child was alive. They mentioned that some houses, hoping to gain the child's trust, delayed telephoning the parents or state institutions from which the child had run, putting the house in jeopardy for harboring a minor. They told of runaway houses which followed the letter of the law and informed parents, taking the risk of alerting abusive parents to their child's hiding place.

Undoubtedly, they told the Secretary that runaway-house counselors became entangled in all the trappings of adolescence. The dangers which free-wheeling children plunged into like shoplifting, panhandling, hitchhiking, sexual situations, and drug experiments came with the youngster to the house. The issues between child and house and house and parents were complicated. But without the houses the solution to the footloose child could become lethal.

More than a year after the Houston case, Secretary Weinberger spoke of the murders as the turning point in his accepting runaway children as a national issue. The Secretary said: "It was the Houston tragedy and my not having realized the extent of the runaway problem before. I think I became interested in runaways most of all because of the resigned acceptance of the parents in Houston. Their kids had been gone for a year and they did not know where they were. I wondered how in the hell your kid could be gone for a year and you would not make a report to the police. The kids were being murdered and no one seemed to care much about it."

Obviously the Secretary had more faith in the Houston Police Department than the citizens of Houston did. The Texans rejected the police story of negligent parents and delinquent boys when they voted the mayor and his chief of police out of office.

"It is a crime still to run away," the Secretary said, unaware that running away is a status offense, not a crime.

In spite of, or because of, his convictions about runaways, Caspar Weinberger got a list of twenty cities where the runaway problem was gravest. Then he asked the Office of Special Mental Health Concerns of the National Institute of Mental Health to undertake a demonstration program in behalf of runaways. By the end of fiscal year 1974, the National Institute of Mental Health was to spend $1,500,000 worth of federal money for runaway projects

For fiscal year 1975 the Office of Youth Development in HEW would continue what NIMH had begun: the development of services for runaway children and their families. About $2,500,000 would be allotted to several agencies within the Department for various programs. The Office of General Counsel would study the legal rights of runaways through a survey of state statutes. The Office of Planning and Evaluation would research the national incidence of runaways and determine their geographic distribution. The Social and Rehabilitation Service would begin a two-year project to assess the services offered from state to state. The Office of Education would inform school-teachers and administrators about the problem, alerting them to their responsibilities in detecting possible runaways. NIMH would study the effectiveness of runaway houses and counseling centers which were granted federal funds. Besides sponsoring regional conferences on the issue of runaway youth, the Office of Youth Development would be responsible for coordinating the studies.

If the President signed the juvenile-justice bill into law, the Department of Health, Education, and Welfare would lose its jurisdiction over delinquency prevention to the Justice Department. Only the runaway program would remain at HEW. Officials at HEW asked the President to veto the comprehensive bill, arguing that HEW had the money, the experience, the organization, and the compassion to carry out the anticrime assignment. The confusion over the moral stance of HEW versus that of the Justice Department reflected the government's uncertainty over what a runaway was: a social problem or a juvenile delinquent.

The argument had shadowed the Runaway Youth Act from the beginning. If the runaway child was a social issue or a mental health problem, he belonged at HEW or its division, NIMH. If the runaway was a delinquent or predelinquent, he needed the control of the Justice Department. Who he was still bothered those who had decided what to do about him.

To the professional the runaway was an anomaly. Because he could not be classified he cracked the myth of expertise in family matters. He belonged to the majority of healthy adolescents, as the Shellow Report concluded. He rarely committed delinquent acts, as studies like the Shellow Report and the second national survey of youth by the Institute for Social Research showed. Indeed the question was not how to pay for his care, but why should we pay for him? Why should we interfere in a family affair? For the government, temporarily, the Houston case answered the questions. A family affair had developed into a national issue and a matter for the President.

President Gerald Ford signed the revised, all-inclusive Juvenile Justice and Delinquency Prevention Act of 1974 into law on the September evening before he pardoned Richard Nixon. Since he had called inflation the enemy of the people, the President announced that he would not ask Congress for all the money the bill provided. Not, he said, "at a time when the economic situation demands across-the-board restraint, especially in the federal budget."

As Congress appropriated only half the money necessary to the Runaway Youth Act, the future for runaways remained uncertain. Once again children had succumbed to institutional restraint. If President Ford had supported the bill boldly and had paid special attention to runaway children, he would have dignified their cause and pardoned them for running away in America.

14. The Runaway Tragedy

"She left home because she thought she was going to a fuller, exciting, worthwhile life. Instead, she ran to her death."—Dr. Lucile E. St. Hoyme, associate curator of the Department of Physical Anthropology, the Smithsonian Institution.

When I began my investigation three years ago, I read in the papers about a rare find for the Smithsonian, the national museum, in Washington, D.C. The treasure the curators had added to the anthropology collection was the skeleton of a runaway, a fifteen-year-old North American female.

I went to the museum to see for myself this proof of the runaway tragedy. Stored in a drawer and labeled simply New Jersey Skeleton 1972 were the bones of an unidentified girl. I talked to Dr. Lucile E. St. Hoyme of the Department of Physical Anthropology, the skeletal specialist who analyzed the remains for information that might lead to her identity. Dr. St. Hoyme told me the story as she had heard it from the police who brought the bones to the Smithsonian.

They belonged to a girl who had left her home, hitchhiking, in the spring of 1971. Six months later they were discovered in New Jersey near U.S. 30. Two hunters stumbled on them in a gravel pit. They called the New Jersey State Police and the police began an investigation based on a motel key found in the pocket of the girl's blue jeans. They traced the key to a motel near the highway and the room number to a man who had stayed there with a girl for two days in June.

He told them what little he knew about her. He had picked up a slender girl between Hammonton and Egg Harbor, New Jersey, on June 1, 1971. She told him that her name was Sandy and she was on her way to Atlantic City to get a job for the summer. He guessed that the name was as new as her bleached hair. She carried nothing with her, only the clothes she was wearing.

Quiet and withdrawn, Sandy did not talk about her family. She mentioned having friends in the District of Columbia and she spoke of crossing the Delaware Memorial Bridge. She agreed to spend the night with the man who gave her a ride. He seemed kind, and she needed a place to stay. He bought her clothes, bell-bottoms and shirts, and pleased, she tinted her hair back to its natural dark brown color.

In the mornings he drove to work, leaving her at the motel to wait for him. Early in the evening of June 3, she was seen walking toward a restaurant. Since she carried the room key, the police thought she meant to go back to meet her friend. Instead, she died, mysteriously, a few feet from the highway.

When the man arrived at the motel that evening, he was surprised that Sandy had gone. The motel records proved that he waited two days for her. Then, deciding she had run away again, he returned to his routine and forgot about Sandy until New Jersey police confronted him with the fact of her death.

After questioning him, the police were convinced that he had not killed her. He had cooperated with their investigation completely although he did not know much about her, no facts to place her in a family or give her a real name.

As the police publicized their discovery, dozens of worried parents telephoned them. They thought they recognized their runaway daughter from descriptions of the tattered clothes and the wristwatch woven into a wide leather band which the police had also found. Like the parents who would respond to Dr. St. Hoyme's story of the runaway, these parents were relieved to learn that the dead girl was not their child. Their daughter's physique did not fit Sandy's skeletal features. Her height, her perfect teeth, narrow hips, and prominent nose ruled out the probability that she was theirs.

After six months of investigating the murder of the runaway girl, the police from the New Jersey Major Crime Unit drove to Washington, to the Smithsonian Museum of Natural History, with the bones of Sandy. They turned them over to Dr. St. Hoyme and Dr. J. Lawrence Angel, curator of the Department of Physical Anthropology. These scientists would examine the skeleton for clues to how the girl died and who she was. They would keep the remains in the museum and, if she was not identified within five years, the Smithsonian would catalog the bones.

I asked Dr. St. Hoyme why they wanted such a macabre sample of twentieth-century civilization.

"Young people are relatively rare in the collection," she said. In the department, drawers from floor to ceiling were filled with specimens of twentieth-century man, of men and women who had lived a full span of years. Sandy was to be the exception.

"Teen-agers are an abstraction," Dr. St. Hoyme said. "Until you know one, as I know Sandy, they are not very real to you. But here is a specific girl, an unhappy girl, bugged by something at home or at school. She left home because she thought she was going to a fuller, exciting, worthwhile life. Instead, she ran to her death."

Like Dr. St. Hoyme, I had touched on an abstraction and found it real. For me the abstraction was not teen-agers, whom I knew and liked and thought I understood, some of the time. The abstraction was the death of childhood by violence, the ending of misunderstanding by flight, the rebellion against loneliness by coupling with a stranger. The discovery at the museum late in the summer of 1972 was my introduction to the tragedy occurring between American parents and their children.

I sensed the tragedy then as I understand it now. The runaway tragedy was a drama of the conflict between generations. Parents and children were caught by circumstances which they tried to control. They expected so much of each other that failure was inevitable. They struggled against each other for power in a world that was indifferent to their private misery. In the child's desperate fight for autonomy, and in the parents' futile stand for authority, they often lost what was most important to them, the love that bound them to each other. At times they lost more than love. If their fights became hateful and demeaning, they lost the chance for reconciliation. Sometimes, like Sandy, runaway children did not go home.

In searching for the meaning of the runaway tragedy, I looked for someone to blame. First, I accepted the parents of runaways as the natural villains. I imagined them as ineffectual men and women who were also ignorant of the realities of contemporary adolescence. They refused to understand the amorality of the era. In their own homes they shut their eyes to the influences and pressures of the times, while they bore them, matter-of-factly, in their daily business lives. They accused their children of criminal deeds like possession of marijuana while they admitted that men in high places have always been crooks and manipulators. Their shock at the peccadilloes of children was graver than their disapproval of federal corruption. They accepted the wheeling and dealing of tycoons and presidents with equanimity, but raged at the faults of children.

When parents of runaways quarreled with their children, they aimed for the jugular. They accused the children of foul deeds and wretched behavior. Instead of a constructive argument, which Dr. Stierlin described as a "loving fight," they waged battle with blame and guilt.

It was no surprise to me that parents could be vicious, even cruel, to their children. The sense of parental possession is strong. Parents think of a child: "He is mine." They can do with him, and to him, what they wish, for the laws make them the masters. When runaways told me of beatings with belts and cords and fists and feet, I believed them. To admit such violence against them by their own parents was humiliating. What kind of monsters must they be if their mothers and fathers despised them enough to beat them?

I came to see the children as victims, because they lived in a time of extremes and did not know whom to believe. "Live and let live" became "Everybody's doing it." "Everybody's doing his thing" became "Anything goes." For children the confusion was doubled. Their friends urged them to enjoy. Their parents insisted on the achievements of childhood: success in school, courtesy and common sense, clean living and a wholesome appearance. When they chose to be like their friends, their parents floundered.

When I talked to the parents, they surprised me with their innocence. They were victims too—of their own belief in absolutes. Many had held dear to one way of raising children, one idea about the nature of children. They felt society erupting around them, but the fortress of the family would withstand the turbulence, they reassured each other. For their parenthood they had followed the customs of the country. The sentimental past dictated the limits of their experience and circumscribed their roles. When, suddenly, without warning, they were exposed as unjust because they were authoritarian, they were stranded on an ancient beach, fearful of the sound of change and the echoes of mutiny. Their own cries for direction mingled with those of their children. The worst of it was they could not explain themselves. They were as inarticulate as children. They expected understanding without making the effort to be clear. Love, they had thought, was enough. Tradition would carry the day. The responsibility of parents for children was to be matched by the loyalty of children for parents. No matter how the world turned, they believed children and parents would stay close and comforting. They watched the indecisiveness of the schools, the confusion of the law, the inability of government to govern honestly, and they still believed that the family was immutable!

Slower than other institutions to acknowledge change, the family abided by custom. Although it saw the flaws in power, it clung to authority. Instead of being helped by the combined wisdom of the social order, the family was misled by old assumptions. Because of ethical blind spots, parents overlooked the idea that there was little connection between how much money they had and how their children behaved. Society's assumption that the poor needed support in rearing children but the middle class could control its own rebelling young confused them. No matter who they were, parents of runaways did not know what to do with the child who refused to go along with them.

Middle-class parents heaped ashes on themselves by pushing their children toward goals they had found wanting. Although they called it desirable, the pattern of college, career, marriage had not insured contentment for everybody. Men and women proved their disillusion by breaking the design through divorce or separation, by quitting their jobs and pursuing endless change. In asking their children to repeat the pattern, they went after the second chance vicariously and foolishly. The children wanted to discover the meaning of life for themselves.

The children of wealthy and powerful parents ran away for reasons similar to those of middle-class children. The rich, running children I knew clarified the runaway tragedy because their parents had won what the middle class sought. Their parents' theme of great expectations and boundless ambitions wore the children down. They ran for relief, to escape for a time the apparent success of their parents and, by contrast, their own failures. Claudia, daughter of an important statesman, was to tell me: "The way the upper class abuses its children is subtle. The parents devise implicit pressures rather than commit explicit acts. They compel us to success, not directly, but by their example and their words. We are their children, but what can we prove? We can never surpass what our parents have achieved. For upper-class kids the American Dream is dead. We're looking for a reason to live."

I went to visit Claudia, who was a former student of mine, at her college in New England. Four years after her last episode, I wondered how her periodic runaway experiences had affected her. When she was a junior in high school, she had run away. Again as a senior, the year I taught her, she had jumped into her car and driven off to the countryside. She slept in the car and worked at drive-in restaurants. After three or five days when she felt the tension ease, she returned to school and family. Then, I thought she was unstable. Now, I knew she was running from expectations which she could not fulfill, those she had imposed on herself and those inherited from her parents.

"I'm still the runner," she admitted. "I'm no different at twenty than I was at sixteen. The feelings that promote the running are still here. Anger. Insecurity. Tension. I wonder, is what I'm doing worth the effort? Do people care about me as much as I care for them? I run instead of exploding."

Men and women were caught in the same vise that twisted children. High hopes were tightened against the pressures one accepted to achieve them. Ambition scraped against frustration. Love, which was meant to bear all things, was screwed against change, which promises to better all things. The tension was tight enough to break any part of the whole, any single person in the family, to split the whole itself. The runaway child was only one symptom of despair.

Wherever I went and whomever I talked to about the runaway tragedy, I asked the same question. Why is it happening? Why are so many children running away from home? Why has Huck Finn's trip become the answer for thousands of children? How has a political maneuver become a private revenge?

The answer revolved around the state of the family and the

condition of the state. Once again parents became scapegoats for
a society that wanted instant remedies. The family was no longer
strong, all agreed. Each member was too concerned with his own
pursuit of business or pleasure to contribute to an effective unit.
Experts announced that the family was no longer extended by
grandparents and aunts and uncles who in times past assisted as
sages and child tenders. The family was nuclear and could be
separated. The family as once imagined was defunct because men
and women no longer wanted to spend twenty or twenty-five
years of their lives devoted to the home. Women wanted to contribute to society rather than to children and husband. Men were
workers first, husbands and fathers second. The family was sick
and dying, the critics claimed.

Those former strong supporters of the family, the church
and the schools, swelled with criticism of parents. The rector of
a church in Washington's Georgetown neighborhood told me of
the parents who talked to him about their runaways. "They came
on as self-righteous, wronged. They'd done everything for their
kid but turn him over their knee to say we don't behave that
way." A Boston priest bemoaned the fact that suburban parents,
parents of runaways who streamed into the city, had told him to
leave their children alone and they would go home. The un-
attended children had become heroin addicts, he said. One Western minister threw up his hands, and his parish, in frustration.
He talked of the hard business of family relationships. He announced: "If you love your kid, you have to learn to let him go to
hell if that's what he chooses to do." Hell was preferred, he
implied, to parents' meddling in the sacrosanct ritual of growing
up.

Educators explained the erratic behavior of children by
blaming the parents. Children in trouble, runaways, potsmokers,
young alcoholics, shoplifting youngsters, vandals, poor students,
came from homes that were shaken by divorce or separation, they
insisted. They came from homes where the pressure applied to

children to succeed was so intense that the child did not function intelligently. They came from homes where mother worked, or drank, and father traveled or stayed away from home sixteen hours a day at his job. The troubled youngster lacked an attendant mother, a visible father, the school counselors mourned. Without them, the school recommended counseling, therapy, psychological help. And when the psychiatrist decided that a child required treatment, he asked that the whole family participate in the therapy.

As traditional protectors of children, the police turned against the family because the numbers of rebelling children were overwhelming. They were not baby-sitters, they argued. They could not chase down every runaway in the county, or the city. The law shrugged off its mantle of paternalism. With justice, lawyers and judges claimed that running away from home was an offense against state statutes that did not belong on the books or in the courts. It was a family affair. "Strengthen the family" became the rallying cry for institutions. Although they seemed to be accusing parents of negligence, they knew the issue went deeper than name-calling. On their part it was a revolution in attitudes.

Men and women who know runaways well—adults who see them daily, like runaway-house counselors, probation officers, policemen in the juvenile division, street workers—are experienced enough to know that blaming parents is too easy to be true, too simple to be valuable. As adolescents who have chosen to act decisively by leaving home, runaways are approaching maturity. They are acknowledging participation in the family and a share in its unhappiness.

Everyone I met during three years cited "lack of communication" as a primary reason for the breakdown of the family. "Lack of communication" was the underlying, not the immediate cause of a child's running away. "We can't talk. We can't get along," many runaways complained about their parents. "She never talks to us," their parents explained. "I don't have anything to say to my parents," one of my nonrunaway students told me.

During her appearance at my school Margaret Mead called the generation gap "a funny ditch," which was too deep to repair. Since the explosion of the atom bomb, the event which she claimed divided the generations, the anthropologist believed that the common ground under the elders and their young was blasted away. She exaggerated to make a point about the generations, but for runaways and their parents the ditch was deep. For them the familiar charge that communication was impossible was not an excuse. It was a genuine reason for anguish. The conditions necessary for dialogue had disappeared, and they failed to explain themselves to each other. How could the parents discuss school with their children if they did not know what was taught? How could parents discuss the social life of their children if they disapproved of its content? Crossing the ditch, like going into space, was possible only with the determination and planning an important venture requires. Millions of parents close the gap with their children daily. Parents of runaways can emulate their success.

Parents of runaways can become youth advocates. At first within the home, then outside it, they can listen and learn as they expect their children to. They can disapprove if they do not also accuse and hurt. Without assuming that children already know, they can explain the basis for their decisions, clearly, not loudly. They can tell children why they feel as they do. They can respect and dignify their children by behaving as they wish to be treated themselves.

Parents of runaways can fight for justice for their children. They can refuse to acquiesce to the judgment of institutions which control the lives of their youngsters. They need not bow to the wisdom of the ruling system. Because in their desire to be efficient, institutions are always practical. Police take runaways to detention centers, then to juvenile court. The judge places repeating runaways on probation and supervises their behavior.

Schools insist on their undergoing psychological counseling. All strive to define, classify, categorize, and organize. That is their work. It is not the family's.

Please do not misunderstand me. The runaway tragedy is a complex national sorrow, and I do not have a simple solution for runaways and their parents. Many children must leave home, and they should not return. They must have other choices besides living with their parents. If they are sixteen or seventeen, they can become *emancipated minors* with the approval of their parents and the law. They are allowed to live independent of a home setting. Radical runaways should also be able to live in group homes or foster homes, m boarding schools or in other settlements of youngsters who learn and work together.

For the reluctant runaways, the majority who want to go home to their parents, we must yield. We must forgive them because they are inexperienced, and frightened of adult power. We must have them help us recognize what is happening to them. We must realize the reasons for running away and admit that we are the victims of our own emotions where our children are involved. If we do, we will accept the complexity of growing up in the final quarter of the twentieth century. Then, we will have a chance to love our runaway children wisely.

Index